HERO

Vince McKee

This collection is a work of non-fiction. All the events portrayed within are a true account according to the author. Some of the names contained here within have been altered or changed to protect the real person's identity.

HERO

Published by V Peter Press
Cleveland, Ohio

First Print Edition: October 2012

PB ISBN-13: 978-1479281053
PB ISBN-10: 1479281050

HERO

I would like to dedicate this book to my Uncle Peter DeLuca. Your guidance and belief in me from a young age gave me the strength to grow and become a man. May your soul forever rest in peace.

I would like to thank my loving wife Emily for always believing in me and giving me the confidence in myself that I lacked before we met. My parents for their guidance and encouragement my entire life. My brother Don and sister Abbie, your enthusiasm in this project is what kept me going from the very beginning when I had many doubts I could finish. To my cousin Jim who sacrificed his time to edit every word until it fit the story perfectly. My friends David Murphy and Joey Graham for sticking by my side for twenty plus years. Bill Meyers, I could have never coached this team without your help. My Uncle James Deluca, for motivating me to put what I had in my mind on to paper. My friend Ty who was the first person to lend a hand when I was ready to give up on my dream. Thank you to the parents of the players for making it easy on me and never losing faith. To my players, for always believing in our dream of winning the championship and never giving up until we did. To Bill Wheeler and Karl Kubb for installing the love of the game in me. Most importantly my lord and savior Jesus Christ, it is through your light that all work is done.

Table of Contents

Words from the Players

"Despite missing so many games due to my vacation, feelings of distance with the team began to dissipate and I was so glad to be able to contribute what I could with everyone. I didn't realize at the time how those experiences with the team and the whole deal were contributing to my character.

My most vivid memory of that season was sitting in the grass in that circle with that trophy being passed around. It was an exciting and neat moment that I won't forget. In addition to the whole season and summer in general. It wouldn't have been our season without Coach McKee being the coach he was."
~ Nathanael Dolesh

"It's crazy how life has passed by for me, well probably for all of us. One day I'm putting in work wearing clients on a baseball field and the next min I'm putting in work wearing boots in Iraq. What I've always took from that summer was that we bonded like brothers and worked like warriors. That type of thing doesn't happen very often. I am extremely grateful to have been a part of it. Oh and on a side note I still never knew what Andy Barth was doing."

~ Kyle Keller

Introduction

As the umpire yelled the final words and the championship game concluded, there was only a certain amount of people who truly understood the sacrifice that it took to get there. The courage and belief in one another had risen above any obstacle set in the way of fourteen young men in a summer of dreams.

A simple baseball diamond can bring a person's world into peace. On that field nothing else matters except the game being played and the players on it. It's a time when you are surrounded by your teammates and opposition yet you can still feel alone. It is a time when the baseball gods work their magic. On that field no one care's how you got there or where you are going when you leave. The only thing that matters is the next out, the next pitch and the next moment in time that can change a life forever.

In the spring and the summer of 2000 my team of little leaguers and I would go on the greatest journey anyone could ever dream of. In a time when I truly needed something to believe in, a group of ten year olds would provide exactly that.

I was eighteen and had just graduated from high school with the rest of my life ahead of me to decide what I was to become and where I was headed. Little did I know that it was going to take this group of amazing children to show me that life was worth having something and someone to believe in.

Chapter 1
The Seed is Planted

"Anyone can give up, it's the easiest thing in the world to do. But to hold it together when everyone else would understand if you fell apart, that's true strength."
~ Unknown

I was born on January 14, 1982 in the middle of a blistering winter. My parents named me Vincenzo Peter McKee. My name was a tribute to my great grandfather on my mother's side. It was only mere hours after an airplane crashed into the Potomac River. There may have been sadness in the world but pure joy was the only emotion my family shared that day.

I was the younger of two boys. My older brother Donald who was almost four years old, jumped up and down on my grandparent's bed shouting, "I have a baby brother, I have a baby brother." It was also that day that the love of baseball was born inside of me.

The doctors had told my mother several times that she would not be able to have me. She suffered from severe epilepsy and the chances of her having children were slim. After beating the odds with my older brother my parents took one more chance. It was a good thing that they did because if not I would have never came along. It was an early sign that life would be filled with uphill battles and challenges at every turn. From day one I was ready to defy odds and make living count.

My tool for enjoying life came every time I picked up my glove or swung a bat. It was baseball that would bring the greatest challenges but also the most positive rewards. As a young toddler the only toys I would play with was a cushioned baseball and soft cotton bat in my crib. I showed interest in the game at the age of three when my parents could sit me in front of the television for several hours with a game on the screen. I didn't comprehend what was going on at such a young age but the thrill of what I was seeing was there.

We grew up in West Park Cleveland, just a stone's throw away from downtown and the heart of the city. Donald who was named after our father was my only sibling and that allowed us to be close and spend plenty of time together. The age difference never stopped us from getting along great.

I knew early in life that I would like sports and in particular baseball. When a child is little he learns how to talk, walk, then almost always learns how to throw. Most children tend to always want to pick something up and throw it. I was so anxious to throw a baseball that I threw anything I could get my hands on. There was one time at the age of two that I chose to scale my refrigerator and start throwing eggs all over my parent's kitchen. It was an early sign that doing things out of the ordinary wouldn't be uncommon for me.

When I was about five years old, my dad took me outside our house and taught me to play catch. I had watched him play many times with my older brother Don and I was eager to join in the fun. Playing catch in the yard with Don and my dad became my new favorite thing to do. It wasn't long before my dad would get home from work with his sons waiting at the door to play catch.

My whole life my dad has been there for me and taught me pretty much everything I know. He worked for a bus line located in northeast Ohio. From his humble beginnings as a bus driver he rose up to become the main supervisor of one of their busiest warehouses. I was lucky enough to have a father who came straight home from work every day to spend time with his family. I have seen that not all families enjoy the same privilege. Dad made it a point to spend as much time with his children as possible. His job allowed him off every day by 4 pm and he would spend every night spending time with his family.

My mom comes from a huge Italian family with three brothers and four sisters. We were lucky enough to be two of twenty plus grandchildren, so we also got a lot of attention from aunts and uncles. There wasn't a Christmas that went by without plenty of toys under the tree. Family came first in my life, with baseball a very close second.

My Grandfather on my mom's side took over the responsibility of teaching us how to hit the ball. He had three sons and had coached all of their baseball teams when they were growing up. One of my earliest memories of my Grandpa Deluca was the time he first tried teaching me how to hit. He came over our house regularly because he and my Grandma lived two blocks away. The night he came to teach me how to hit, I had visions of hitting home runs out of Cleveland Municipal stadium. Grandpa came over with a bat and little plastics birdies that people use for badminton, my hopes were quickly dashed. He taught me that it was about hand speed and hand eye coordination. The point was to pick up the birdie when it left the pitcher's hand and hit it with the bat. It seemed kind of odd at the time but I quickly learned what he was trying to teach me.

Another great drill he taught Donald and I was hitting the ball off a fence from two feet away. The other player would toss a ball up from kneeling next to the hitter. This is a drill that is actually used by big leaguers today. It teaches the importance of making contact with the ball as well as developing a level swing from the hips.

Between his teachings and those of my Dad, I was eagerly ready to play the first chance I could get. When my kindergarten year ended and the summer of 1988 had begun my brother and I were both chomping at the bit to get on the field and play. My brother had been able to sign up for overhand fast pitch because he was four years older then I. I had to settle for tee ball.

For some reason we did not need a team sponsor at that age, so each team was given the name of a Major League ball club. I wore jersey number twelve of the Milwaukee Brewers. I wore that jersey twenty four hours a day seven days a week, only taking it off to swim and bathe. There wasn't a team in the league called the Indians, to keep any of the kids from being jealous I presume. The Brewers were fine by me because I always liked the colors yellow and blue.

It would anger me that we never had practices for tee ball. It was bad enough that we had to hit off of a wimpy tee. I would always go to my brother's practices and shag fly balls when they let me to make up for the lack of practice time my team received. The cool thing about tee ball league was that they matched you up for the most part with the kids you lived near. I got to play on the same team with a couple of my best friends from school. It was also that summer that I chose to start the tradition of sleeping with my glove every night before a game.

Although I have a great memory when it comes to anything baseball, I don't remember too much about that season other than a few key events. Our second game of the season was against the Phillies. It was the only game of the season that my Dad was lucky enough to catch on video camera. Tee ball only consisted of a few things. Each team would get up to bat once until every player had their turn at bat. The whole game would only last one inning.

I stepped up to the plate for my at bat full of hope that I was going to knock one right to the sky. My first swing was a miss. I couldn't believe it! Who misses the ball in tee-ball? Well, sadly I did as I swung with everything I had and completely missed. I had swung so hard that I spun around completely in a circle and almost tipped over. My dad even said out loud as he is taping "He swings like a banshee. You don't have to hit a home run just make contact". In what can only be described as pure irony I hit a home run on the very next swing.

I rounded third base and the ball was nowhere close to the infield yet, I would surely be safe by a mile. That did not stop me from sliding into home plate and knocking over the tee. I always wanted to slide and nothing was going to stop me. When I got back to my feet instead of running to the dugout for my teammates, I ran up to where my parents were standing to tell them what I just did as if they hadn't seen it. I quickly turned from them and went into the dugout for the support of my teammates. It is a cool memory and one I will recall for the rest of my life. I should also mention that my brother Don was there to slap my hand.

When I wasn't on the tee-ball diamond, I was going to watch my brother play. Donald played for a team called Harper's Hardware. The team wasn't very good but he didn't seem to care. He got to bat first in the lineup because of his great speed and great eye at the plate. The most vivid memory about going to those games was that their coached yelled all the time. The man was insane and was constantly screaming at everyone and everything. I was lucky enough to never have a coach like him. Yelling and screaming at children so young can never have a good effect. It is okay and much needed to be stern with them, however it must be done in a positive way. This is crucial for the coach to do if he expects to gain the support of his team.

The great thing about the summer of "1988" was that it didn't matter where you went, as long as you came home for dinner. Things were safer back then and Donald and I would play baseball in the neighborhood all day, if not with other kids then with each other. On the truly hot days we would play slip and slide running bases. The game consisted of throwing the ball off the roof of the house. Meanwhile the other player goes running and sliding on the slip and slide before you can catch the ball and tag him out.

One of my happiest memories of playing in the yard with Donald those summers growing up was our classic whiffle ball games. For some reason he would always want to be the Houston Astros and I would be the Atlanta Braves, wearing my Brewers jersey of course. However, for some reason I would never say Atlanta Braves, I would always say Atlantic Braves. The Atlanta Braves would go on to be my favorite baseball team along with the Yankees and Pirates growing up. It didn't matter who was playing, if baseball was on I was watching.

At the time the Indians were always the worst team in the league so it was really easy to get a ticket to watch them play at the stadium downtown. My Mom and Dad would take Don and me to a few games each summer and I was always thrilled to be there. Usually the Tribe would lose but it did not matter one bit to us. To a little boy everything seems so big. The outfield grass seemed to stretch for miles. The crack of the bat seems so loud. Everything down to that beautiful sound of the ball hitting the catcher's glove was surreal at that age. I loved the sound of the ball ripping the glove and the umpire yelling "strike." Even the sound of the venders in the stands yelling only helped to the surreal feeling every time I stepped into a big league stadium.

One fateful night the Indians were having a promotion in an effort to draw more attendance. It stated that any child who signed up for a library card would get two free tickets for that night's game. Dad took me up to the library so we could sign me up for a library card and get two free tickets. The librarian who had been working there for years pulled Dad and myself in a side room and proceeded to tell us all the rules and responsibilities of having a library card. The lecture went on for at least thirty minutes until my Dad finally told her that we understood and needed to leave.

That night we went to the game and had a fun evening with all the thrills of a big league game. My dad had set the books on top of the dresser by a window that was open. On our way home from the game it started to poor down rain. When we got home the books were completely water logged and ruined. Not

7

wanting to face the wrath of the mean librarian my Dad had to think quickly.

He waited until the next night when the library was closed to spring his plan into action. He took the books with him up to McDonalds and bought a large strawberry milkshake. He went to the side of the library where the night drop off box was located. He then took the lid off the milkshake and poured the entire milkshake down the chute to ruin all the books that had been already dropped off along with mine that he set in there as well. That way the next day when they opened up the shoot they would never know that my books were already damaged and that way we couldn't get in trouble.

I was blessed that my parents put a little money aside for us to do these things as a family. We were never spoiled with material objects, but the love we received from our parents was worth a million dollars.

Growing up we did not have video games but we did have plenty of toys and fun. Don and I were constantly creating new games to play. In the winter we had to find something to do inside which wasn't always easy for two kids who loved to be outside. We managed to invent a game with our baseball cards, a pencil and a marble. It was better than any fancy store bought game. The game consisted of holding your pencil while sitting on the floor. The opponent would roll the marble and you would have to try and hit it with your pencil and not have it roll over any of the nine position cards on the floor. If it did it would be an out. The nine position cards consisted of real life player cards that we had collected. As with anything else Don and I did together, we were highly competitive with this game.

There was nothing wrong with being competitive with one another. Growing up coaches always preached winning. Sure they wanted us to try hard and have fun, but make no mistake about it, winning was the number one goal. It is a shame as to how much things have changed over the years. Little league games would never end in a tie. If you lost a game you would cry and be upset for the next hour at least. There was no such thing as orange slices and a juice box after each game. The closest thing we ever got to a treat was ice cream if we won. That was only reserved if we won the championship. I had it drilled in to me at a very young age that winning was important, not by my parents either, but by my coaches growing up. There is nothing in the professional sports world that angers me more than when a player on a team loses and he's smiling. I'm not saying that little children shouldn't have fun, but they need to want to win. This is a lesson that has to be taught at an early age. A person needs to have that attitude that winning is important. It will help them do better at school, work and there your social life. It teaches a child to want to be a better person and strive for the best.

On the other side is that you don't want to overdo it. A person can put far too much pressure on a youngster and totally turn him off to the sport all together. The parents who stand behind the dugout and yell and scream at their son are better off not even coming to the game. The coaches that make it seem like it as all about them are better off not coaching. A coach needs to find the perfect blend of desire to win and ability to have fun, two things that are mandatory when it comes to coaching. The players need to try their hardest and leave it all on the field. It is great if that results in a win, if not, than no big deal because they tried their hardest. That is the most important thing a coach can ask from his players. They don't always need to love you, but they need to play hard for you. Show them respect and they will want to be successful. I have had a bad taste in my mouth after a win because of the lack of effort shown on the field, as well as pride in a loss because my players gave it everything they had.

I was lucky enough to have parents who knew how to motivate me, without making me feel over pressured. I was also lucky that my parents came to every game I played in. Sometimes it would be rough because Donald would have a game at the same time. My parents would still make sure that one of them was at each. Donald was great about it too. He would come to every game I ever played in once he finished playing. He even took stats for me and was always my biggest fan from tee ball on up.

When the summer of 1989 rolled around we did not play. There were numerous reasons as to why we didn't play. My parents were trying to sell their home and provide a better life for us. We lived in a decent area of Cleveland, but my Dad and Mom had been saving money and wanted us to live in the suburbs. We also lived by Hopkins Airport which was planning to buy out all the land anyway within ten years. With all the pressure and work that comes with selling a house, they simply did not have time. I remember being sad but quickly getting over it. When you are seven years old it doesn't take much to improve your mood. We

9

spent that summer again on the street playing street ball and on the slip and slide.

My love of the game had not diminished that summer by any means. Just because a person isn't doing something does not mean they can't still love it. Just because you aren't with someone doesn't mean you can't still love them. Baseball is a love that is pure. It doesn't let a person down and it is not going to leave them.

One night in the middle of the summer when my parents were showing our house to potential buyers, I decided that rather than sticking around I would go up to the fields and catch a game. I didn't tell a single person I was leaving and snuck out the back door when no one was looking. Not an hour went by before my parents came up to the fields looking for me and to make sure I was safe. Maybe I didn't want to move and this was my way of recovering against it. It was the start of a trend I developed growing up during stressful times. If I ever had a lot on my mind I can go to a baseball field anywhere no matter who is playing, and whatever problem I have at the time seems to disappear. Everyone vents feelings in a different way. It is safer and less expensive than any drink or drug.

As another long winter turned into spring in "1990" I was chomping at the bit to play baseball. With the house still not sold my dad was quick to sign Donald and me up for teams to play on that summer. My parents did not want to rob us of the joy of playing despite the uncertainty of if we would be moving suddenly.

That is when I met the man who would end up being the greatest coach I ever played for, the man who showed me what baseball was all about. This man ate, slept, and breathed the game. He knew what was going to happen on the field five seconds before it happened. If ever there was a coach who I modeled myself after it was this man. His name was Bill Wheeler. He was set to light the fuse of a fire that would burn for many years to come.

Chapter 2
Razor Sharp

"Whether you think you can or think you can't, you're right"
~ Henry Ford

It was a cold and rainy day in late February when dad drove Don and me to baseball signup's. We would be playing in a new league this season called Tri League Four Corners Baseball. After the summer off and the cold winter to follow Don and I were eager to get back on the field and play. We heard many good things about this league and went into it with high hopes. When we arrived at the place signups were being held, my Dad quickly saw someone he knew. His name was Bill Wheeler and my dad had gone to high school with him years earlier.

They attended West Tech High School. A very rough, tough school located in one of the worst parts of Cleveland. They were friends in school but had not kept in touch since. They began talking and realized that they had sons who were the same age. He had a son named Kevin and planned on coaching his team this season. Mr. Wheeler told my dad that he would be sure to pick me to be on his team. He also assured my dad I would learn a lot and have fun. He said that practice would begin soon, which brought music to my ears.

As we drove home my dad mentioned that it might be a good idea to get me a bigger glove to use because the one I had was a cheap plastic one. I quickly objected to the idea because I felt a certain sense of loyalty towards the one I had been using. He explained to me that this would be different from what I was used to. He explained there would be a lot of practices, in the game they would actually be keeping score and we would have records. Hearing these things brought more music to my ears.

Practices started at the first sight of green grass when the snow melted off the diamonds. On my way to the first practice I was excited but also a little nervous to meet my new teammates. Our team consisted of eight and nine year olds. It mainly had eight year olds on it. Being one of the younger guys was fine by me because I was used to playing with Don and his friends in the neighborhood already.

The practice consisted of mainly the basic drills of

11

fielding, catching and throwing. We also covered base running but not hitting of any kind just yet. Mr. Wheeler had a great approach with the kids of being firm but not shouting. He made it fun and challenging all at the same time. What I remember most about that first practice was playing catch with Matt Paulett at the end of it. Until this point things had been going well. We started playing catch and I quickly realized that my hand was really starting to hurt. As always dad was right and my cheap glove was not correct for this type of action. I did not want to let my new teammate know that I was in pain. So after about ten or so minutes I asked him to start throwing me ground balls instead.

When practice ended Mr. Wheeler gave us a talk about working hard and wanting to win every game we would play in. He explained because we had so many eight year olds on the team that we might be overlooked, but he still thought we could win. He told us our goal that season was nothing less than a league championship. Hearing him say that was very inspiring. It showed that he had confidence in us right from the start and that he believed we could be as good if not better than any other team.

Mr. Wheeler had a way of making the game fun and interesting. He did not shout very much but he still commanded respect. He treated all players the same no matter the talent level, which is something we don't see very much of at all these days at any level. The other great thing is that he never singled out his son for any reason in front of the other players. That is something seldom seen anywhere else regardless of the sport. He had a way of getting his point across without making us feel dumb. He would make a player do the same thing over and over again until we got it right.

On the way home from practice Dad and Don were both anxious to hear all about it asking me various questions. I was hesitant to tell them about my hand hurting but I eventually did tell them. My dad suggested that instead of going home we should go to the sporting goods store and purchase some new leather. The glove we bought was black with a tiny red patch on it. To me it seemed the coolest thing in the world. When we got home we quickly put a ball in it, wrapped it with string, then put oil on it and let it sit overnight. We did this to get the glove loose and ready for playing.

We had many practices that spring and our team quickly took shape and looked good. I had a chance to play many positions, but felt that I liked playing infield the most. Second base seemed to be where I felt most comfortable. I have never been a fan of playing the outfield, however, because I felt like I was just too far from the action. When playing in the infield I felt as though every ball was going to be hit to me. In the outfield it was always hard for me to judge the ball position in the air and it gave me too much time to think about dropping it. A player doesn't have the time to be nervous in the infield because the ball comes at him so fast it as all about reaction.

The first game was rapidly approaching and because of all the great talent we had on the team there would not be a place for me in the infield. This was tough news to take at first and I was a little sad about it. But the fact that I would still be in the lineup made me feel better. I was put in center field and I was fine with that. I was just happy to be playing on a team that summer. Some players would be discouraged about not getting to play their favorite position but I saw this as motivation to become better.

Getting ready for my first game I was about to put on my uniform when my dad came in to my room and told me to put this on. He tossed me a box with a cup in it, and not the kind of cup that you drink out of. It was an athletic protector, the most uncomfortable thing any guy can wear. I remember staring at the cup then looking back at my dad as if to say "Are you serious?" When my dad closed the door so I could get ready I knew that he was. I wore it to my first game, then hid it under my bed the rest of the season and never wore it again that year.

The cool thing about the new league was that I got to wear spikes and stirrups just like the big leaguers. Mr. Wheeler also bought black out for the all the guys to put under their eyes. Blackout is used to protect the player's eyes from the sun, it made us feel like the big league players. My uniform that year was red and white with solid blue pants. We had to have a sponsor to help pay for them and ours was "West Park Sports Bar". The number twelve was taken by an older player on the team so I had to settle for two.

Before opening night all the league teams got together for a parade down the streets of West Park. I will never forget riding in the back of one of the coaches' pickup trucks with four other players. We all were screaming at the top of our lungs. It was a blast, one of the things that made me love playing the game so much. Having happy times such as these can only increase the enjoyment for any youngster getting involved in Little League for the first time.

The games took place at Terminal Field in Cleveland. The park consisted of four diamonds. One even had a homerun fence which I thought was really neat. It also had a snack stand set up for the parents and friends watching the games. It was a fun atmosphere for everyone involved. The umpires were all adults and we even had real scorekeepers. The park was set up behind a Holiday Inn Hotel on West 150th Street. People staying at the hotels would often come watch some of the games. I sometimes would pretend that famous people staying at the hotel may have been in the stands.

We played our first game against a team called John Hancock. They had to call the game in the fifth inning because we were ahead by twenty runs. The one thing I remember about that team is that they had sharp blue and white jerseys. Their jerseys looked great even if the team did not. I caught both balls hit to me in the field, however, I went zero for three at the plate. I was not too happy about that at all. Worse I struck out swinging all three times. I kept swinging hard and taking my eyes off of it. I remember crying on my way home because I was so upset with myself. My grandparents had come to the game as well, so I felt as though let everyone down.

Two really great traditions did come out of that game. The first was to make the sign of the cross before every at bat. That was something I saw a player do one time for the Indians and I decided to do so too. The other was one brought on by Mr. Wheeler in the pre-game huddle. In an effort to get the team pumped up for the game he gathered us all up and we would chant one time very loud "RAZOR SHARP, BAD TO THE BONE, LET'S GO TOUGH!" It worked really well and put us in the proper mindset for the game. The other teams would hear us chanting this and it gave us an early psychological edge.

Later that night sitting in our room with Don watching the NCAA championship game between Duke and UNLV, we sat and talked about my baseball game. Don was quick to boost my confidence and said not to worry about the strikeouts. He said that it was a part of the game and it happens to everyone. I still was not happy with what took place and I vowed to not to let it happen again.

It was a sixteen game season that year and we had our

share of blowout wins. It was a nine team league with everyone playing each other twice. I was able to improve drastically by improving my batting average and cutting down on my strikeouts. We jumped out to a seven win and zero loss record. We were flying high when it came time to play our rivals Brooks and Bebee. They were the only other team in the league that was unbeaten. They wore black and red jerseys and had some huge players on their team. They consisted mainly of eight year old players, but like us they were very good. During that first game against them it was the first time I saw Mr. Wheeler lose his cool and he was ejected in the fifth inning for arguing with an umpire. We went on to get blown out 18-9.

Because it was my first loss as a player, on the way home I cried once again. I hated losing and getting blown out was even worse. I was in a bad mood the rest of the night. Mr. Wheeler called everyone that night to inform us we would be having practice the next day. It was unusual because in little league a team doesn't have many practices during the season.

Up until that point I had been doing a decent job in the outfield. Mr. Wheeler said that he saw something in me and wanted me to play in the infield. However, it was not at second base or third. I was much too short to play first base and our shortstop Kevin Fix was the best player on the team. Instead I was put behind the plate to handle the pitchers. He said he wanted me there because I had a strong arm and was one of our outspoken leaders on the team verbally so I'd be good at helping the pitchers. I was a little standoffish at the change but took to it quickly when he told me I could talk to the batters. That was a lot of fun, something that I could do quite well. I was not much of a trash talker but I knew how to get in the hitters' heads when needed.

We kept on rolling by winning our next seven games setting up a showdown with the unbeaten Brooks and Bebee. We had a great record sitting at fourteen wins with just one loss, but we knew that we had to beat them to feel good about the season. The game went on much the way the first meeting did with another blowout loss complete with Mr. Wheeler being ejected from the game for arguing with the umpires. It was discouraging but this time I did not cry on the way home because I was too angry to do so.

The regular season had ended and the playoffs were coming up. I had adjusted well to my new position while my hitting had dramatically improved. My brother Don had kept track of my stats and I batted over 300. I was happy with that as well as happy that we were listed as the two seed for the tournament. If we won our first two games we got a rematch with our hated rivals.

We beat Clock and Tickers in the first round of the playoffs handily. I had three hits in the game and even threw out a batter trying to steal second base. The entire team looked ready to do well. We knew that playoff games were what we worked hard for all season. Mr. Wheeler had us ready to compete and win.

The semi-final match up was against a team called Schwab Bike Shop. It was a decent team that gave us two very good battles in the regular season. They were known for their pitching and sharp defense. We were confident that we could beat them but also made sure not to take them lightly.

The day of the game I was very sick spending my time in bed resting. I had stomach flu and was drained of energy. I laid in bed all day trying to sweat out the sickness. I felt terrible and did not want to move let alone play. I refused to get ready and begged my parents to let me stay home. This was so out of character for me to act this way but I was truly ill. My parents did something that night that I will never forget, I still thank them for it to this very day. They made me go to the game and play. They said that I owed it to my teammates to be there and that they did not raise me to give up and quit. They were right to do so. I don't believe in missing games for any reason. If someone is in a wedding or someone close to them dies and they have to be at the funeral are the only two excuses I can tolerate. In the eight seasons that I played little league I never missed a game. In fact, during the two years I played for Mr. Wheeler no member of our team ever missed a game. If I was severely ill I know my parents would have taken me to the hospital. This was a case of summer heat with some bad food in my system.

My parents filled me with medicine and Gatorade to do whatever they could to ensure I was in playing shape. They said that once I got to the field and if I was still sick, I wouldn't have to play but that the excitement of the night would make me feel better. Sure enough they were right as always. About two minutes after arriving I was ready to play.

It was a tight game for a while but we eventually got up by eight runs going into the last inning. In the top of the last inning

Mr. Wheeler took me out of the line up as catcher and put me back into the game at second base. He took out his own son so I could finally play the one position I had coveted all season long. I think he felt comfortable enough with an eight run lead to chance it. Still, he did not have to do it but he did anyway. It shows what kind of man he was.

With two outs and no one on base and still up by eight runs the game was just about over. The player on the other side swung at the first pitch and smashed a grounder right to me. I picked it up and threw him out at first base. The game was over and we were going to the championship. Our whole team went wild with Don running onto the field from the stands as I jumped into his arms. It truly is one of the fondest memories of my life and something money could never buy. Thank God my parents let me play in that game or I would have never had it.

The other tradition we had that season was that after every win the team would take one lap around the bases. I'm not sure how it started or why teams did it. I don't honestly see the point to it at all, but my teammates loved it so it was fine with me. By the time we finished running the bases that night I was exhausted. I remember my dad offering to buy us ice cream but I said no. I just wanted to go home and crawl back into bed at that point. It is funny how the body works. I felt no pain during the game at all, but the second it was over I was ready to collapse. I think the adrenaline has a lot to do with it.

There was a major upset in the other half of the bracket. Brooks and BeBee had been knocked off in the semifinals against Weinbrewer Motors. That meant we would not be getting our rematch but instead playing a team that we narrowly beat twice that season. They wore orange and black jerseys that looked menacing. Our team was pumped up and ready to play them for the gold trophy. We had worked all year to play in this game and nothing would stand in our way of victory.

Despite the fact that the team consisted solely of nine year olds, we still had beaten them twice that year and felt good about our chances. In the second inning I was back behind the plate and tried to do whatever I could to get in the heads of the other players when the umpire stopped the game to shout at me. He stated that if I opened up my mouth one more time he would kick me out. Mr. Wheeler stuck up for me but there was not much he could do at that point.

17

It was a bad game and little went right that night. We ended up losing ten to two in what some felt was a minor upset. It was a bitter end to what was an otherwise great summer of baseball. I didn't cry on the way home that night but I wasn't thrilled either. The only thing that made me able to stomach the loss was the silver medal we won for taking second. Knowing that our team did consist of mostly eight year olds and that we would be back the next year helped improve my mood as well.

Sometimes the best motivation for winning is experiencing the agony of losing. We hated losing in the championship game to a team we felt we were better than. If we had rolled over them with an easy win than we may have not came back with the same fire the next season to win. By losing to them proved that we still had parts of our game to work on, it also kept the fire burning inside of us to focus harder. We were determined to make next year better and not stop working hard until we hoisted up the championship!

I went to bed every night for the next several weeks thinking about ways to improve my game. I wanted to make sure that by the time practices began again I would be ready to perform at my best. I knew that coming back for a second year I would be looked at as one of the leaders. I was determined to do everything I could to not only be a better player but also a better teammate.

Something happened later that August that would jeopardize my ever playing for Mr. Wheeler again. It was such a major change that all my dreams of coming back and winning a championship seemed to vanish. I came home from playing at the park one day to see a sign in our front yard that said, "sold."

Chapter 3
Bad to the Bone

"Every strike brings me closer to the next homerun"
~ Babe Ruth

It is been said that you must learn to lose before you can win. To truly know the thrill of victory that one must first encounter defeat. No one likes to lose, but it is how they handle it that can make someone a champion or a pretender. It has also been said that it doesn't matter how many times you get knocked down, what does matter is how many times you get up. That summer of 1990 had plenty of wins for our baseball team but it was the three losses that would mold the team of 1991.

That night we returned home to our cozy house on the corner of Midvale. As I sat on my bed and shined my silver medal, I couldn't help but think about the post-game talk given by Mr. Wheeler. He let the team know that no matter how bad it seemed to lose the big one, we would be back. He said that our team had more heart than any other in the league. He commented that next year we would work every bit as hard and take the next step. He told us to be proud of ourselves for what we had done that season but not to forget that the main goal was to be the best. It was a solid message, and one that I took strongly to heart. I was going to have something to look forward to all fall and winter.

A few weeks after the championship game my parents finally sold their house. It was their dream to move out of Cleveland into a safer, nicer area. It also looked like it would be a good ten years or so before the airport bought it. The move would bring big changes for us as we were set to move to North Olmsted. It was about fifteen minutes west of where we were living. We had to wait for the bank to close on the house so it wouldn't be until the last week of September that we actually moved into our new house.

Excitement about moving also caused me panic when it finally dawned on me that I couldn't play for Mr. Wheeler anymore. We would be moving outside the city limits which meant I couldn't join a Cleveland team. When my dad broke this news to me I was devastated. I was so upset that I begged and pleaded with him for days not to move. I asked if I could live with my grandparents so I might stay in Cleveland and play for Mr. Wheeler. I carried on for days and days until my parents finally gave in. They said that they would find some way for me to play for him one more year. My wanting to play for him was only part of it. The other was that I wanted to beat Brooks and Bebee, win a championship, and erase all the bitter memories of last season. I wasn't sure how my parents were going to make it work but I believed in them when they promised me they would find a way. It was just one more sign of how much they loved me and their willingness to make things right when they could.

We moved at the end of September 1991. It was a Sunday afternoon and our entire family chipped in to help out. Don was really upset about moving. I did not seem to care because I knew I still could play baseball that summer. I was excited to be living somewhere new and looked forward to meeting new people.

The biggest difference was that this house had a tiny backyard and that we lived on main road so playing in the front yard was out as well. It was a huge change from the nonstop back yard ball we had grown accustomed to. Two things offered a saving grace. First we had a park ten houses down the road with two baseball diamonds. The park was named Little Clague Park. Anytime we wanted to play, we just had to walk a short distance and we would be there. The down side to that is that unlike Cleveland, when boys were outside all day during the warm months, the boys in North Olmsted were inside playing with their fancy toys and video games. I felt a huge culture shock at first.

The other major difference between the two homes was that the new one had a basement. My dad spent weeks down there before we moved in, furnishing it and making it one of the finest rooms in the house. It had everything including a bumper pool table, a television set and a couch. Most important it had a green shag rug in the middle of the couches that I used to play with my action figures. I spent all my time in that basement; it quickly became my favorite place to be. I spent so much time there that my Uncle Pete nicknamed me "Cellar Rat."

The biggest change was the new school that I was attending called Maple School Elementary. It was one of six schools for the first grade through the fifth. It even had a mustang as its mascot. This was ironic because my skinny and lanky legs and ability to run fast, prompted my Uncle Pete to also give me the nickname of "The Colt".

During my first couple of months there I was picked on a lot. To say a lot is putting it mildly because I was picked on almost every single day that entire year. I never breathed a word of this to my parents because I did not want them to reconsider moving and feel bad about it. The simple fact was that I was the new boy. It did not help that I was short and skinny. It really did not help that one of my ears was bigger than the other; students were constantly calling me "Dumbo" and picking on me.

About half way through the school year when the weather turned cold and we started playing football at recess, I met my first real friend. His name was Dave Murphy, we would become best friends. He said that we they were getting a team together to play against some of the other third graders that formed a team at recess. It was the first time during the entire school year that I felt accepted by someone. We went on to play football at recess every day for the rest of the school year. Through Dave I was able to make some more friends and things got much better as the year went on.

My parents signed me up for year two of Tri- League Four Corners Baseball in West Park Cleveland. Like last year I would be playing under the direction of head coach Bill Wheeler. My dad pulled it off somehow and in some way he has managed to never tell me exactly how I got to play for him that second summer. My guess is that they used our old address, but whatever the case was it didn't matter to me because I got to play for the coach and team I wanted. Dad took me again to St. Vincent de Paul's church basement for sign ups and Mr. Wheeler was happy to see me. He said that I was a "warrior" and that he wanted me back on a team full of "warriors." He used this term because the high school that he and my dad attended had the symbol of a warrior.

Two days before practice began my mom took me to the eye doctor to get glasses for the first time in my life. I was so worried about this because I didn't want the other players on my team to see me with glasses. I thought they would make me look like a wimp. My mom promised me they would not and that I could pick out my own frames. She also said that if I did this she would take me to the toy store where I could pick out one or two starting line up's.

My mom was great about that kind of thing. Mom always made me feel like I was handsome even though I knew that I wasn't. She was a great person in her own right. She overcame epilepsy and had two kids when the doctors never thought she could. She went on to hold down a job and obtain a driver's license. She is a true inspiration.

Mr. Wheeler started off our first practice with these words: "Gentleman, we have one mission and one goal this year, win the whole thing and beat Brooks and Bebee along the way. Is that understood?" It was very much understood and the reason I came back for that second summer of 1991. Our whole team felt the same way. Our goal was to win that championship that had eluded us a year ago. We were determined and knew that nothing else would be tolerated or accepted. I desired something that I had never felt in my heart until then. The fact that every boy on the team shared the same feeling just made us a stronger ball club. I believe that a person should have to want something and want to be the best at everything you do. Mr. Wheeler had put the will to win in us that first season as well as the love of the game. He made us believe that we could be good enough to win it all and that should be our only purpose that season. For the first time in my life I felt pressure, but I liked it.

It takes skill to be good at whatever you do, but it also takes heart and desire. You must have those two things as well or you will never truly achieve anything. God blesses you with talent, but you need the desire and will to win to ever truly fulfill your talent. I feel that whatever I may have lacked in talent in my playing days I made up in heart and hustle.

Mr. Wheeler always had a look about him that was uncanny. He was a bigger man but not overly towering by any means. He just had a presence about him that made people pay attention when he talked.

The team was still in the eight and nine year old league with all of our eight year olds were returning from last season. We were all nine years old now and felt as though we walked on water among the younger kids we had picked up. We also had a good lineup coming back lead by our phenomenal shortstop Kevin Fix.

As we practiced for the beginning of the regular season, Mr. Wheeler said he had another position for me that I was going to like even better than playing catcher. He thought I did a great job in the infield the few times I had gotten a chance to play there last season. He wanted me to try playing pitcher's mound. I would stand next to the other team's coach as he threw the ball to the opposing players to hit. If the ball came back to me I would have to field it and throw him out at the proper base. I was ecstatic to have a new position in the infield. It was a great feeling to know he had the confidence to put me at such an important position along with his all-stars in the infield. We stayed after practice the last couple weeks before opening day to get me ready. Not only did he hit me countless ground balls but he also grilled me mentally as well on game situations that might came up.

I loved my new position making it easier to become really good at. In all my years of playing sports, no matter what team or position, I can honestly say I was better at that position than any other I ever played. After a school year of getting made fun of and teased, it was nice to have something that spring to feel good about. When I became the pitcher's mound player I felt as if I had achieved something. When I became very good at that new position I felt as though my teammates were proud of me as well. It erased the bitter memories of the boys back in North Olmsted because I was accepted by the kids who truly mattered.

I was getting dressed for game one, season two when I decided that no matter how uncomfortable it might be that I should wear my cup. I had an infield position and the probability of a ball hitting me in the groin was much higher. This was much unlike the previous season when I went out of my way to hide the protector. That year we had yellow jerseys with blue trim, we also wore blue pants. I decided to wear number nine that year. My thinking was that I was nine years old so I should wear the number nine.

The uniforms were paid for by our team sponsor that year American Funland. The place itself was filled with batting and fielding cages. It also had an ice cream stand and go karts.

That year the league had grown to sixteen teams. Yet the season would only feature twenty games so we would not have to play each team twice but only some teams twice. It happened to be that Brooks and Bebee was one of the teams we would be playing twice. That gave us two chances to knock them off.

Our first game that year was against the team that had taken our sponsor from the previous season. They wore powder blue jerseys with black trim and had a female coach that Mr. Wheeler referred to as "Big Red".

Big Red hated Mr. Wheeler for some reason, much like most of the other coaches did. They call that the price of winning. It is much the same as to why the New York Yankees' are hated as much as they are. When a team wins often the opposing teams tend to build anger towards them.

Big red was a tall lanky woman, the only female coach in the whole league. She had long red curly hair and was always chomping on a red pen. She also would shave off her eyebrows and paint them back in red ink. She would jabber during the whole game and try to rattle the cage of Mr. Wheeler and it worked like a charm. At times it was funny to actually see him get rattled. As intimidating as he was, this did not happen often. We won that game by a large margin. All the trash talking did not seem to matter at all in the end.

We did not run the bases after that win, nor did we run the bases after a single win that entire regular season. That season had one focus and we all knew what that was. It is not to say that we did not have fun that year because we most certainly did. We took things a slight bit more serious. We didn't hope to win games that season we expected to win games that season. There is a big difference between the two. There is a fine line between being confident and being cocky. We walked that line but made sure to never cross it. Mr. Wheeler would not let us cross it. He made sure we stayed humble in victory after victory.

We had gotten off to a quick twelve and zero start when we met our hated rivals Brooks and Bebee. Not surprisingly they were also twelve and zero. The entire league turned out to watch the game that day. The feeling of respect you get when boys your own age turn out to see you play is unreal. It makes you feel truly special and makes the outcome seem much more important. The stands were packed and other people were standing all the way past the outfield fences. There was not an open seat in the house. The night had that big game feel atmosphere surrounding it. I remember being nervous for the first time ever before a big game. Don could not make it because he had a game himself that night at another park, so that was on my mind as well.

The game itself turned out to be pretty good and I made a few nice plays in the field. We could never seem to get out on top and trailed the whole game. Late in the game Mr. Wheeler got thrown out for arguing calls, the third time in two seasons that this had happened. All three times we had played them he had got thrown out of the game. We ended up losing by a few runs.

The schedule was odd that year because we played them again the next week so we knew it wouldn't be long before we had another chance at taking them on. Our next game was played against an all green and yellow team called Holiday Inn. They were a decent team but I remember this game clearly because it became the best game I ever played in my entire life in any sport. I went three for three at the plate and made several great stops in the field. My first time up to bat I hit my only home run that year and the last I would ever hit, bringing my career total to a stellar two.

It was a great way to get rid of the bad memories of the recent loss to Brooks and Bebee while getting our momentum back for the rematch. I was so proud of how well I did in that game but knew that tougher games would be coming soon. With our rivals next on the schedule it didn't give us much time to relax.

It had been one week since we played them last and not much had changed since then. They were still undefeated and we had just that one loss to them. The fans packed the stands yet again for this showdown. It would be high drama at Terminal Field that evening. The stage was set and the showdown was near. It was time to grab a seat and cold drink because the best two teams in the league were about to show why they were the envy of the league. It was a rivalry steeped in hatred and venom for one another. It seemed that when the two teams met on that field the world came to a stop.

The game proved to be another close one with some tight action on the field. One of my jobs as pitcher was to cover home plate in case there was a play there. Our new catcher Mark Antonelli was not very good and Mr. Wheeler wanted me to cover the plate on anything close. Sure enough there was a play late in the game at the plate. Kevin Fix was the cutoff man and turned around and launched the ball to the plate. I went to tag the runner but he was able to slide right under my tag. It was my own fault because I tagged him much too high. I felt bad about it and was not happy with missing the tag. We caved in under the pressure that night. We played flat and didn't have the same fire we usually did. It was as though we were playing not to lose instead of playing to win. It may sound like the same thing but it's not. When a team plays to win they are more aggressive and take chances. When they play not to lose they are playing nervous and without the confidence needed to get the mental edge.

On the way home it was just my dad and me in the car because. As we sat there I expressed to my dad the anxiety I had about missing that tag at the plate. He said not to worry about it and that in baseball you almost always get a second chance. I wouldn't have to wait long to realize his words coming true.

We wrapped up the regular season with an impressive eighteen and two record. Both losses were to those daunting young men in the red and black jerseys. For some reason lacking any common sense at all, the league proceeded to put us on the same side of the bracket as Brooks and BeBee. This meant if we got past our first round opponents that we would have to face them in the second round. The tournament consisted of sixteen teams with us being the number two seed. It made no sense at all for the second seed to possibly have to play the first seed in the second round. I remember getting home from practice and telling Don about it, he was as angry and confused by it as I was. Meanwhile my dad just sat back with a huge grin on his face and said "This just means that you guys get to beat them a little earlier than expected."

The first round game was against W.S.P.B. and Big Red herself. A game that was supposed to be a blowout turned out to be one of the most unforgettable games I ever played or coached in. Our team was so consumed by the fact that we would be facing Brooks and Bebee in the next round that we looked right past her "Redness". These were only seven inning games and in the sixth we were losing one to nothing. As the top of the seventh inning was approaching with us set to get our last chance at bat against a team we beat twice that year by twenty plus runs Mr. Wheeler called us in a huddle outside the dugout. He told thus that he quit, that he couldn't take how poorly we were playing and that maybe we would play better if he wasn't around as coach. He then lit up a cigarette and pulled up a lawn chair and parked himself in it. As we stood there in shock as to what just occurred, we suddenly got angry ourselves. We proceeded to score twenty runs in the top of the seventh inning and go wild doing it. Mr. Wheeler in his own crazy way had done it. He had motivated us by angering us. It worked like a charm. By the time we got up by about fifteen runs he came strolling in the dugout with a big grin on his face as to say he had fooled us and he did. After the win our next game would be against our rivals.

Sometimes for a game hype is not even needed. It is not often you get three chances for redemption in a single season but on this night we would. It was time to get the monkey off our back. It was time to put Brooks and Bebee in its place once and for all. It was time we claimed our rightful place on top of the little league world. Sports need great rivalries and this was certainly one of them. By this point it was starting to take on that David and Goliath feel and we were certainly about ready to sling our biggest rock.

But the game provided no drama at all, we proceeded to stomp on them all game long and win nineteen to four. The game was called in the fifth inning due to the "mercy rule." We had out played them all game. We fielded any ball they hit and we hit any ball thrown to us at the plate. We played with confidence and no fear. Here was this team that we respected but wanted to beat so badly we could taste it. After the game I remember there was very little celebration at all. As great as it was to finally beat them, it was more important to us to win the whole thing. After the game in his post-game speech Mr. Wheeler reminded us that this was just step one and that step two would be hoisting the championship trophy.

Our record against them wound up being one win and four losses but that one win ended up being the only thing that mattered in the end. It just goes to show that everyone is beatable and to never give up on yourself or your teammates.

The semifinals were against the Holiday Inn team which had a fairly good record and produced a decent challenge to us. They played hard and took the early lead, although we were able to catch up on get on top. Late in the game, in the bottom of the sixth inning, with us up by three runs and them at the plate an interesting play occurred. A player on their team bunted the ball and I fielded it cleanly and spun around to throw it to second base where Kevin Wheeler was covering. I made a good throw right on the money to get him out. When Kevin went to apply the tag to the runner sliding into second base, the boy kicked his cleat right in the nose of Kevin busting him wide open and Kevin dropped the ball. You cannot do that at any level anywhere. You cannot kick the second baseman in the face on purpose when you slide so that he drops the ball. Kevin didn't even have to tag the runner in the first place because it was a force out. He bent down to tag the runner out of habit. It still does not justify the other boy to kick him in the face.

Mr. Wheeler exploded out of the dugout at full speed for his son who was lying on the ground bloody. Mr. Wheeler picked up Kevin and took him to Fairview hospital to get stitched up.

We went on to win the game and make it to the championship. It was a bittersweet win because we were worried about Kevin.

We had one day off before we did battle in the championship game. I woke up early that morning and quickly went outside to throw a tennis ball off my garage. I did this all day long, taking short breaks to eat and rest a little. I would throw the tennis ball off the garage as hard as I could and field it after one bounce. It was both good practice and fun. It also helped calm some of the nerves heading into the next nights championship game.

It was our second championship game in two years and we were ready. On August 2, 1991 the American Funland squad was set to do battle with Roman Fountain Pizza for the league championship in front of some two hundred people. People were hanging from the rafters to take in the scene. Every team in the league along with parents and coaches turned out hoping to see us get beaten.

Roman Fountain Pizza was one of the worst teams in the league and truly had a great underdog run in the tournament to make it as far as they did. We were the solid favorites going into the game. Sometimes this is harder than being the underdog because the pressure you have on your shoulders to win is doubled. When no one expects you to win, it easier to play loose because you have nothing to lose. It also puts a chip on the shoulder of the underdog team as they can feel disrespected, which will motivate them to prove everyone wrong.

In the pre-game huddle, Mr. Wheeler gave us a simple speech saying that this was what we worked for all year long. He reminded us of that first practice game in spring and how far we have come. It was a speech that said just enough and didn't over hype the game at all. Sometimes a team can get too pumped up for a game, which can backfire.

Kevin Wheeler, was back all patched up and playing at second base, allowing us to have our whole line up intact and prepared to win. To the surprise of many it turned out to a tight game early on and stayed that way. I had four plate appearances that game and hit fifth in our lineup which was the highest I had hit all season long. I remember Don being very proud of me for my spot in the batting order. I managed to get four singles with my plate appearances and was able to score on all four trips. I felt good about my appearances' at the plate but it was my play in the field that I remember the most.

In the fifth inning, clinging to a one run lead, we had two outs and they had a runner on second base. The hitter drove the ball into shallow center field. Our center fielder quickly grabbed it after once bounce and threw it to Kevin Fix. Kevin turned around and launched one to the plate where I was waiting with baited breath. A player about twice my size was steamrolling to the plate and we would have him out by a mile. The whole time in my head I was thinking tag low, just tag low. The only problem was he was not about to slide. So I braced myself for the upcoming collision. I was so pumped and ready for him to slam in to me that by the time he did it felt like a bag of feathers and I tagged him out. The crowd went wild as I looked up at my dad in the stands. Dad just looked at me and had a huge smile on his face. His words came true, and I took advantage of my second chance to tag a runner out at the plate.

The play of the night came at the end in the hands of our best player. With one out in the top of the last inning and one base runner on second base, we were clinging to a three run lead. The hitter drilled a line drive that Kevin Fix dove for and caught. The runner at second base edged too far off the bag so that Fix tagged him to turn the unassisted double play to win the game. It was one last great play made by a great player to end a season that could only end one way.

Our team stormed onto the field and the party was on. We piled on top of each other in the middle of the diamond. When I look back on it years later my heart still races when I think about how great that moment felt. It was one of the happiest days of my entire life.

After the game we each received a gold medal. It was a nice upgrade from the silver one from the year before. My dad bought a frame and put both of them in it. I knew in my heart that it would be my last game as a player for Mr. Wheeler, yet I was fine with that this time. It is how I wanted my last memory to be. I couldn't think of a better way to end that chapter of my life.

The next season would bring on a new team with new challenges, but until then my teammates and I felt like kings. It just goes to show that when you really want something bad enough, when you work hard enough for something you can achieve it. Never stop believing in yourself and you can do anything you set your heart and mind to. These are all popular sayings but until you live your life that way you never truly realize just how true they are. I had won my first championship which led for the quest to win more to begin.

Chapter 4
Glory Days

"Perfection is not attainable, but if we chase perfection we can catch excellence."

~ Vince Lombardi

It's amazing how a song can make you think of something or someone after hearing the first two notes. The song "Glory Days" by Bruce Springstein is my favorite song because it makes me think of playing little league baseball growing up. It was playing on the radio on the way home from the championship game. The great thing about fond memories is that they never leave despite how many bad times a person may face. While driving home that day little did I know how many more glory days would lie ahead of me.

With a great summer behind me it was time for me to start another school year in a very snooty community. I imagined that this year would be different, that I would not let the words of others affect me so much. The first major change this school year was that I already had friends. That made a nice change of pace and continued throughout the school year.

Dave and I had plenty of time to kill during the winter while we waited for the snow to melt and the green grass to sprout. I could not wait to hear the umpire yell, "play ball" and the crack of the bat one more time. In North Olmsted teams are not allowed field time to practice until April 15.

Baseball signups were held at North Olmsted High School in mid-January. My Dad and I figured that it would only be about a month before we got the call for my first practice. We did not realize the rule of April 15.

As we walked out of the school that day my Dad also told me that we would have a new person living at our house. Excited at the thought of possibly having a baby brother, I learned something even better. We would not be having a baby but an Uncle Peter instead.

Uncle Peter DeLuca was a three sport all Ohio letterman in high school. He was the starting shortstop in baseball for John Marshall High School, as well as its starting quarterback. Standing a mere

31

five feet six inches, he had a rocket for an arm. He was also the state runner up for the 1973 State Championships of wrestling. The man who beat him, Mike Chin, later went on to win a medal in the 1976 Olympics. Peter not only had incredible talent on the sports field but also had incredible talent with his artwork. He could draw and paint every bit as good as he played sports. However, despite his many talents he had fallen on tough times. Because of this he needed a place to stay for a while and my dad as always was gracious enough to let him live with us.

Peter had a brilliant mind when it came to baseball. His moving in with us was one of the best things that could have happened to me. We would sit up for hours talking about baseball and on how I could get better at it. He knew much about hitting and fielding. He showed me exactly how to stand at the plate and turn into the swing. He got a round weight and tied it to a short rope. He showed me how pulling up on the rope with my hands helped to build wrist strength. The most important lesson he taught me was to always stay on the balls of my feet rocking back and forth in the infield. He said that a player needed to be ready to spring anyway instantly and to never ever be flat footed. He was a wealth of knowledge when it came to baseball. For the rest of my playing days I could always hear Pete's voice before every single pitch in the field "Balls of your feet, Balls of your feet, Vincent."

As March rolled in and there was still no call for baseball practice to begin, Pete and I took matters into our own hands and went to the park as often as we could. The coaching sessions helped every aspect of my game. Pete never had a child of any kind, but I could tell from my time around him that he would have been an amazing father. He even went as far as to buy me a new bat. He was constantly doing nice things for Don and me.

When Peter and I were not talking about baseball or playing it, we were watching or talking about "Rocky." I think we watched that movie at least fifty times in the six months he lived with us. It got to the point that we watched it so much that we would begin to quote things from the movie at all times to each other.

He was such a great human being that words cannot even do justice what he meant to my family. Pete was the kind of person who would give the shirt off his back to someone if they were cold. Working for a pizza company while living with us, he was constantly bringing home pizza for Don and me.

While Uncle Pete mania was going on, baseball practice still hadn't begun as we entered April. With Don no longer playing, I was left to wonder why no coach had called to inform me that I was on a team. It didn't make any sense because I was so used to practicing much sooner.

It wasn't until mid-April when the phone call came informing me that I had been picked by Mr. Kubb to play for his team that summer. Not knowing a thing about the man or his team, I went to school that next day and asked Dave if he knew him. Dave proceeded to tell me that Mr. Kubb routinely coached the best team in the league every single season and that I was lucky that he picked me.

I quickly learned after the first practice how right Dave was about Kubb's team. The players had been together for three seasons and had not yet lost a single game. The roster was virtually set in stone, which is why they didn't have many practices. The only reason I was picked for the team is because a player moved away and they needed a new player. I had played on championship caliber baseball teams my whole life so this would be no great change of pace for me. I was eager to show my teammates what I was capable of doing.

The practices Mr. Kubb ran were fun but also hard and challenging. He coached in a different style Mr. Wheeler did but he still got his point across. He had a loud deep voice that you could hear from the outfield if he was talking in the dugout. He was a classy man who coached a classy team. While Mr. Wheeler had that lovable subtle craziness about him that kept you on your toes and always pumped up, Mr. Kubb always remained calm. Despite the fact that he had a loud voice, he never raised it or his temper. They were two completely different men and two different coaches, but they shared the same common interest. That common interest was winning!

I didn't know a single one of my teammates because almost all of them went to a different elementary school across town. North Olmsted had five of them and this one was located on the better side of town near the rich housing development called Brenton Ridge. I felt like an outsider all over again, however, my teammates were kind to me and that feeling quickly disappeared.

The major difference between the two coaches was that Mr. Wheeler focused on having fun and learning the fundamentals along the way, while Mr. Kubb was more concerned about running plays and going through scenarios. This was overhand fast pitch so players were allowed to steal bases. One play involved a situation when the other team had players on first and third base and they tried to pull a double steal. The conventional thinking was to hold onto the ball and let the player steal second base because we didn't want the player on third to take off for home plate. Mr. Kubb showed us how the catcher would get up as if he planned to throw to the shortstop covering second base but instead throw it to the actual second baseman running in on the play that would quickly catch it and throw the runner out at home plate. It worked more often than it didn't.

He also taught us the squeeze play in which the runner from third would steal home and the batter lays a bunt down the third or first base line. He did not originate any of these plays but he did teach them to us. At the end of practices there were no pep talks or anything like that. This did not mean he wasn't a great coach, it just meant he had a different style from what I was used to.

Mr. Kubb was a good coach because he knew so much about the game on many levels and kept us focused. He was a very smart man and a good teacher of the game. The biggest difference between his style and the Wheeler way of doing things is that Mr. Kubb focused more on being classy and winning with style.

The uniforms in this league looked different as well. They were not t-shirts but actual jersey tops, a nice silky feel to them and looked great. Our jerseys were dark navy blue with white lettering and white trim. They looked amazing with our red hats and red stirrups. I also wore batting gloves for the first time in my life. The uniforms were complete with black sun glare and white pants. This again showed how classy things in North Olmsted Hot Stove Baseball were taken. Mr. Kubb also supplied several donuts for the baseball bats. A donut is a small weight with a hole in the middle that is placed on the bat in the on deck circle. When it comes time to bat the player will take off the donut and the bat feels lighter allowing you to swing more quickly.

The team was sponsored by the gym that assistant coach Mr. Cook owned called Work "n" Out. It was fun sponsorship to have and made us sound tough. Mr. Cook's son Ryan served as our star pitcher. Though he was only 10 years old he could really throw the ball hard. He was clocked at 60mph one practice. We had other effective players as well. Though the team was stacked full of talent, I can honestly say that I held my own. The problem was that I was new and didn't really enjoy much playing time in the infield. This was a huge change from the two years I played for Mr. Wheeler every inning of every single game. I did not whine or complain about this but continued to show up for every practice and every game. Mr. Kubb was a very fair coach, he had the starters he was used to playing and it was the right baseball thing to do. He never let me sit the bench too long by making sure I always got in the game early and often.

As I look back on it, I do not blame Mr. Kubb one bit for not starting me. These players had been together for three seasons and were rolling along nicely. He knew what he had with them and knew he could trust them. I was an unknown and he didn't k now what I could do just yet. The thing about Mr. Kubb that was so great is that he never made me feel left out. He always showed confidence in me when I got my chance to play. He was like Mr. Wheeler in that he treated his all-stars the same way he treated his bench warmers. I was lucky enough to have such great baseball coaches back to back. I was blessed to be surrounded by such great influences during my early years.

I needed to stay humble, and keep my mouth shut and just play hard when I was given the chance to play in games. A little boy is easily discouraged, but it is how he handles such challenges and adversity that can shape him into the person he becomes. The bottom line that summer was that I was doing what I loved and that was playing baseball.

It was after Memorial Day when we finally played our first game of the season. The league consisted of eight teams with nine and ten year olds. Ours was a team filled with ten year olds. In this league after your team played a fourteen game schedule, the first place team was declared league champions.

The biggest difference between Tri Four Corners League and North Olmsted Hot Stove was the level of fun involved. This was evident from the very first pitch of the very first game. During those seasons played for Wheeler, our crowds were extremely loud, and cheering for every single pitch that was thrown. The players on the bench became involved just as much as the fans. There was cheering and yelling and screaming. The parents bought hot dogs and chips from the snack stand. Each team had chants before, during and after each game. It was such an enjoyable time for every single person involved.

In the North Olmsted league things were drastically different. Fans did not cheer at all for anything that happened. No matter what occurred on the field, there was no cheering of any kind. Instead, the parents would sit in the outfield bleachers and either read a book or listen to the radio softly. Instead of snacking on hot dogs and soda pop, they drank wine and ate cheese. It was as if my family had entered a strange new world.

It wasn't all bad because the park was located a short distance from our house and it provided a short walk home. I would usually get home from a game, doing whatever to kill time until Peter called from work to see if we had won or lost and how I played. Because he had to work almost every night, I didn't see much of him at night and he was unable to make it to most games.

The worst thing about the summer of 1992 was that it rained most of the time. As I mentioned before, we only had a 14 game season and they were constantly being rained out. We never played more than one game in a week so that we ended up only playing twelve. It was just a lackluster summer when it came to Little League.

When the regular season had ended, we were undefeated league champs for the nine and ten year old league. It provided no drama and was extremely different than the previous year's championship. It did mean that we qualified for the state tournament for all league championship teams in Ohio that summer. This was as a statewide tournament consisting of the best teams the state had to offer.

Mr. Kubb worked for the Ford automobile plant, was about to take his annual summer vacation out of town. The other assistant coach, Mr. Metz, would be going with him as well. That meant that our team was in need of two new coaches for this all important upcoming tournament. Mr. Cook, the acting manager, asked my Dad to help out. I think he asked my Dad because he had attended every game to watch me play. Despite the fact that I didn't play that much, he never complained and never missed a game.

The other new assistant coach was Mr. Pecatis, who had a son named Steve that played on the team. Steve and I had become great friends that summer. He was shorter then I and very chubby.

He looked like Curly from the Three Stooges. We made a funny pair because I was so skinny and we just looked goofy standing next to each other.

Steve and I spent a considerable amount of time together that summer when Dave wasn't around. He became my second true friend in North Olmsted. When he came over we played everything from action figures to back yard baseball. Steve was a very fun person to be around and we got along very well.

When both of our dads were asked to be assistant coaches, it was a big deal for us. After the practice when our dad's starting helping out it was the first time all summer that I felt excited about things on the field. They had put me at third base and pounded grounders at me for a couple hours straight. It was a great fun and provided me with much needed work.

The summer was looking up with my new position set for the biggest game of the year. I had a new friend in Steve and also a best friend in Dave. I couldn't help wonder how my old teammates were doing at that time. We didn't go and watch any of their games that summer because it would have been too hard for me to just watch without playing.

The morning of the state tournament game I woke up to find a note sitting on my dresser from Uncle Peter, who had already left for the day. It simply said "Dear Cellar Rat, Play hard and always hustle. I'm proud of you. Love, Uncle Pete." It was the best way to start one of the biggest days of my life.

The game was played in Spencer, Ohio, which was about a forty five minute drive from my house. On the drive out there, we car pooled with Steve and his dad. I remember being both nervous and excited for what was to come. This was my first chance all season to play in the infield so I wanted to be sure to make the most of it.

We arrived at the fields which were glorious looking. The park consisted of six fields. Each field had an underground dugout just like the big leaguers. They were made out of cement and looked amazing. They protected the players from seeing any fans and just being able to see the field in front of them so they can focus. There was also a home run fence on each field. They truly looked like the real thing seen at big league ball parks. The atmosphere was electric as the best sixty four teams from the state showed up to play. Unlike North Olmsted fans these people were loud and followed every single pitch that was thrown from start to finish. It reminded me of my Terminal Field days all over again.

We were the home team and took the field first. It didn't take me long to see action as the first two batters smashed ground balls right at me. I cleanly fielded them both and threw the runners out at first base. I felt as though I could have walked on water at that moment. It was a drastic difference from sitting on the bench watching other players do it. I would have more opportunities as the game went on to show my skill at the hot corner.

The game proved to be a tight one with both sides displaying great defense and pitching. I honestly felt that the other players on our team underestimated the team from Grafton, Ohio. In the bottom half of the last inning, we trailed 2-1. We had two outs with a boy named Nick Nevel on third base. Nick represented the tying run and we just needed to get him home to extend the game. James Steele dug in at the plate in an effort to score Nevel. James was our best hitter so the confidence that he would get the job done was high. I was on deck, batting fifth that day behind James, who was in the cleanup spot. He was an excellent hitter so I had no doubt that he would hit in Nevel and tie the game. I expected to bat next and drive him in to become the hero. That thought would come crashing down as the next pitch flew over the catchers head and Mr. Pecatis sent Nevel home to try and score. It was a close play, but the umpire called him out and the game was over.

It was an odd way to end the season because we were still league champs. On the car ride home I did not feel like a champion, but it did not matter. Once we got back home Steve and I proceeded to beat the tar out of each other with a Nerf ball and bat. Our dads had a cookout on the grill to take some of the sting out of losing. The great thing about being a child, is that it is easy to accept things if they don't go your way. I struggled with that many times; however, this time it didn't really trouble me much for some reason. Perhaps it was because I didn't care all that much about my teammates. While playing for Wheeler we developed respect for one another and cared about each other on the field. For one reason or another, this team just never had given me that same feeling. I still got to play my beloved game and became good friends with Steve in the process. Our team had achieved the league championship which was a big honor; however it wasn't nearly the same feeling as winning it in a tournament would have been.

A few weeks after the loss Mr. Kubb returned from his vacation and called a team picnic at Little Clague Park. He used the chance to hand out our league champion trophies. I got a kick out of that but I still thought the medals looked better. He told the team that he was proud of us and thanked everyone for a great season. He said something nice about each and every player then we all signed a team ball and gave it to him. It was pretty standard end of the season proceedings. He made a little speech about how great my parents were and how I had never missed a game or practice. It was kind of him to do that even though he didn't have to. He also said that starting next year the team would be broken. In the ten and eleven year old league a coach can only freeze seven of his players while the rest would enter a live draft. That comment made me nervous and I only hoped I would still end up on his team. Mr. Kubb was a great coach and I hoped to play for him again.

That season made me realize that sometimes we can gain victory from defeat and defeat from victory. In all the games that we won that season, I did not play that much, which made me feel defeated. In the one game that we lost I played the whole game and played well which made me feel like a winner. I was proud of myself because I had worked hard all year and never quit trying. It would have been easy to do so but I never did. It was a combination of good coaching and good parenting that never let me give up on myself.

After a long cold winter cooped up in the basement, we once again waited for the call to come in to let me know when baseball would begin. When the phone did ring my worst fears came true as the coach on the phone was not Mr. Kubb.

Chapter 5
The Other Side

**"Our greatest glory isn't in never failing, but rising every
time we fall."
~ Confucius**

In the spring of 1993 things were going very well. I made friends
at school and was completely at ease living in North Olmsted.

Fortunately I was making friends because my Uncle Pete
had moved away and I had lost my partner in crime. It was tough
not having him around, but it taught me that people I become close
with often end up leaving me. I prayed for him every day,
retaining all the knowledge he had taught me over the past few
months.

My grades in school that year improved as well. I made
the honor roll every quarter making Mom so proud of me. She
always took the time out of her schedule to help me with any
homework or project that I had. Towards the end of the school
year we took part in a huge fifth grade ceremony in which the
school board handed out academic awards. When I won a stack of
awards, my mom cried because she was so proud of me.

When the call finally came that baseball season was about to
begin, I was excited and ready to play. The only downside being
that it would not be for Mr. Kubb. I was picked by another coach
in that year's draft named Mr. Chambers. He was a first year coach
with zero experience. It was the recipe for a long summer.

By the spring of 1993 playing baseball was something that I
related with winning. I had played three seasons of little league
baseball, only having the bitter taste of defeat six times. It was
never an issue of if my team would win but always a question of
by how much. During all those victories that my teams had piled
up, I never considered how the other teams felt. In the summer of
1993 I was to become very familiar with the feeling.

Mr. Chambers was a pleasant man who seemed to be a
pretty decent person. He never yelled at the boys. The problem
was that he knew absolutely nothing about baseball, which became
crystal clear in the first two minutes of the initial practice. In his
first speech to the team, he compared playing baseball to playing

Nintendo. He said that if we knew how to play Nintendo we could then become great baseball players. Not only did my family not own a Nintendo but even if we did his point made little sense.

My other major concern was that he selected players based on who his son hung around with at school. His son Jim was in his first year of playing and his inexperience showed several times. Jim had a favorite baseball player named Carlos Baerga who played for the Cleveland Indians. Jim insisted on wearing number nine and playing second base because it was the same number as his hero. For every ten balls hit his way he was lucky to field two cleanly. I felt bad for him and tried to help him with advice on fielding, but my words would just fall on deaf ears every time I tried.

Our practices consisted only of batting practice thrown by pitchers who could barely get the ball across the plate. Mr. Chambers wanted his pitchers to toss batting practice because he thought it would be good practice for them. The problem was that our pitchers were horrible so it barely did any good. We needed steady pitching during batting practice to get our swings down for the season. By not having the routine of steady practice can only affect a player negatively.

Like any black cloud I was forced to find a silver lining in this one. The silver lining was that I was able to play every single inning of every single game. I mostly played third base and really enjoyed it. The biggest difference is that more balls got hit to me on that side and usually a lot harder. I found out quickly why third base is called the hot corner. Right handed batters are more likely to hit that way. I enjoyed playing third base and seldom made any errors. Even when I did it didn't matter much. Making errors seemed to be what our team concept was that season.

I asked Mr. Chambers at one practice if we were going to have any signs. A sign is a hand gesture given from one of the coaches that symbolizes what he wants the player to do. The most common signals are steal, bunt, hit and run, and take the pitch. With Mr. Kubb we used signals all the time and it helped us win. When I asked Mr. Chambers about this he had no idea and went back to his Nintendo analogy.

I felt I was walking into a bizarre world that summer after the well-oiled machine team I had just left. I was determined to make the best of it, taking the good with the bad. The good was I was in the starting lineup and batted second. I was playing third base and was sure to get plenty of action. I looked forward to both of those things despite the fact that the outcome of the season would more than likely be a poor one.

In a cruel stroke of irony our first game of the season was slated against Mr. Kubb's team. After one look at that schedule, I turned to my Dad and just laughed. In what can only be described as salt in the wound, Dave Murphy was picked to play for Mr. Kubb that season. My best friend was getting to play on the team I wanted to be on. For a very competitive child like I was, that was extremely difficult to deal with. Dave and I wanted to play on the same team so bad and this was just dirt in the face of that hope.

We received our jerseys right before the first game and had to change in our parent's cars. As I looked up I could see Kubb's team warming up with the jerseys they had most likely received weeks in advance. As usual they looked great. This further showed how unprepared Mr. Chambers was about everything.

Our jerseys, a solid brown color, looked awful. They had white lettering that said "Temp Team" on them. We were sponsored by a local temporary hiring agency. My Dad said that the jerseys were perfect because watching us play could make someone temporally insane!

I chose to wear number four because it was the fourth season I would be playing little league baseball. I had wanted to wear the number one jerscy but another player had taken it. I wore number one as a player on Mr. Kubb's team the past year so I had originally hoped to continue the trend.

In the entire season that I played for Mr. Kubb, I almost never got dirty playing. Most times my Mom didn't even have to wash my jersey because there was nothing on it. Playing for Mr. Chambers was a totally different story as I came home after every game caked in mud from diving for balls. To me a muddy uniform was the sign of a fun time. The positive thing I can say about that summer is I had fun in the infield. I hated the fact that we kept losing game after game but at least I was playing and getting dirty, which is what little league is all about.

The first game came and went and we were crushed by my ex-teammates. I only made two plate appearances as the game was stopped in the fifth inning due to the mercy rule. I struck out against Ryan Cook and drew a walk against Mike Kubb. I was angry we lost the game but not surprised. After the game Mr. Kubb came over to me and told me that I had played well. That compliment made my night.

Mr. Chambers gave no words of advice in his post-game speech. He simply stated that it would be a long season and maybe we would win the next game. He was just that kind of person. He never made us feel bad about losing and made it seem that it didn't even matter. This was a nice change of pace from the constant pressure of having to win, however; it didn't make losing any easier.

A good coach implies a mixture of both pressure and keeping their players loose. Mr. Chambers kept things much too lose and at times. Mr. Kubb did a good job of always making sure his team was focused on winning. What made Mr. Wheeler such a great coach was that he found the way to do both. Mr. Wheeler stressed that winning was important without taking the fun out of the game for us.

Steve, who was a year younger than I, was picked by a team in the younger league that summer. On nights when he did not have a game he would come to mine and I went to his on the nights I was free. His team was almost as bad as mine. I could tell that Steve was not too thrilled with losing but we made fun of each other all summer which helped ease some of the frustration.

Our second game of the season was played against a team full of twelve year olds coached by Mr. Kerr. They seemed liked giants and crushed us much like the Kubb team did in game one. Mr. Kerr's team went on to win the league championship that season. They were a solid group of players led by their excellent pitching.

There is one thing about the game against Mr.Kerr's team that I will never forget. I was playing third base and we were getting crushed. Between one inning a boy I went to school with named TJ, who just happened to be up at the park watching the game, took it upon himself to tell me that I sucked. It really made me angry and I wanted to punch him in the mouth. When we took the field, I ran to my position just hoping that a ball would be hit to me so I could make a play and shut him up. The first player walked, then stole second base and finally third base. The next pitch was lined directly at me. I swiped it in the air and calmly stepped on third base to turn the unassisted double play. I looked at TJ and mouthed the words "Take that!" It made losing the game a little easier to handle. We lost the game when it was stopped in the fourth inning due to mercy rule by a final score of 41-0.

In the middle of the season something happened that changed my life forever. Amazingly enough I owe it to Mr. Chambers. He called me on the phone one evening towards the end of the season. He talked about the team and asked how I thought we could improve. Here was this man in his forties asking an eleven year old for advice. It was one of my first real conversations on the phone with someone at length that I wasn't related to.

I ran by him many ideas on how the team could improve during the hour long conversation. We discussed baseball mostly, until he turned to the topic of everyday life. It seemed so odd to me to have a conversation with someone outside of my family or friends on the phone. But I was talking with Mr. Chambers as if we had known each other our whole lives. At the end of the conversation he said something that would change my live forever. He said "Vince, you will make an excellent coach if you choose to do so." He was the first person ever to recommend that I coach someday. I thought about his suggestion to eventual coaching but chose to keep it to myself. I was still at a very young age so I didn't want to focus on anything other than playing and improving.

He slowly tried to instill some of my ideas into the team, but the season was too far gone by that point, so we continued to lose game after game. Our team did improve but we still kept our perfect record intact until the final week of the season. With two games left we were well on our way to losing again when he put me in to pitch.

I had never pitched in my entire life or even showed any interest in it. We were down by ten runs so it was worth a shot. The umpire that evening was Mr. Kubb. Not only was he a coach but also the head of the umpiring staff. It was a sharp conflict of interest but Mr. Kubb was an honest man so not too many people questioned how he was able to do both. It was weird for me to be making my pitching debut with a man I admired behind the plate calling balls and strikes. It made me more nervous than it would normally have. Mr. Kubb had to umpire because one of the umpires called in sick and he couldn't find a replacement. This was not something he normally did.

I pitched well but not enough to make a difference. It was our fifteenth straight loss. We were staring at a winless season. Our last game was slated for Saturday night under the lights at North Olmsted Park where the high school team played. They let each team play one game a season there under the lights and this would be our chance to do so.

The Saturday of the game we had a family picnic to attend. It was held in the valley and a lot of fun as all my cousins were in attendance for it. Family parties consist of plenty of food and fun with this providing plenty of both.

My Uncle Jim took all the grandchildren onto this big field and proceeded to hit us fly balls. I went to grab a ball when it bounced short and sprang back up to hit me directly in the forehead. It hurt badly leaving a huge knot on my head. It looked as though my head was trying to hide a large softball in it.

My aunts all gathered around and put ice on my head to try to stop the swelling. I remember being more embarrassed than anything else. The other thought dancing in my head was that I had never missed a game and worried that my parents might not let me play. My Mom thought it was not a good idea for me to play and recommended to my Dad that I should sit this one out. My Dad agreed with her and I immediately began to panic. I talked them into letting me play if I promised to take it easy and just sit and relax for the rest of the picnic. Ten minutes later I was back in the field going after more fly balls until my Mom caught me and made me sit back down.

A couple hours later the picnic was over and we left for the game. I sat in the back seat holding an ice pack to my head the whole ride there. I was hoping that the swelling would go down in time so Mr. Chambers would not notice and let me play. He didn't notice and I was back in the starting lineup at third base.

I still had a ringing headache when I stepped into the batter's box for my first at bat of the game. I made sure not to tell anyone because I didn't want to come out of the game. The first pitch was a fastball that hit me directly in the head. I dropped to the ground like a bag of sand. But I got right up and ran down to first base. I refused show any discomfort because I did not want to leave the game but inside I was screaming in pain.

Needless to say we ended up losing the game and finished the season with a spotless 0-16 record. I had played for the best teams in the league and now also the worst. The summer was fun despite the losing because I played all year in the starting lineup and tried a few new positions. It still did not change the fact that I hated losing. Mr. Kubb's team failed to win the championship that year so I didn't miss out on a trophy if I had played for him. That was one small consolation.

It was an enjoyable summer with a few great memories along the way. I had learned the importance of trying hard at something even when the individuals around you are not. This was a valuable lesson that I have retained into adulthood. We didn't hold a lead for a single pitch that entire season. Still, I never quit playing hard and never quit hustling. It was a summer of both growth and pain.

The following fall I entered North Olmsted Junior High and went from a school with 500 students in the entire school to one with 500 students in my grade alone. I hadn't been picked on in years but entering sixth grade brought on new bullies who had not yet met me. It wasn't as bad as it was in third grade but there were boys that still gave me a hard time because of my height and ear size.

I hoped and prayed all school year long that the summer of 1994 would find me playing for a better team with a decent chance at winning. A month after baseball signups we received a call from my baseball coach. My prayers were answered because the man on the phone, talking with my Dad was Mr. Kubb. He managed to return me to his team for the summer of 1994. He also got to keep Dave on his team as well. Things were starting to look up. Little did I realize just how much the following summer would resemble a rollercoaster ride.

Chapter 6
Return to Dominance

**"It's not so important who starts the game but
who finishes it."**
~ John Wooden

No one should ever underestimate the importance of having self-confidence. Without confidence it is hard to achieve anything. When children are young it is vital that they have confidence in themselves and avoid negativity at all costs. During the season when I played for Mr. Chambers, I never lost confidence in my ability to play the game that I had grown to love. Despite losing, I did not let it detour my passion for the sport and my will to win. I had a great season of hitting and fielding despite the poor ball playing around me. Most importantly I never lost confidence in myself when it would have been so easy to do so.

In the game of baseball it is important to have confidence in your skills at all times. Once a player starts doubting himself he falls into a slump. When a hitter is standing at the plate he has to truly see visualize himself hitting the next pitch and where he wants the ball to land. If he stands there and can only think about striking out, he will almost always fail. In the field a player should want every ball hit towards them. The moment a player begins to doubt his ability in any way, they begin to fall apart. Most times it takes them a while to restore his confidence.

I speak of confidence because in sixth grade I slowly started to lose it. Perhaps the number of students in school helped make me feel like just another face. Perhaps the children were cruel and telling me I sucked because I just came off a team that hadn't won a single game. Whatever is was it took away something inside of me which I didn't recover for many years to come.

North Olmsted had five elementary schools that had about 100 students in each grade from first to fifth. On my first day of school in sixth grade, I felt that I had traveled far away to a strange distant world. We had lockers and more than two teachers. We even had gym class where we had to change clothes in front of other boys. These things were all new and scary for an eleven year old boy to handle.

But as the year went on I quickly adjusted and grew to like my new surroundings. I especially liked the eighth grade girls. I was on the edge of puberty so that seeing these new girls, who were much older than I with figures starting to develop, was all my hormones could handle.

I would be rejoining my teammates once again from Mr. Kubb's team and things would pick up. The only problem was that I quickly realized that those same boys I played with two summers earlier were mostly jerks. It didn't take long into my sixth grade year for me to figure out they were as stuck up as their parents had been on the sidelines. It was my first real experience of how people are not always the same when removed out of the original environment I met them in. At practice I fit in with them but at school they did not even know my name.

Children can be cruel even if their insults are completely harmless. I was lucky enough not to get picked on all that often once I got to junior high and high school. But that doesn't mean that I don't remember the times that I did. I don't hold grudges such that if I was to see some of those boys today, I would only say pleasant things to them. I don't condone what they did, but simply mean that no one truly knows why they acted the way they did. Who knows what they may have been facing at home either. It's all right to tease a little bit and I'm no stranger to joking around but not to the point that it hurts someone's feelings.

The one constant in my life that remained throughout all the changes was baseball. Once again I was counting on it to either make or break my summer. The fact that Mr. Chambers was no longer coaching allowed me to be available to be drafted by Mr. Kubb. I had mixed emotions because it meant I would have a great coach and play on a winning team. It also meant a strong chance of spending time on the bench. I was not okay with that this time and wanted to prove badly that I belonged.

I was coming off one of the best seasons of my life as far as production went. I had knocked the cover off the ball and fielded my position well. So I was determined to show the coaching staff and my teammates that I belonged and was not just enjoying the ride.

Dave Murphy was on the team this year, a huge positive. Having my best friend around helped in many ways. He was my only friend on the team and I was glad to have him there. His parents were great people as well and it meant that I would have more than just one set of parents cheering me on. Dave and I were competitive with each other and that helped both of our games. He was much better than me at basketball but I felt that I held the slight edge on him in baseball. Dave was a good ball player however. He was the fastest runner on our team and smart at the plate. Like me he was slated to spend some time on the bench due to the stacked roster.

Our first practice consisted of drill after drill and plenty of running the bases. Our focus that year seemed to be speed on the bases and quickness turning the double play. Mr. Kubb had the same school of thought as Mr. Wheeler when it came to scrimmaging there would be none! He felt that practice was meant for practice, and he was right. I would come home from those practices exhausted, but a better ballplayer. I did not get a single chance at playing infield, however.

Walking home from the first practice with Dad he asked how I thought the team looked this season. I told him we were as good as the first time I played for Mr. Kubb. I also said that the difference was that this team seemed to be cocky and too sure of themselves and that might lead to trouble. Dad told me to just keep working hard and not to let the cocky attitude of my teammates annoy me.

In the two years' I played for Mr. Wheeler he never let us become full of ourselves and believe our own hype. I cannot say one coach was better than the other because they were both excellent. I can say this, "The Wheeler team would have crushed the Kubb team if they ever met." The reason I see it going the Wheeler teams way, is heart and desire. The talent level on each team appeared almost the same. The coaching level on each team seemed the same. The biggest difference was that the Kubb roster had no heart while the Wheeler roster did. That is not Mr. Kubb's fault in any way. He coached with all his heart but for some reason the players just never seemed to get it. On Mr. Wheeler's team if we got down in a game, we almost always recovered to win. We were pumped up to play harder and want victory more. On the Kubb team, whenever we fell behind they just flat out quit trying.

As our practices continued, the big leagues were beginning their season and this year the Indians had made some moves and looked like they were about to turn the corner. It was fun to have a big league team to cheer for that actually won games. They opened up a new park called "Jacob's Field" after the owner Dick Jacobs. The first pitch in the new park was thrown out by President Bill Clinton. It was a good time to be a child in Cleveland.

At the final practice the coaches announced the starting lineup for the first game. I was to start in right field, the least coveted of all little league positions. At least it meant I was playing. I was going to approach it the way I did everything else, that was to play hard and just keep hustling.

I would have plenty of cheering fans for that season. Don had taken a job as Steve's official babysitter for the summer. This meant, Steve would attend all my games and sit with Don and my parents cheering loudly. That was a great support system to have. My best friend played on the team, with my other great friend sitting next to my brother and parents in the crowd. It always helps to look into the crowd and see familiar faces supporting you.

Our schedule lined up for our team to be tested early by the best teams in the league. This was a league with rosters of eleven and twelve year olds. Our team, which had all twelve year olds on it, was picked to win the championship by most people. Our first two games would be played against teams with all twelve year olds on them. The first game was scheduled against Mr. Bobko's team, the second against Mr. Lasko's team. The danger with playing good teams early in the year is that if your team is rusty and not yet ready to play, the chance of losing is much higher. You always want to play the best teams when you are in mid-season form. The positive side is Bobko's and Lasko's teams were likely to be rusty too.

The morning of our first game I was standing at the bus stop on the corner of my street waiting for the school bus. At the bus stop with me was a child named Bobby Simmons. Bobby, who was a year ahead of me in school, had not said a word to me all year. This was basic rule because the students in the higher grades never spoke to the younger students no matter who you were. It wasn't that he was mean to me in any way, it was just a standard junior high rule that we all followed.

As we stood there waiting for the bus, he leaned over to me and said "We are going to crush your team tonight!" Bobby was in the seventh grade but had a late summer birthday so he was only twelve years old, allowing him to still play in the younger league with fifth and sixth graders. I wasn't caught off guard by this because I was so used to playing for great teams that everyone else gunned for. It has been said before, "It can be lonely at the top." I took that as a compliment when all the other team's sole purpose is to try and beat my team. It simply meant that we had everyone's respect.

Major league ballparks across America that are struggling for attendance look forward to when the New York Yankee's are coming to town because they know that the fans will show up in droves. They are so hated but so respected for always being great that whenever they come to town fans want to see them beaten. When teams play eighty one home games a year with only three sellouts it usually meant that those three sellouts occur only when the Yankee's come to town. Fans hate the Yankee's, much like they hated the Wheeler and Kubb teams. There is nothing wrong with that because it motivates teams more than anything else. No team wants to be considered as an easy win, so when a team looks at their schedule and circles your game as the biggest of the year, only take that as a compliment.

On the bus ride to school that day Bobby actually sat next to me for the first time all year and we enjoyed a good conversation. I remember other boys looking at him as if he was crazy to be sitting with a sixth grader. I thought that it was really cool because I was getting noticed the by older students. Bobby was a nice boy when I got to talk to him, I noticed that even know he was trying to get in my head that he was just being friendly. The one thing he did make a point of telling me was that he was a pitcher and if he got the chance he would try to strike me out.

The entire day at school all I could think about was that game. I wanted 6:15 p.m. to arrive so badly that I could taste it. I kept telling myself not to strike out if I faced Bobby that night. During The ride home from school there was more trash talk. I tried to not let it get in my head any more than it already had.

That season our jerseys were dark navy blue, they almost looked black. They had white trim with white numbers on the back. The stirrups were navy blue while the hats were scarlet. My number was "1" that season because it was the smallest jersey and

I was the smallest boy on the team. It made sense for me to wear it and I didn't mind. I was also in a good mood because both my parents would be there as well Don with Steve. My grandparents also   attended the game as they usually did when we played bigger teams.

The game took place at Little Clague Park, ten houses down from my home. This was the same field where we held most of our practices and where half of our games would be played. I had played and practiced there so many times that I knew every inch of the field. The only downside to opening night was that I was scheduled to hit last in our lineup. I wasn't too thrilled but there was nothing I could do about it.

On the mound for Bobko's team was the coach's son Sam Bobko. I was surprised not to see Bobby on the bump to start the game, but I knew it would only be a matter of time before they put him in. A little league game is only scheduled for seven innings and a pitcher is allowed to pitch four innings in a game during the regular season. I knew it would only be a matter of time before I got to face Bobby, I relished having my chance to crush one off of him.

After two innings of play the game remained scoreless and our team was still looking to breakthrough with something to get us started. Sam Bobko, who was pitching well against us, seemed to have good command of the strike zone. When it came to the bottom of the third inning and the game still remained scoreless, I was surprised that Mr. Bobko replaced his son in favor of Bobby Seibel.

I was up first in the bottom of the third and looked to make a statement right away. I dug my cleats in the batter's box and coiled up ready to tear into the first good pitch I saw. As I stared down the pitcher as I normally did I could tell that Bobby knew I was ready for him. He looked at me with the same face he had that morning at the bus stop, as if to say "I'm going to strike you out!"

His first pitch was a fastball right down the center of the plate and I crushed it as hard as I could. The ball went flying ten feet over the left fielders head as I flew out of the batter's box as fast as my legs would take me. Rounding first and heading into second base I looked up at Mr. Cook who was screaming at me from third base to keep running. I made the turn at second base and was heading for third base as the ball was flying in from the outfield to try and get me out at. I heard everyone screaming "slide!" I slid feet first into third base, as the third baseman applied the tag. I was out by a mile, but the umpire yelled "safe!" The normally quiet stands came unglued and began to cheer loudly for me. I got up and dusted myself off as I tried to catch my breath. The third baseman was mumbling under his breath that it was a terrible call. I was agreeing with him silently in my mind but sure not about to say anything. My heart was beating so hard I felt like it was going to explode. I didn't have much time to recover because the very next pitch was wild so I stole home scoring our team's first run.

I jumped into our dugout and pounded my fists against the fence. I was so pumped up at that moment I felt like I could have lifted a car above my head. It started a huge rally and we ended up batting around in that inning. By my next time at bat in that same inning we were up 7-0 and Bobby was still pitching. I again swung at the first pitch and hammered a single into shallow center. He eventually got the next batter out and the inning was over, but we made a huge statement. We had woken up and were ready to play.

Two innings later with our team ahead 9-4, I singled off Bobby Simmons again. I was a quick three for three against a good pitcher. Every time I got on base that game I was able to come around to score.

A mercy rule is declared if a team was up by ten or more runs after the fifth inning then the game would be called. After the fifth inning we were winning 16-4 so they called the game and declared us the winners. It was a far cry from the previous season playing for Mr. Chambers. We had gone the entire season without enjoying the lead a single time. The mercy rule was mercy shown to a group of young boys getting crushed. They also had the rule to prevent four hour games from occurring.

Walking home after the game that night I was on cloud nine. Don and Steve were also excited and let me know that they were proud of me. Mr. Kubb had given out two game balls after the game. I received one for my three hit effort while James Steele also earned one for hitting the cycle. The cycle is when a batter gets four hits including a single, double, triple and home run. It is one of the hardest things to do in sports and rarely ever happens. To be in the same class with James for one night was a big thrill for me.

I arrived at the bus stop a little early the next morning. For the first time all year I was looking forward to going to school. Bobby arrived about two minutes before the bus showed up but did not say much to me other than "good game." I could tell he was embarrassed and didn't feeling like rehashing what happen about twelve hours earlier. His sister Erin who was in the eighth grade also rode the bus with us took the opportunity to tell me "nice hit." It was like rubbing salt in an open wound for Bobby to hear that.

At school that day numerous people told me they heard about the triple. It was really cool to have my classmates show me some respect for once. I was finally starting to get some much needed popularity. Unfortunately there was just one week left in the school year. Sitting next to Ryan Cook in science class, we talked about the game all class long. I told him I was happy that we won and looking forward to playing the boys from Lasko later that week.

Going into the Lasko game I was still thinking about the triple a few nights back. I couldn't seem to get my mind off of it. This game would be played at the field behind Spruce Elementary school in North Olmsted. The field at Spruce school was just one diamond and covered by a dark forest on each side. It was a shady park with very little room for sun to peak through. It differed from Little Clague which had two diamonds and all kinds of room to move around. This was a typical mid spring night in Cleveland, cold and damp. The mood before the game was tense and I realized my teammates were a little anxious.

Don, who had been writing a story about our team for the high school newspaper, chose this game to write it about. Mr. Kubb let it be known to the players, which turned out to be a mistake. It was awesome that Don picked us to write about it, but it would have been better to find that out after the game. It just made everyone nervous and it showed early and often. We were playing what many considered the second best team in the league and we knew that a win would pretty much set us up to dominate the rest of the season.

With the weather adding a sharp crispness to it, the ball was not jumping off the bat. This game saw few big hits and shaped up to be a pitcher's duel. Ryan Cook was pitching for us while Mike Lasko took the hill for them. I was starting in right field again so the chances of my playing infield were slim to none.

In my first time at bat I singled and came around to score. I was a quick four for four to start the season. Our team took the early lead and never looked back. By the fifth inning we were up 8-0 and had the Lasko team on the ropes. I had one more at bat but could only draw a walk.

In the top of the sixth we put Mike Kubb into pitch but he was not on his game that night. He was nervous because of Don's writing for the paper. He promptly walked in batter after batter until the score was 8-6 before the inning was over. The problem our team suffered is that it never really had any team spirit or heart of any kind. When the inning finally ended and we walked back to the bench not a single player went up to Mike and offered him support. I decided to tell him "Hey, don't worry about it we will get those runs back."

In the bottom of the sixth Nick Nevel ended up hitting a three run homer to put us up 11-6. From there we ended up scoring one more time and taking a healthy 12-6 lead into the final inning. Dave Ashton, who came into the game to pitch the final inning, set down the side in order. Our team enjoyed two wins and zero loss start against our two toughest opponents. The next fourteen games looked like a cake walk.

After the game the team was in a somber mood because it wasn't the usual blowout they had been accustomed to. I personally didn't care, feeling that a win was a win no matter the score. The attitude shown by the rest of the team was also one of relief. They were relieved that the toughest two opponents were out of the way, thinking that an unbeaten season was a sure thing. I couldn't have disagreed more because I have never thought any game should seem like an easy win. The second a team lets' its guard down is when it gets stung with an upset loss.

Summer was about to begin as I looked forward to it more than ever because Steve was practically at my house all the time. If I ever got tired of him I could always go over Dave Murphy's. Steve's mom would send him over with a week's worth of junk food that we would usually be consumed in the first two days.

Hanging out with Steve and Don was a nice relief from the pressure of the season. We had gotten off to a four win zero loss start. The problem was that in the two most recent wins I had gone zero hits in eight at bats and had suffered seven strikeouts. All of a sudden I started choking and could not hit the side of a barn. To make matters worse, Don was keeping track of the team's stats that year and I could see my batting average plummeting. I was four for twelve and fading fast.

By the time the fifth game had rolled around I was really pressing. I remember that on the day of the game, I prayed for rain so I didn't have to play. I was losing all confidence in my skills, a sure sign that a slump will continue.

The game that evening was played against Mr. Coffey's team. We jumped out to an early lead and were cruising along. But even with the team doing well I was still slumping as I went a zero for two with two more strikeouts. It was the worst slump of my life which made me feel horrible. I was coming off the best season of my life and I couldn't figure out how it went bad so quickly.

I was standing in right field yelling at myself in my head when a ball was finally hit to me. It was the first one all season and it looked like it was going to drop in for a hit. I ran as fast as I could to try and track it down. When I held out my glove I could feel the ball bounce right in the web of my mitt. Only for it to bounce right back out again and land on the grass for a base hit. It was one of the worst feelings in my little league career.

I didn't have much time to think about it as the very next pitch was hit to me in right field. It looked as though I would have to charge at this one too. I stuck out my glove along with my other hand to make sure the ball would not pop loose this time. I caught the ball and made the throw into the outfield to hold the runner at first from advancing. It was the first thing I had done right in weeks, a huge relief. One of the oldest rules in baseball is always use two hands when catching a ball. Take your free hand and cover the glove with it after the ball hits the leather. That way you have extra protection against the ball coming loose and dropping it. Because I had failed to follow that golden rule, it came back to bit me in the rear.

My next time at bat saw me so desperate to get a hit that I swung at anything thrown. I had two strikes on me and I swung at a pitch that was eye level. It was terrible pitch to swing at and I deserved to be benched. I remember sitting on the bench and burying my head in my glove. Mr. Kubb came over to me and said, "I want you on that field." He refused to bench me no matter how poorly I was playing. He was such a good man with a totally different attitude from most of the players he coached.

That night when we got back home I was in my room trying to think about anything but baseball when the phone rang. It was Mr. Kubb calling to say, "He was proud of me for catching the second fly ball." Saying that "it took courage to come right back after making an error and make the very next play." It was a kind thing for him to do, something he didn't have to. It helped cheer me up after what had been a rough night.

I remember both the good times of my playing days and the bad times too. I had to experience each to grow and become better. My Dad, who saw this as well, made a phone call to an old friend.

The day after the game Dad came into my room the second he got home from work and said, "Grab your mitt boy, there is somewhere you need to be." I had no clue what he was talking about because we did not have a game that night. He refused to tell me where he was taking me and said I would find out when we got there. About twenty minutes later we arrived at Impett Park in Cleveland. It was the park my brother had played at when we lived in Cleveland. I never got to play there because we moved by the time I was old enough.

It looked as beautiful as it did years earlier; exactly the way I remembered it. It was only 4:30 in the afternoon so no games were going on. In the middle of the diamond stood the man who installed the love of the game in me initially. Standing in the middle of the diamond wearing a green jersey and orange hat was Mr. Bill Wheeler.

I went up to him and shook his hand. His first words out were "So I hear you been playing like crap. We will have to fix that!" Mr. Wheeler hadn't changed one bit and I was glad to see that.

We spent a good hour of field time before teams started showing to play that night's games. We used this period to have him hit me countless ground balls and pop flies. I then took batting practice and he zipped in some serious fast balls to try to get my timing down. It was a tough workout that left me drenched in sweat. It helped a long way in restoring my confidence and letting me have fun again.

After the mini-practice he pulled me aside from my Dad and gave me a little speech. He told me not give up on myself and keep working hard so that things would get better. He said that years prior I was one of his favorite players to coach, thanking me for my countless efforts and team spirit. He also called me a warrior. It was great to be around him again and he did wonders for my confidence.

As our practice wound down, the players starting arriving for that night's game. It was awesome to see all my old teammates and friends once again. I didn't realize how much I missed playing with them until I saw them on the field later that evening. They were every bit as good as when I played with them. It was a shame that their league did not enter the state tournament. I felt if they did they could have won it. It was a great night, one that I owe to my Dad and Mr. Wheeler. Between that night and the phone call from Mr. Kubb I felt as though I had something to build on.

The night before our next game I slept with my mitt as I usually did, but this time I also slept with my entire jersey on minus the cup. Baseball players are constantly doing crazy things to break out of a slump. I was willing to try anything to turn my luck around. The day of the game I played with my action figures all day just to try to relax and not think about the game that night.

By game time I was ready, willing and eager to bust out of my slump. In my first at bat I drew a full count walk. I didn't even care that I didn't get a hit, I was just happy to finally get back on base. My next at bat I lined out hard to the third baseman. Again, I was not thrilled to be out but at least I made good contact and that was a step up. In my third at bat I lined a single into left center field. I felt as though a hundred pounds had been lifted off my shoulders. I did not get a fourth at bat because the game was called due to the mercy rule. We had won by a wide margin pushing our record to six wins and zero losses.

When I got home that night Dad insisted that I call Mr. Wheeler and let him know that I broke out of my slump. I felt weird about annoying the man with my news but Dad insisted that I call to thank him so I did. He was happy to hear the good news and I made sure to thank him repeatedly.

To celebrate my new found hitting streak Dave spent the night. We stayed up all night playing with action figures and trading cards. It was the perfect way to unwind after what had been a stressful week. Dave and I had the habit of staying up the entire night during sleepovers and not going to bed until seven in the morning.

Over the course of the next several weeks our team began to steamroll the competition. We ran off nine straight wins and brought our record to a flawless fifteen win and zero loss mark. Our last game was played against a team that had only won two games all season and was filled with eleven year olds. It should have been an easy win and the team was looking past them onto the state tournament. The fact that we had already clinched the league championship did not help matters.

It was nice to win yet another league championship. It was the third time in four years that I had been on a team that won a league championship. This one seemed to lack the luster of the first two because we didn't have many close games. In addition I had suffered from the slump. Plus anytime you don't win it in a tournament it just isn't the same. It doesn't have the same feel. Winning a tournament has the fun and excitement to it. It gives players a sudden death feel and makes every game they play in a must win.

The team we played against was coached by Mr. Lekan. He did a great job motivating his players into thinking they could beat us. They came out guns blazing and shut us down for the first six   innings taking a four run lead into the bottom of the last inning. I remember sitting on the bench thinking to myself that this was finally happening. The boys I had played with all year long had been cocky so it was finally catching up to them. Mr. Metz called us together for a huddle and said "ok, guys, gut check time." There wasn't too much more to say other than that.

The first batter to the plate was Sean Kaza, who struck out on three pitches. I was up next and walked on four pitches. It was my fourth walk of the game in four trips to the plate. The next batter was James Steele. He crushed the ball but it was caught by the diving center fielder. It was one incredible catch for a little leaguer to make. The team exploded in cheers and they had every right to do so. I was angry that we were about to lose, but I couldn't help but feel happy for the boy who caught it. Up next was Ryan Cook who promptly struck out on three pitches. The Lekan team had beaten a team filled with boys older than them with more talent because they showed more heart and desire. Sadly, despite all our talent we lacked both of those traits.

After the game Mr. Kubb told us not to worry about it because we were still league champs. He also informed us that we would have a practice before the state tournament started. Not much was said and my teammates didn't even seem to care. The only player on the team besides myself who seemed to let the loss anger him was Dave. The two of us had strived for perfection all season and came up just shy.

I was able to walk home that night because the game was played at Little Clague Park. I was eager to

get home and stop thinking about the loss. It helped that the Major League All Star game was on. It would be the perfect fix to my depressed mood. I hated losing and this was no exception even though it didn't seem to affect most of my teammates. I have watched every All Star Game since I was six and it is one of my favorite nights of the summer.

That year's all-star game was even better than usual because the Indians finally had more than just one player in it. They had a great team that year and were represented well in the mid- summer classic. The game itself was a thriller and went into extra innings. The American League lost by a narrow margin. It was the last All Star Game ever held at Three Rivers Stadium in Pittsburgh. Years later the Pirate's would move into the finest stadium in all of baseball called "PNC Park". Located on the shores of the Alleghany River, it looked amazing all lit up at night.

On the next day the biggest tournament of the year began. Our team was set to play in Spencer, Ohio, as we had years earlier. I was excited to return to those fields that I had daydreamed about ever since first seeing them.

As happy as I was about going back to the big dance, I realized that for the first time all season I would not be starting. The state tournament rules prohibited four outfielders and I did not make the cut. I would be our first player off the bench if we needed someone. I experienced mixed emotions about not getting to start, but I kept my mouth shut and just soaked up the experience the best I could. I made sure to be ready if I was called upon. I had played lousy most of the season and Mr. Kubb was correct in not playing me in such a pivotal game.

Our first game of the tournament was played against a team from Macedonia, Ohio. We were able to beat them rather handily; however I did not get the chance to play. It marked the first time ever that I did not play in game that I dressed for. That was a bitter pill to swallow.

Our second game was played against a team from Solon, Ohio. We defeated them by 13 runs when the game was called in the fifth. Our team was on a roll and looked as if we had a strong chance to make it to the State Championship game. I was able to get a perfect view of it from the bench. I don't blame Mr. Kubb for benching me because I had a sub-par season and he needed his nine best on the field.

Our team had made it into the field of sixteen and the games were about to get tougher. In the third round we played a team from Medina, Ohio. It was a close game and we never led by more than two runs. In the bottom of the last inning we enjoyed a two run lead. Ryan Cook walked the bases loaded when Mr. Kubb pulled him and put in Dave Ashton. We were clinging to a narrow lead, but the other team had the bags loaded with nobody out. Dave struck out the next three batters in a row on nine straight pitches. It was a huge win for our team as we headed for the final eight. Once again I did not play but was happy to see my team get the win.

The next game would go down as the weirdest one I have ever played. I have coached in stranger games, but this was by far and away the strangest one I ever played in. It was a warm Sunday morning in early August. We were scheduled to play the same team from Grafton, Ohio, that had beaten us years earlier. Win, lose or draw, we could already stake are claim as one of the top eight teams in the entire state.

During warm ups I was standing in right field shagging fly balls when I noticed my Grandparents had showed up to watch me play. It felt great to see that they had driven so far to support me. Then I realized that they had driven all that way just to see me warm the bench. Up to that point I had not played a single inning in the tournament. My anxiety grew when I saw that my Uncle Pete made the trip with them.

This was the first game he attended since he had moved away from us. I had mixed emotions on seeing him. On one hand it was great to see him and I really missed him. On the other I felt even worse about sitting on the bench because Pete had taught me better than the way I had played that summer.

The game began with Mike Kubb on the hill. His first pitch was hit for a solo home run and the other team never looked back. It didn't help that the umpires were squeezing Mike all day.

When an umpire squeezes a pitcher it means he doesn't call it fairly. He makes the strike zone tiny and hard to hit. Calling every pitch not swung at a ball. Mike was clearly rattled and the blowout was on. This game also marked the first time I ever saw Mr. Kubb scream at an umpire about a call or strike zone.

In the top of the fifth inning we were down 17-0 and the mercy rule would soon be in full effect. There were two outs and the bases were empty. Ryan Cook's pitch was popped up into shallow right field. Running from right field was Jeff Metz. Backing up and trying to make the catch was second baseman Dave Ashton. This was clearly the right fielder's ball and his job to call off the second baseman. The problem was that Jeff was too unsure and didn't say a word. Meanwhile Dave wanted to make the grab and kept charging hard. They collided with Dave's mouth smashing into Jeff's skull. Dave's two front teeth had dislodged and jammed into Jeff's forehead. It was one of the scariest things I have ever seen on a baseball diamond. Both players were rushed to the emergency room for medical care.

I was inserted into the game to play second base for my injured teammate. The very next pitch was a line drive right at me that I grabbed for the third out. It felt nice to make the play even if the game was more than likely over. I was taught to play hard no matter what the score was.

The pitcher from Grafton was on the cusp of throwing a no-hitter. The only player to reach base all game was Dave Murphy. Dave had the incredibly bad luck of getting hit in the head in all three of his at bats. He never played little league baseball again after that game. However, a struck batsman does not count as a hit, so this opposing pitcher still had his no-hitter intact. If it wasn't for his zest to throw the ball at my best friend's head the boy could have had a perfect game in the works.

I was set to bat third in that inning and unless our team found a way to come up with eight runs to stave off the mercy rule, this would be our last at bats of the season. The two players in front of me both grounded out to the pitcher for two quick outs.

I remember walking to the plate and seeing all my teammates in the dugout beginning to pack up their gear. I looked in the stands when I saw the parents doing the same thing. It made me furious. The only people in the crowd cheering me on were my own relatives. I gripped the bat as hard as I could and looked right into the pupils of the opposing pitcher. I knew he was throwing a no-hitter, and I also knew I wanted to be the one to end it. His teammates knew he was throwing one and the fans of their team sure knew. I looked right at the pitcher and thought, "I'm going to wreck it!"

Mr. Wheeler and Mr. Kubb taught me to always look at the first pitch and let it go; unless it was a perfect strike then it was okay to swing. The first pitch was right down Broadway, and I wasted no time hammering it into deep center field for a standing double. I could hear people from the stands booing from the other team because I broke up the no-hitter. Meanwhile the few people actually paying attention still on my side started going crazy in the stands cheering for me. Mr. Kubb yelled out from the dugout "at a boy, Vince, big hit baby!" I was so pumped up I could have run a mile without breaking a sweat.

The next batter struck out looking and they game and season were over. We finished in the top eight which is a very hard thing to do. They gave us each a really cool patch to remember our finish in the tournament.

It was a wild way to end a long season. Our team had gone 18-2 and hoisted another championship trophy. Despite the winning I still had the hunger for more. I hoped that the summer of "1995" would bring more winning but also more fun. It wasn't going to take long to realize that the following summer would be one of the best in my life.

Chapter Seven
Simply the Best

"One thing you will discover that life is based less then you think on what you have learned, and much more then you think on what you have inside you from the beginning."
~ Mark Helprin

Driving home after the last game many emotions and thoughts ran through my head. I was proud that I had broken up the no hitter when everyone else had abandoned hope. I was also depressed that baseball was finished for another summer. The mixture of emotions that I felt hit me unprepared. It made me realize the cold hard fact that little league baseball might be the farthest I might ever go. Playing against the team from Grafton made me hunger for the days when I played for Mr. Wheeler. It also showed me that no matter how good I became at something, there is always going to be someone better.

The drive home also allowed me to reflect on what had been a good summer outside of baseball. Just being a youngster allowed me to have fun with my friends and family despite how good or bad my baseball team was. I realized that no matter how little or how often I played that my family and friends would still love me. By the time the fall of 1994 rolled around, I was well adjusted to junior high with my seventh grade year off to a solid start. I continued to make more friends and things were looking very good for me socially. I even attended my first dance that fall. My first slow dance took place with a girl named Stacy Witt. She agreed to be my girlfriend; however, I never saw her again the rest of the school year. We did not have any classes together and I never got her phone number.

Despite the dancing fool that I was becoming, I also made another close friend named Paul Hut. Paul was the only boy I knew who was skinnier than I at that time. Paul was such a pleasant person and maybe one of the nicest individuals I have ever met. He wore huge thick glasses to cover this big jagged scar over his left eye. He had a tumor as a small boy that was removed. I think this is what made him so humble. I stuck up for him when other boys would pick on him. Remembering years past when children picked on me, I didn't want to see it happen to Paul. It was another example of children being cruel to someone who is different.

Don was in his tenth grade year and met his first serious girlfriend. Her name was Jenny and she was the first girl to come over our house on a regular basis. I hated this new change and was not even close to accepting it. He was spending all his free time with her and leaving me in the dark. I don't blame him now but at the time I was not happy.

I will never forget that Christmas when we got done opening all our gifts and Don left to go over her house to spend time with her. Christmas was reserved for us to spend all day playing with our new toys in the basement. I gathered that my parents approved of him dating because instead of his usual gifts of games and toys, Don received cloths and colognes that year.

After a long winter with plenty of laughs and good times, the weather finally turned warm and spring time arrived. This meant baseball practice and another new team. The league that year consisted of teams with thirteen and fourteen year olds. Mr. Kubb stopped coaching when the league said he was unable to be head of the umpires and a coach at the same time. It was a cause of too much conflict in scheduling and too many parents had complained saying that his team received unfair calls from the umpires. I truly believe that the parents were worried about nothing and that I personally never saw Mr. Kubb get calls in his favor. The only questionable call that I ever saw came when I was called safe at third base in the Bobko game when I thought I might have been out.

Mr. Cook, who took over the team, decided to not pick me for the team that summer. I was okay with it and looked forward to the chance to play with another team as long as my teammates wanted to win.

The coach who took a chance on me was Mr. Hurley. He was a kind man who also happened to work with my Dad at RTA. He had been coaching the same group of boys for seven summers and they were indeed a solid team. The team consisted of mainly fourteen year olds and I was one of only three thirteen year olds on the team. The other two were a boy named Casey Kalawinski and my friend Joe Graham. It was cool having my friend Joe on the team and being on a team that was mostly older children because it made me believe we had a chance to be good. That dream was crushed when my Dad came home from work one day and told me that Mr. Hurley told him they never had a winning season yet.

The weird and amazing thing about baseball is that all it takes is one good swing to turn everything around. The summer of "1995" would go on to become my favorite as a child and it would have much to do with that team.

We started practice the first chance we had and used every practice to keep improving and getting better. We practiced drill after drill on hitting and fielding and our mission was to be well rounded at both. I could tell early on that these boys were ready to start winning and cared about the results on the field as badly as I did. In fact I was rather impressed at the talent level of many of them and couldn't figure out why they had lost so many games in seasons prior.

Our third base coach was Mr. Bell was very smart and knew how to handle any situation that arose on the field. He did more strategy work then the actual head coach because he made every lineup all year long. He was big into having signals for almost any situation that arose.

The team had many fans that would attend every game and cheer us on to victory. However, the biggest fan of the team happened to be Jerry Hazard. He was part boy and part man. Jerry Hazard was the biggest eighth grader on the planet. He had muscles bigger then my head. He resembled a college freshman though only fourteen. In fact he was so big that the league did not allow him to play. I never thought that was fair to him. After all, it wasn't his fault he was built like a brick house. The coolest thing about Jerry was that despite his superior size, he was good natured, humble and never bullied anyone. He was friendly with everyone on the team and came to every single game.

With less than a week before the season started Uncle Pete came over my house for a few days to visit. He had taken time out from his church work of feeding and clothing the poor at St. Malachi's to spend some time with me. We picked up right where we had left off a few summers ago by watching Rocky. The next day we went to the park where Peter drilled me in new drills that I never even knew existed at that point.

For two solid hours we played a game/drill called pepper. Simply put, Pete just tapped the ball with the bat to different sides of me. I had to pick it up cleanly with my hand or glove and set myself to make the throw. Instead of throwing it to a base I would gently throw the ball back to him and he would clip it with his bat so that I would make play after play. It is nonstop action and is amazing at getting you into shape and great for hand to eye skills. It teaches the player to be quick on his feet and ready to shift to any side to get the ball. I loved playing this game with Pete because it was far and away the best thing he ever taught me.

After practice Pete took me to the sporting goods store to buy me a new bat. It was a silver and blue Easton. At the time it was costly to buy a brand new bat and I know Pete most likely did not have the money to spend on it but he did. It just shows what kind of man he truly was.

When the time finally arrived for our first game that season our team was more than ready and willing to play. We would need to be because our first game was scheduled against the defending champs from that league the year before, Mr. Kerr's team. They had won the seventh and eighth grade league with a team packed with seventh graders. One year later, as eighth graders, they were the team to be feared. They had not lost a single regular season game in five years and were the back to back state tournament champions. Every team in the league aimed to beat them but none ever did.

I could tell going into that game that my teammates let Mr. Kerr's team intimidate them. They took one look at the schedule and said "We are going to start the year 0-1". It was odd to see that in what otherwise seemed like a group of confident and hungry players.

When competing, players must let their own fear drive them to stay sharp and try harder than they normally would. They must let fear cause them to be hungry and dangerous. Whenever a team or player lets fear weaken them it has a crippling effect.

While getting dressed for our first game I couldn't have been happier. Our colors that year were solid blue tops with white lettering and numbers. They had yellow trim along the sleeves and lettering that looked amazing. They were easily the best looking jerseys I have ever worn in any sport I have ever played in!

Our sponsor was a company called Andrew's Heating and Cooling. For the second straight year I wore number one. For the second consecutive year I was the smallest boy on the team but it did not bother me one bit. My teammates never gave me any grief for being so small. I was thankful for that.

I was able to tell by the third inning of our first game against Kerr that we were going to lose. We were only down by 3 runs when the fourth inning began but our team made things feel as if we were down twenty. We just had this look of defeat on our face's right from the start. In the bottom of the fourth inning we committed several errors. The next thing we knew we were losing by thirteen runs. We folded up quickly in the top of the fifth and it was game over.

On the way home I was furious. I screamed, yelled and almost wanted to quit. It could have not been very pleasant for my parents to hear my whining but they grit their teeth and didn't kick me out of the car. I was angry because my team quit on itself at the first sign of trouble. It reminded me of playing for Mr. Chambers and for Mr. Kubb when things didn't start well.

I clearly remember storming into my room when we got home, ripping off my jersey and just throwing it against the wall. I never liked to lose and this was no exception. I was upset because I believed our team was better and that my teammates were just going to accept losing all year.   As much as I hated losing when I played for Mr. Chambers, I almost grew to accept it that season because I knew our team was terrible. This time I knew that was not at all the case.

Hours later I sat on the edge of my bed and reflected on the game. I thought about the night in general and what I had to do to stay upbeat. I reflected on that fact that I got to play on the biggest diamond for a Little League game I have ever seen. It was even bigger than those at Spencer, Ohio, for the state tournament games. I'm speaking of the fields at North Olmsted Park, the same fields that the high school teams play on. Once I started thinking about that it did much to cheer me up. I closed my eyes for a quick second and pictured possibly playing high school ball. The thought of it gave me goose bumps. The image brought me back into the reality that it was a long season and that this was only one game. I returned to the living room and apologized for screaming at my parents. They understood

Game two would be played two nights later at North Olmsted Park where all the contests that year had been scheduled. It was against the team coached by Mr. Stone. It had been the second best team in the league everywhere coming behind the Kerr team. Again our players had a bad attitude about it, feeling as though a loss was certain. I felt our team was talented and that we stood a good chance at upsetting this team.

By the third inning we were losing 5-0. Then in the bottom half of the fifth inning we fell behind 11-0. With no one out and a man on third base I drew a walk. The next batter was our leadoff hitter Matt Holian, who hit a two run triple and brought us to within nine. This meant that we would avoid the mercy rule and get to play the sixth inning at least. After Mark Grasskemper drew a walk it was up to Mike Gray to drive them in. He promptly smashed a three run homer. The next thing we knew we were down only 11-5. Before the inning was over, we received key hits from Steve Bell and Timothy Malik, cutting the lead to 11-7.

In the top of the sixth inning Steve was throwing heat and mowed down the order with three straight strikeouts. Our once morbid team became a house of fire. Every player was on his toes and cheered their teammates with no one sitting on the bench when we returned to the dugout for our at bat. A four run deficit was a steep hill to climb but for the first time all season we had the confidence that we needed.

Leading off the bottom of the sixth we quickly had one out from Casey Kawalinksi. The next batter was Craig Penny who doubled and the rally was back on. Soon we were down 11-10 with only one out and the bases loaded.

At the plate was one of only three seventh graders on the team. He was my future good buddy Joe Graham. The third baseman crept up close to the plate in order to prevent Joe from bunting as well as fielding the ball to throw home if need be. The count quickly went zero balls and two strikes. He then worked the count full by taking three straight pitches outside the strike zone. With the count full and our hearts in our throats, Joe calmly popped the next pitch up over the third baseman's head to tie the game. If the third baseman had been playing at the regular spot it would have been an easy out. However, Joe did a great job at placing his hit in the perfect spot to drive in the run.

We were back at the top of the order when Matt Holian hit a base clearing double that put us ahead 14-11. We had battled all the way back to take the lead, a remarkable comeback that still needed closing out in the top half of the seventh.

When the inning ended and we grabbed our gloves for the top of the seventh, Mr. Graham's dad came over to the bench to tell his son "good job!" This was the first time I ever heard him speak.

The top of the seventh was not without more drama. Timothy Malik had come in to close the game out with Steve switching to catcher. Anthony put two men on base with only one out. It was high drama at the ball park that night. Steve, as he often did, went to the mound to settle down his pitcher. Steve was always the first person to pick someone up when they were down. The next pitch was a pitch out and Steve gunned the runner down at third base trying to steal. Just like that we had two outs and just one shy of victory. The next batter hit a long fly ball that the speedy Mark Grasskemper easily tracked down for the final out.

This was a big win at a crucial point in the season, a win that our team badly needed at the time for many reasons. It changed our whole outlook for the rest of the season. I remember that after the game, we mobbed each other with high fives and back slaps. It's amazing to say that I have played and coached in over a one hundred Little League games but that victory was easily one of my favorites.

Our win showed that the team was better than most people thought. It proved that a game is not over until the last pitch is thrown and we should never give up hope. It gave us one of the biggest weapons any team can have at any level. The weapon is called confidence.

My car ride home that night was a much different atmosphere as I was thrilled about the big win. Earlier that night I had talked my Mom into letting me attend the game instead of going to an honor student awards banquet at school. Because I had earned honors that year for my high grades, that night I was invited to attend a banquet honoring the students. My Mom and I had fought all day about going. She wanted me to attend the honor ceremony. I told her firmly that I was not about to miss a game for the first time. Up to that point in my Little League career I never missed a single game and I was not about to start.

The summer of 1995 was becoming the best of my childhood. It seemed as though it never rained and the sun was always out. Days seemed to last forever and nights were always as fun as the days. This was mainly because the Major League baseball strike was finally over, and the Indians went back to their winning ways.

Much like my team's comeback win over Stone, the Indians made a habit of winning in the last innings with one miracle play after another. They had the most potent lineup in baseball causing Jacob's field to sell out every single night. They had even added the presence of future Hall of Famers Eddie Murray and Dennis Martinez. One addition was that of my favorite player Orel Hershiser. It was great to have the best team in baseball reside in our town. For Cleveland fans it was long overdue.

While the Indians were dominating in the big leagues, my team started dominating in Little League in much of the same fashion. We got off to a red hot start at 6-1, with four wins coming from behind in the late innings. Each game seemed to have a new hero while the ball just kept rolling our way. The biggest thing that made our team click was that we all got along with one another. The older boys treated the younger boys with respect. Despite the deficit in any game we knew we could still win, fighting back until we took the lead for good. It reminded me so much of those summers when I played for Mr. Wheeler. It was the most enjoyment I had playing ball since we had moved to North Olmsted. I could tell my parents in the crowd were enjoying it as much as I.

At mid-season we were 7-1 and in second place behind Mr. Kerr's team. Our next opponent was the "Workin Out" team coached by Mr. Cook. It was the first chance I had to play against my former teammates since that horrible Chambers team from a few summers back.

The evening before the game I could not sleep and spent the entire night awake tossing and turning in bed. I wanted to win so bad that I couldn't relax long enough to fall asleep. When I woke up that morning I quickly went outside and started throwing the tennis ball off the garage. It was a Sunday so I had to eventually stop to attend church. When I got home from Mass it was almost time to leave for the game. I didn't do or say much before leaving because my nerves were high. My parents knew that I was nervous so they said little to me on the car ride to the field.

Attending that game were my grandparents and Uncle Pete. It was the only game Pete had a chance to attend all year, which increased the pressure. Also in the crowd were my two best friends Dave and Steve sitting next to Don. I remember my brother patting me on the back before I took the field in the first inning, saying "Just relax out there and have fun". I must hand it to Don because he was always there for the biggest moments in my life and never put any pressure on me that I couldn't handle.

The problem was that I was too nervous to be on the field and do well. It was the first and last time in my Little League career that I didn't want the ball to be hit to me in the infield. Normally when I played infield I wanted every ball hit to me, but this time was different. For some reason I just could not shake the nerves.

In the second inning with the game scoreless and a runner on third base, the ball was slowly hit to me. The runner was charging for home and I knew if I fielded it cleanly I would have to make a strong throw to get him at the plate. I was so worried about making the throw that I bobbled the ball and didn't even have the chance to throw it. Our team was down 1-0 and it was my fault.

Later that same inning with the bases loaded and only one out, the ball was hit my way again. This time it was a high pop up to shallow right center field. I backed up perfectly and called off the right fielder Mark Grasskemper to make the catch. I was so relieved to do so I didn't realize Mike Kubb was darting for home plate. I recovered in time but still rushed throw to the plate. A good throw with my arm would have had him out by a mile. Instead I rushed it and sailed the ball to the backstop allowing him to score easily. I had made two errors in five minutes letting two runs cross the plate. I felt so low I could have slid under a rock.

That is the game of baseball. It is unpredictable; it can pick you up and it can also crush you. Despite the many good plays before that inning, none of them mattered now. I was ready to just curl up in a ball and die. From the stands I heard a voice yell "That's okay, Vince, it was a good catch." The voice came not from anyone on my side of the field; it belonged to Mr. Kubb who was sitting in the stands with the rest of the opposing team's parents. Mr. Kubb was always so kind to me and here was another instance of many examples.

When the inning was finally over I ran back to the dugout as fast as I could. I sat down on the end of the bench and just buried my head in my glove. I was so upset with myself it took everything I had not to cry. I felt like the world's worst baseball player who had let everyone down. Mr. Hurley came over to me and said he was going to sit me down the rest of the game. I couldn't blame him. He had every right to bench me. I was playing horrible and did not deserve to be out there.

As I sat on the bench my Dad came over to me and tapped me on the hat. He didn't say anything and he didn't have to. I knew he still loved me and that was his way of saying "It's okay to screw up even if it doesn't seem like it right now." While sitting on the bench as my team took the field for the next inning Mr. Kubb left the stands to come over to me. He said "You will make a better throw next time, I know you can". The memory of his saying that and my Dad tapping me on the hat is so vivid it seems like it happened yesterday.

The game became another close one that came down to the final inning when we trailed 3-2 in the bottom of the seventh. We had two men on base and Brian Strang at the plate. He hit the first pitch from Ryan Cook half way to the street behind North Olmsted Park to win the game. In my six years of Little League, it was the first ever walk off home run I had ever seen hit. Our team mobbed Brian at home plate helping erase the hard feelings of my horrible plays earlier that day.

It was great to beat the team that I had played for in the past. I almost felt vindicated that they didn't pick me and that I ended up on a much better team that summer. I also vowed that I would never let nerves control me as badly as they did that game.

After that game the team just kept on winning. We went from coming back in the end of games to just plain dominating right from the start. We ran our record to 13-1 with two games left. Sadly, Mr. Kerr's team was even better at 14-0. Our next game would be against them meaning that a win could cause a one game sudden death playoff game for the league championship.

The biggest difference between coaching a big game and playing in one is the feeling of pressure. When playing in big games I only had to worry about what my role was going to be that night and fielding my position. I always had confidence in my teammates and believed in them. When I coached I was a nervous wreck on game days because I needed to think about every position on the field. If we lost when I played I was most likely never going to receive sole blame. As a coach you receive most of

HERO

the attention when you lose and very little when you win. As a coach it was much easier to second guess every decision I made throughout the game.

The difference in emotion is also drastic. If I liked winning as a player then I loved winning as a coach. If I disliked losing as a player then I hated losing as a coach. The feeling that everything I did, whether it was good or bad, was magnified tenfold as a coach.

The night the game took place was a drastic change in the way my team had looked in the first meeting of the season. We had developed a confidence and a swagger that let the other team know this was not the same group of players they saw the first time around. We had rattled off thirteen straight wins and lost only one. We knew that a win that night could force a one game playoff for the league championship providing we both won our last game of the season. The drama was so high that many players from other teams came out to watch this one. It reminded me of the earlier years playing for Wheeler when we faced Brooks and BeBee. Events like this explain why I loved that summer and that team so much.

There is an expression "Second verse same as the first". That particular night that saying became true and enforced. All year long our team had made a habit of getting down early but battling our way back into games. For some reason on this night we never seemed to recover after they grabbed the early lead.

After the third inning we were already down 8-2 and it wasn't looking good. We managed to stave off the mercy rule and keep within striking distance but never got closer than three back. We lost by a final score of 11-8. I was proud of our team despite the loss because we had come a long way since the first meeting. We had grown as a team and showed heart all year in any situation. I wasn't happy that we lost but I coped with it better than I thought possible. The next night we blew away our opponents and closed the regular season with a record of 14-2.

I was on the bench one inning late in our last game of the season when I said to Mr. Bell, "That boy is going to ground out to short". Sure enough he grounded out to our shortstop Craig on the next pitch. When Mr. Bell asked me how I knew this would happen, I explained to him that Mike Gray was a ground ball pitcher. The batter had grounded out to short the last time he was up and

74

that judging by the way he was standing in the box the odds were strong he would do it again.

I sat by Mr. Bell on the bench the rest of the game and pointed out many things I was seeing and different reasons why I thought certain things would happen. He asked me why I paid attention so closely. I told him "Because I love this game and its fun."

After the game was over Mr. Bell came up to me and said, "Son, you will make a great coach someday." He was the second person to tell me that. After hearing those words from two of my baseball coaches I should have started thinking about it more but I still didn't for some reason. When I was young, playing baseball was all I ever thought about. I never thought about the future because I felt as though the present was never going to end. Maybe back then I had the urge to coach, but it never entered my mind until many years later.

Our team still had a chance to hold up a championship trophy if we could win the post season tournament. We were more than ready to do so. We were listed as the number two seed in a field of eight. Mr. Cook's team was listed as the seven seed meaning that if they won their first round game and we did then we'd meet them in the semi-finals.

The first round game took place against Mr. Miller's team of first year players. We jumped out to a big lead but seemed to lose focus. Once we got up by ten runs in the third inning we took our foot off the gas pedal. Instead of putting them away, we started talking about how bad we were going to beat Mr. Cook's team. We started fooling around too much on the bench with the girls who would come to watch us every game. The next thing we knew the game was tied going into the fifth inning.

Mr. Bell lit into us louder than he had done that   season. We finally woke up and got back to work. We ended up scoring three runs in the bottom of the sixth and holding onto the lead in the seventh for the win. It was the first time all season that we lost our focus and it almost cost us a chance at the semifinals.

One more win meant a chance to play for the tournament championship. Moreover this game would be played against my former teammates. I was not as nervous as I was the first time but I can't say that I was exactly loose for this one either.

Our team was confident and took the game seriously. We jumped out to an early lead but were unable to hold onto it. By the third inning we were actually down 5-3. The umpires for this particular game were poor. Nothing seemed to go our way during the whole game. We didn't get a single favorable call and it seemed as though our pitchers had to throw the ball directly to the center of the plate to get a called strike. I normally would never blame poor play on an umpire but on this particular night we were getting robbed. I remember vividly that my teammates grew increasingly upset with everything the umpires called.

The problem with North Olmsted baseball is that it had teenagers umpiring the games. In the Cleveland league it was always adults. These young men let coaches intimidate them into making bad calls. On this night that was exactly what happened. The Cook team could do no wrong and our team couldn't get a call to go our way.

The umpire should never cost a team the game. When they do it is clear to everyone involved. A team should lose because they got out played that night not because they had bad call after bad call against them. This is the first time I can say that bad umpires cost us the game. It drained all of our steam so that we just never recovered. Our first base coach Mr. Penny was actually tossed out of the game for arguing calls.

Down by two runs in the sixth inning we had the bases loaded with only one out. Matt Holian grounded a ball back to the second baseman that fielded it and threw to the plate to get Timothy Malik. Malik was charging full speed and plowed into the catcher causing him to drop the ball. The umpire called Malik out and ejected him from the game for a dirty play. Anyone who knows anything about baseball can say that it was perfectly legal. The umpire did not see it that way and Malik was out. Any momentum we had left the park at that moment.

We went quietly into the night in the seventh inning and were bounced from the tournament without even getting to play the championship game. It was a terrible ending to a great season. I was not happy for my former teammates either. I felt even worse for my current teammates because it was their last ever Little League Game. All would go on to play high school ball but they deserved a better send off. They had played their butts off all season long so that I hated to see them come so close and lose.

After the game ended none of my former teammates came over to me to say anything. So I made a point to go over to their bench and say "Good luck in the championship." I received no reply. The only person who spoke to me was Mr. Kubb who was sitting in the crowd. He walked over to me after the game and said "Great game, be proud." I thought it was a nice thing for him to do, something that he didn't have to do.

Because that day was also Mr. Hurley's birthday, one of the mothers had brought the team a huge sheet cake. We all sat around after the game and ate cake and ice cream. Normally I don't agree with celebrating after a big loss but this time I didn't mind. As angry as I was about losing to players I didn't care for, I was pleased because my team had played well all year and deserved to celebrate. They had grown from a losing team to become one of the league's best.

Shortly after the season, Don found happiness. On August 22ʼ 1995, he met a young lady named Abbie. Don would go on to date her for eight years before marrying her in the summer of 2002.

At first I wasn't happy about Don having yet another girlfriend because it meant more time he could spend hanging out in my basement. It did not take long to change my mind about Abbie because she was very nice and loyal to Don. It was one more part of growing up. While I wasn't thrilled at losing valued basement time, at the same time it was nice to see him happy.

It is crazy to think that a year when my team failed to win the championship would remain my favorite. That I liked and respected the boys I played with helped a great deal. We had no pressure on us to win all season, yet that is just what we did more often than not. When I saw my teammates in school that spring of 1995 while they were still in eighth grade, they treated me no differently and were still friendly to me. A couple years later in high school nothing had changed and they still treated me well. It was a far cry from the boys I played with on the Kubb team.

The only regret that I have about that summer of 1995 is that I lost my friendship with Steve. My parents had told me that I could take one friend with me to Geauga Lake theme park. I took Paul instead of Steve which made him angry. It was a stupid thing to argue about but another part of growing up. I would soon learn that not all things in life are fair. The following summer would be much different than the great one I just had.

Chapter 8
Father Knows Best

"My father gave me the greatest gift anyone could give another person, he believed in me."
~ Jim Valvano

The man that I have been able to call Dad has truly been my personal hero. I have looked to him for guidance and encouragement my entire life and he has never lacked either. Growing up without their father around can be traumatizing to children. Fortunately my Dad was always around allowing my brother and me to soak up every moment.

I can never understand why some men don't go straight home from work to be with their families. I will never understand men who go to the bar after work instead of home. I always felt that having a wife and children would be a blessing for any man. Luckily for Don and me our dad realized that and never strayed from us. The importance of having a male figure around helped us in many ways. It kept Don and me in line and out of trouble. It also gave us a person to joke around with in a way that we could not do with Mom.

In high school Dad was a star athlete in wrestling. He had won scholarships to college before he tore his shoulder during his senior year. Despite his amazing ability at athletics he never pushed Don and me too hard to get into sports. Rather he helped us once we chose to play. I also had three uncles who all wrestled. Between the three uncles and my Dad, I had the pedigree to become a good wrestler if I had chosen to do so. Looking back on it I wish that I had chosen to wrestle at a young age and stuck with it instead of playing basketball. I often think about how much better I could have been at wrestling. I don't have many regrets in life, but that is surely one of them.

What is amazing about Dad was that he came from a broken home. His own father served in the Korean War. When he came home from it he was completely messed up in every possible way. Grandpa McKee would come home from drunken tirades and beat up my Grandma McKee right in front of the children. He would tie her up and beat her. Witnessing this should have traumatized my Dad. Instead it made him the complete and total opposite. He also made it clear that hitting a woman was wrong and that we should never do such a horrible act.

Dad came straight home from work every day, never stopping off at the bar for a drink. He learned from the many mistakes his own father had made. This is why Dad remains such a strong level headed person to this day.

Because of how disturbed my Dad's family life was, we seldom had contact with that side of the family. This fact combined with the fact that my Mom's side was so loving and fun seemed to go hand in hand. Don and I basically grew up with one set of Grandparents, which was fine with us.

Before my Grandfather McKee passed away in the summer of 1992, I had only met him two times that I can recall. My Grandmother McKee remains in a nursing home and I have only seen her about six times in my life. It was important to my Dad to keep us away from that dark side of living.

Having the childhood that he went through makes me respect him more so than I can even describe. He could have used that as an excuse to act badly his whole life but he never did. Now a day, every time I hear about some lunatic going off the deep end and killing someone, there is a sob story that goes along with it. Sure enough the person had a rough childhood which caused him to turn to a life of crime. I am so sick of hearing people use rough childhood's for an excuse to do wrong things when they know better. If anyone had an excuse to turn to a life of crime it would have been my father and instead he took the high road.

He met my mother a few years after graduating from high school when he went to a wrestling tournament to watch my Uncle Pete wrestle. He noticed the huge family that the Deluca's had and quickly wanted to be a part of them. After many times of turning him down, my Mom finally agreed to date him. This again shows the kind of man my Dad is because he knew full well of my Mom's health issues and over looked them.

Dad has he kept together a marriage, and raised two boys. Dad has been also able to hold down the same job for thirty years at R.T.A. In today's day and age of corporate America it is rare to hear about a person holding down the same job for thirty plus years.

I wanted to speak about my father because I feel that he is instrumental in the person I have become. The same can be said for Don because both of us have been able to stay on the straight and narrow path.

Don started coaching seventh grade basketball at St. Brendan's school. Don was not yet eighteen but had someone forge the paperwork allowing him to coach the team. Don was a natural basketball coach. He looked as natural as a fish in water. He had played and watched it all his life and had a love for the game.

Don had never had any success playing basketball because he was always on St. Brendan's which were known for losing. Don quickly changed the attitude of that, turning his team into a competitive group of players.

The boys really took to Don as their coach and he seemed like a natural fit. Watching Don coach was intriguing to me and I was proud of him. My family would go to all of his games to support him.

It was at one of those games watching Don when my Dad and I got to talking about coaching. Dad said to me, "You may like coaching baseball someday. Have you ever thought about it?" It was the third time that someone had told me that I should coach baseball. They say things tend to occur in three's. This was one of those times that it seemed like God was speaking to me through other people to plant that passion in me to want to coach someday.

Watching Don coach that season provided a lot of fun for my family. His coaching gave us many reasons to be proud of Don. It showed that someone who doesn't have a child on the team can coach just as well as someone who does. By the time Don's basketball season had ended the school year was nearly half over.

With the winter ending and the spring rapidly approaching my thoughts turned to baseball as they usually did at that time. I was excited because I felt the Indians would rebound from their disappointing loss in the World Series and recover with another dominant season. I was also excited for my last summer in the sun playing Little League.

With six great Little League seasons in the books not counting tee-ball, I was more than excited for the final one of my childhood to come. On February 1 of that year I began to count down the days on my calendar till April 15 when practice could begin. Uncle Pete had come to visit several times that March and we worked on several things to make sure I was sharp and ready to play. There was only one problem in all of this. I had no clue what team I would be playing for. The boys from Mr. Hurley's team had graduated and were playing high school ball. Mr. Kubb, who was no longer a coach, still remained the head of the umpires. It would not be until April 14 that I found out about my new team.

The night before our first practice a man named Bob Jones called my father to inform us that I had baseball practice the very next day after school. When it comes time to scheduling the first practice of the year it is usually smart to give people a few days' notice. This coach did not believe in doing so.

On the car ride to the first practice snow began to fall heavily. I remember thinking that I needed football pads on instead of baseball equipment. It could have not been more than thirty degrees outside because it was freezing. Normally I would have not cared but this time I hoped for a quick practice because the cold weather was really fierce.

When practice was over Mr. Jones called us all in for a meeting. Mr. Jones explained that he was a first year coach and that many of the players were first year players. I handled this news with mixed feelings. On one hand I thought it was cool because I had been playing my whole life so that I was sure to be one of the best players on the team. On the other hand I thought he might not be able to judge talent because he hadn't spent enough time around the game. By this point in a league consisting of thirteen and fourteen year olds, the players without experience are at an enormous disadvantage.

We had no signs or basic baseball drills of any kind. It was as though Mr. Jones had attended the Mr. Chambers school of coaching. The major difference between Mr. Jones and Mr. Chambers was that Jones did not make anything enjoyable and he would often yell at us. He reminded me of Mr. Merlin, my old basketball coach. He was taller but very wide and badly out of shape. He insisted on drilling balls at us as hard as he could. He had gray hair and looked a little like Santa Claus without the beard and certainly not as jolly.

I showed up to every practice and worked my butt off. In every practice and pre-season game he had me play second base.

Whenever he talked about the possible lineup for opening day he had me at second base. I was willing to put up with his horrendous coaching skills as long as my spot at second base was secure. A welcome change of pace this year was that two of my teammates were smaller then I.

The group of players never really felt like a team and never bonded in any way. It was nothing like I had experienced before in Little League. At least with Mr. Chambers we had some fun. Mr. Jones seemed about as exciting as watching paint dry.

I had learned one thing about bad situations: always find the best in anyone or anything. However, there was something about him that just rubbed me the wrong way right from the start. Real cocky and arrogant, he just had no clue about what he was getting himself into. I think he took the game lightly and the baseball gods would never allow that to happen. The fact that we had a group of first year players should have forced us to work harder. Things went so bad in practice that it became the first time I counted the minutes until it was over.

I knew how important playing time was going to be that summer. The previous season the high school coaching staff attended our games to scout players for the freshman team. I thought this season would be my chance to impress them and secure my spot playing high school ball. I had looked forward to this season extremely. Now this man was ruining it by his horrible attitude.

My Dad quickly realized this and gave me the same advice he had for years. "Just keep working hard and hustle. Things will work out." The normal attitude I felt was to slowly build up excitement for baseball season to come around and enjoy every practice with excited anticipation for the games to begin. Mr. Jones had somehow managed to drain all the excitement out of me before even playing a single game.

The one saving grace amongst his horrible coaching was that he penciled me into the starting lineup as close as two nights before our first game. I counted on this to save my love for baseball despite the horrendous surroundings of a bad coaching staff and teammates who had little to no experience at age fourteen. I had forgotten more about the game than half the team ever even knew.

On the night of the first game I sat in my room on my bed pulling up my stirrups getting ready for the game. Our uniforms that year consisted of all black tops with white lettering. The pants were solid white and the stirrups were black. The black hats had white lettering.

Because black is my least favorite color, this didn't exactly help matters. I didn't like wearing the color black on anything. I would only wear black gloves if they were batting gloves and even then tried to stay away from them. Mom tried buying me black underwear one time but I threw them away the next day. She was furious and said, "No one would see them. Why does it matter what color they are?"

Until that summer I had related baseball to everything good in the world. It meant happiness and fun. It meant challenges and victory. I related it to nothing but great times and incredible memories. In one fell swoop this man had managed to ruin it all for me. When I reached the field for the first game and looked at the lineup card I was not on it. My eyes nearly popped out of my head when I saw this. It didn't make any sense at all, I was so angry I could have spit fire.

I went over to where my parents and Don were sitting and told them. My brother nearly fell out of his seat when he learned the news. To that point in my Little League playing life I had never been benched to start a season. During my two years of playing for Mr. Wheeler, I played every single inning of every single game. The first year with Mr. Kubb I played about half the time but almost always started. With Mr. Chambers I played every single position on the field and never sat out. Even the second year with Mr. Kubb when I went through the horrible slump he still kept playing me until the State Tournament. The previous year with Mr. Hurley I played and started on a great team with boys almost all older then I was. To be benched on a team where I was one of the best players as well as the only six year veteran on the roster was a slap in my face.

Don and Dad wanted to say something to Mr. Jones but I begged them not to. This was my own issue and I was going to deal with it. I went over to Mr. Jones to ask him about the lineup card. I asked him if he had forgotten about me. He said, "I want someone taller to play infield." Since only two players on the team were smaller then I, this meant just about anyone would be playing in front of me.

I spent most of the game on the bench watching my team getting crushed by a team full of thirteen year olds. Not only were we losing, but we were losing to boys younger than ourselves. In my one chance at the plate I hit a single even though I felt ice cold from sitting all game.

It was a very aggravating night for me. I didn't know how to deal with it but I tried hard not to let Mr. Jones get the best of me. In the post-game talk I looked away from him the whole time because I didn't want to let him notice my anger. I did not want to give him the satisfaction of knowing he had completely ruined my night.

On our drive home I had to beg my Dad and Don once again not to say anything at the next game but just let it go for now. Things had changed considerably since the drive home from my first practice on Mr. Wheelers' team when I held my hand in pain trying not to let them see it. As much as things had changed things had also stayed the same. I did anything I could not to let them see how angry I was because I knew it would cause them to be even more upset.

When I got home that night I did not hand my uniform to Mom to wash and iron. There was no need to clean it due to lack of use. Even when I played for Mr. Kubb and didn't get dirty, I still let Mom wash it because I was proud of my team. This time around I was eager to get the jersey off, just sliding it on a hanger in the back of my closet until the next game.

When the second game came around, I actually appeared in the starting lineup this time. I was slotted to play third base and bat third. In the first inning I made a stop in the field and threw the runner out at first base. In the bottom half of the inning I drew a walk. When I ran out of the dugout for the top half of the second inning Mr. Jones called me back in. He said my night was over and to find a spot on the bench. When I asked him why he replied, "Don't talk back."

Looking over at my parents and Don, I could see smoke coming out of their ears. At first I was in too much shock to be angry. As I sat on the bench the rest of the game I actually felt myself growing sick to my stomach with thoughts of quitting running through my head for the first time in my young life. I had loved playing the game so much that quitting seemed insane.

The game was another defeat for the boy's in black but I could care less. After the game I saw Dad walking calmly towards Mr. Jones but still chose to stop him. I knew Dad wasn't a violent man but I still did not want him fighting my battles for me. We got into the car and drove home in silence. We were all too angry to speak.

That night while lying in bed I prayed to God. I remember asking him to give me the courage to endure the unfair treatment and to not allow me to hate Mr. Jones for it. I prayed to God differently than I had in the past. I knew that I could not let this man break my spirit no matter how bleak things looked. If I could just take the field one more time it would prove to be enough. If I was leaving the game I loved so dearly I wanted to go out on my own terms. The best way I can some up what I was going through at the time is with a Bible verse.

To quote Zachariah 4-6: "It is not by strength, not by might, but by in his spirit we have already claimed a victory in our Lord Almighty"

Driving to the game the next day I knew in my heart that this might be the final time I took the field as a player. Both my parents were with me, but Don was out with Abbie and unable to attend. As we drove, I thought back to all the glory days and big wins that I had experienced. The biggest reason for disappointment was that this season had ruined my love of the game so badly I wasn't even thinking about playing high school ball anymore. When I walked over to the dugout I didn't even have to look at the lineup sheet to know my name wouldn't be on it.

I sat on the bench for the first four innings before entering the game in the fifth. Our team was actually wining this one by a couple of runs but I didn't care. I was put in the game at shortstop and was ready to field anything hit my way.

The opposing team had one out and one runner on first base. The batter smashed a ground ball in the hole that I cut off and fielded cleanly. I stepped on the bag at second and threw over to first base to turn the double play. It proved to be the last play I ever made in the field in my Little League career. Dad and I still speak about this game often and talk about that particular play.

When I returned to the dugout my teammates slapped me on the back and said "Good Job." Chris Jones, who was the coach's son, said to his Dad, "I told you he was good." I was immediately benched.

Two innings later the game ended and we had actually won. I didn't receive an at bat that game and was still batting 1-1 on the season. When both teams lined up to shake hands after the game I could not bring myself to do so. Instead I walked over to where my parents were sitting and told them, "I want to go home."

Dad could no longer tolerate watching this happen to his son. I had been a good player my whole life contributing to every team I played on. I had never missed a game or practice in all my years of playing. I was never lazy or a troublemaker. My parents made sure to get me to every game on time to show their support in any way they could. I had played for some of the best Little League coaches the state had to offer. I had been on three championships ball clubs and two runners up teams. As much as I my heart was breaking having to go through this, so were my parents. It wasn't until I reached the car that I noticed my parents were not with me.

I looked behind me and noticed Dad and Mr. Jones nose to nose talking loudly to one another. Dad had approached him to find out why I had been benched and what exactly the problem was. Mr. Jones had the nerve to claim that my Dad was a bad parent because he didn't help coach. He claimed that if Dad had spent more time with me that I would have been good enough to start. He told Dad that I had a poor attitude and that I must have gotten it from my parents.

Hearing all of this was too much for my Dad. It was incredibly insulting because my Dad spent more time around me than anyone else. He and I were very close and have remained so over the years. Dad proceeded to tell Mr. Jones off saying, "Vince will never play for you again." Basically my Dad quit the team for me.

My Dad did all this because he cared about me. Mom cared about me too and was every bit it as angry as Dad was. I hated the fact that my season had ended so quickly, I had no clue if I would ever play again. At first I was angry at my Dad before Mom explained to me exactly what was said. I quickly lost my anger at my Dad and was proud of him.

I had given this season my full effort. I did everything the same way I had done for years prior. I was never able to understand what it was that Mr. Jones had against me. About two years after that season he passed away from a massive heart attack so I never had the chance to meet him again and ask him.

One thing was certain: this one season had completely ruined my hunger for the game. I was fourteen and about to start high school in the fall. Many doubts ran through my head mixed with anger. I had equated summertime with playing Little League. Now all that had been taken from me. It would nearly be four years until I picked up a baseball again.

Chapter 9
Void

"As we grow better, we meet better people."
~ Elbert Hubbard

It was the fall of 1999. Almost four years had passed since I last picked up a baseball. The love of the game had never left me. I was driving home from school with classmate and friend Mike Bell when I asked him to swing by the recreation center so I could apply to coach Little League that summer. Without hesitation he took me directly to the center where I grabbed a sign- up sheet to coach. As I walked into the main office and asked for the form, I reflected on the last several years of my life and feel as though I was finally capturing what I had been missing for so long. It was a long shot that the league would even need coaches that spring, but I was willing to take a chance.

High school had been very good to me. I had met my first girlfriend and even started my first after school job as a cashier at the local CVS Pharmacy. The years had flown by but with the only competition I had coming from Choir sing offs against other schools I knew the return to baseball was needed. With my romance behind me and my job only filling so much time, it was baseball that would once again fill the void in my life.

Since my last game under the reign of Mr. Jones, I had not participated in anything remotely close to Little League. The last four years had been good ones with very little to complain about. I was having fun, growing up and learning plenty. However, every summer between 1996 and 1999 I felt that something was missing. It was as if a part of me had been tucked away in a dark closet where no one could see. I let a man whom I despised steal the thing I loved the most. It was a youthful mistake that I can never regain. By entering the recreation center that day I was taking the first step in the process of returning to the game I loved.

I went into the league coordinators office and asked to speak with him. I introduced myself to him and he introduced himself to me, his name was Fran McNamara. He made me fill out an application explaining why I wanted to coach. At the bottom of the page there was a place to list one reference, much like there is when filling out a job application. The only name I could think to write down was Mr. Kubb. It had been five years since we had last spoke but I was willing to bet that he remembered me if asked.

Fran sat there for a few minutes studying my application form. He reminded me that since it was strictly a volunteer spot, I would never receive any money for my time. I made it clear to him that I wasn't in it to make any money. He told me that that they were not looking for coaches that spring but if anything changed he would let me know. He also mentioned that if by some miracle he called me to be a coach it would be for the ten year old league if there were a large number of players and they couldn't find anyone else to coach. Fran was basically telling me not to get my hopes up. The small window of hope he left open was all I needed. One thing was for sure, I would be sitting by the phone waiting for it to ring with good news. The only question was if the phone would ever ring?

Chapter 10
The Draft

"Success is where preparation and opportunity meet"
~ Bobby Unser

I knew I would have plenty of time before I heard anything about the coaching position I had applied for. My main concern was taking my mind off of it by staying busy with other projects and events. My senior year was lined up with many of them so it wouldn't be hard.

As fall turned to winter, I quickly realized that my senior year of high school had the potential to be my best. I was starting to make more friends than I could count. It was a far cry from nine years earlier when I had only one. What made them so great was that they were all so different. I still had the main group of five: Dave, Joe, Brad, Allen, and Matt. At the same time I continued to branch out and make more on my own. They came from all walks of high school life. Some were jocks. Some were nerds and I even had friends that were into punk music in which I absolutely despised. When I got over their odd choice of music I found out that some were great people.

Mike Bell became one of my closest friends. He chose to wear all black clothing every day. Normally I would stay away from students like this because of their drastic choices in music and television. It turned out that Mike was actually a great human being who loved baseball and wrestling almost as much as I did. He was also known for his gigantic size at 6 foot 8 inches and nearly 300 lbs. He completely shadowed over me.

On our drive homes we spoke about baseball and wrestling the entire time. Mike had a passion for the game that I hadn't seen in anyone for a long time. To look at him but not know him, I would have pegged him for a bouncer at a club or someone whose idea of sport was throwing people around at a punk rock concert. To learn he was as interested in baseball as much as I was became our common ground.

On a daily basis I would talk to Mike about how I planned to coach a little league team that spring. I told him that if he chose to help out it would be a big boost to the staff. Until that point I had not yet thought about a possible coaching staff but I knew that

Mike would be a great addition. I never imagined that his giant size and tendency for wearing all black might scare the children. I just went off the fact that I knew I could trust him and he seemed reliable.

One day in early October while driving home, we talked about our possible team. I told Mike that I was excited for him to be coaching with me but that there was certain rules that he must follow. My main rules were that he show me respect at all times in front of the children and never correct me in front of them unless it was urgent. I told him that I would gladly accept any suggestions he had and most likely use every single one of them. I also stated that we would make the lineups' together and agree on the signals. He accepted all these ideas and did not argue about any of them.

One of my most important rules was that he would attend both practice and every game. I considered him to be reliable in other ways and wasn't worried about his missing practice or game. My final rule was made especially for him that I was worried about bringing up. However I knew I would have to.

I explained to Mike that if he was to help out he had to quit smoking pot. I explained that in no way shape or form that I was going to put up with it. He always asked me to try it and I was always said, "no". I told him that if he was going to be around children that the last thing I wanted was for him to be under the influence. I told him that it could get us both in huge trouble so I would not put up with it. I knew he was reliable but I have also seen people on drugs and I find it to be the scariest thing in the world. The last thing I wanted to do was jeopardize something I dreamt about for so long.

Because he promised me that he would quit, I was willing to give him the chance. Looking back on it years later I realize that I was asking much from him. I believe that when you want something bad enough you have to sacrifice for it. Nothing in life comes easy and almost nothing comes without a price. If Mike wanted to coach as badly as I did then he was going to have to prove it.

As for trying to select the rest of the coaching staff, I decided to talk with my brother about it and see how he felt. I sought Don's advice because he had coached for years and thought he would also be a great asset to the team. Don agreed to help if he could deal mainly with the pitching staff. Don seemed to be extremely interested in pitching. Since I did not have a wealth of knowledge on it I agreed to let Don handle that area.

My decision of who would be my third and final assistant coach would have to wait on until I actually learned that I would be coaching. I didn't want to raise the hopes of three people, only have to have them collapse in case I wasn't allowed to coach.

Until that point I had focused all my free thoughts on waiting for a phone call. Until I received word from Fran saying I was allowed to coach, I had to keep doing fun things not to drive myself crazy waiting.

As the weeks then months went by, I continued to wait for that phone call. Despite my prayers and thoughts, the phone never rang. It wasn't until my birthday, January 14, which I began to give up hope. I thought that maybe Fran was waiting until I was officially 18 to call and offer me the spot. Sadly, as my birthday arrived there was still no call from anyone in charge of assigning coaches.

The next night after my birthday my friend Liana threw a party for me at her house. It was on this night at Lianas house that I came across a bible quote that would change my life forever. I was sad because I had not yet been called to be a coach when I walked into her kitchen and saw a tiny sign hanging on the freezer door. It read, Jeremiah 29: 11-12 "For I know the plans I have for you says the Lord. They are plans for good and not disaster. To give you a future and a hope. In those days in which you pray I will listen."

I was touched by the verse and told Liana that seeing it brightened my outlook on life. She proceeded to grab a pink post it note and write the entire quote on it for me. When she handed it to me I thanked her and placed the note in my wallet. Since that night it has never left my wallet for more than two minutes, so I can read it whenever times are tough.

As January rolled into February and the call still had not arrived, I was almost ready to give up. Every time I thought about abandoning hope, I looked at the pink sticky note and my faith returned. Sometimes it only takes a few seconds of peace to re-establish faith in something. I wanted it badly enough and truly believed that if it was meant to be then it would happen.

It was the morning of February 25, 2009, the start of what became one of the most important and greatest weekends of my entire life. I was putting on a crucifix necklace that my Mom had given to me weeks earlier. It was a solid silver necklace with a crucifix on it. I wore it at all times except when I slept. That morning when I put it on I kissed it for good luck.

That night after dinner, I lay down on my bed to pray. I turned off all the lights in my room and just lay there for over an hour talking to God. I was in the middle of praying and relaxing when the phone rang. I could hear my Mom in the next room answer it. She said, "Ok, I will tell him." That was all I heard. Two seconds after I heard her hang up the phone, she was knocking on my door. Until this point I had not told her or my Dad I was thinking of coaching.

Mom entered my room and explained that the phone call was for me. She told me that she didn't want to disturb me because she thought I was sleeping. She then told me that, "The man on the phone said to be at the Rec Center tomorrow by 3.p.m. to choose your team." As my eyes jumped from my head and my heart pounded through my chest, I remained speechless. I was so focused on whipping Brad's butt later that night, coaching was finally the last thing on my mind instead of the first. Mom then asked me, "What in the world is going on? You're not going to try coaching are you? I don't think that is a good idea."

I walked right past my Mom's negative thoughts into the living room to let my Dad know of what I had just found out. To my shock he was against the idea as well, even though it had been his own idea years prior.

The main reasons for their concern were that I would lose focus on school and the friends I had made. They went on to say that "the last year of your school is the best, and my focus should be on doing 18 year old things, not grown up things." They were concerned that I would get angry if players missed practices and games. They explained that times had changed since I was little, and that not everyone had the dedication I did. They worried that if my players didn't go full speed or care about the game the way I did, then I would begin to hate coaching.

Their biggest concern was that I would encounter severe prejudice because of my age and gender. They understood why I wanted to be a coach, but they explained how others might view it.

I agree that an 18 year old male wanting to be around a group of ten year olds doesn't sound completely normal; however, my heart was in the right place and my parents didn't want to see me get hurt. They explained that the other coaches would not allow me any respect and that as my parents it would be too hard for them to watch. They wanted me to enjoy my last days of school and freedom instead of taking on such a huge obligation.

I was angry and just stormed off without finishing the conversation. I was incredibly angry that for the first time in my life they didn't support me on something. I was too young and naïve to realize why they didn't want me to coach. At the time however, I only saw it as a negative and considered it unfair. I felt that it wasn't right that Don was allowed to coach basketball and they had never given him any trouble. Growing up as a younger brother the way I did, sometimes you tend to feel left out or over shadowed. It wasn't just then but pretty much my whole life I felt that way. I knew my parents loved us equal, but being the younger sibling I always felt that whatever Don achieved I had to do better at it to get any attention.

After the heated conversation with my parents over coaching, I went to Brad's house to cool off and hang out with my friends. I needed to go somewhere and clear my thoughts. Dave had just started one of my friends from choir named Julie. They stopped by and it was interesting to see my best friend with a girl I had known and hung out with for several years prior. It was the first time I had a friend dating a friend.

I was having considerable fun that night but I decided to cut it short so I could get home and speak with my parents about coaching before they went to bed. We sat down for about an hour and calmly talked everything out. They told me I was allowed to coach if I didn't let it interfere too much with school, my job and my friends. I was able to live with those conditions. Even if it did interfere I knew never let it be known because I didn't want to admit they could be right.

My parents loved me and were just looking out for my best interest. It was important to them that I enjoy normal teenager things. They pointed out that the prom was coming up in a few months and that things may super cede coaching. I knew that the sacrifice would be great but I was willing to make it.

I lay in bed that night barely able to sleep because of all the excitement the day had brought. My mind raced thinking about picking my own little league team the next afternoon. Months of waiting and wondering were about to become a reality.

The day was February 26, 2000 and it would forever change my life. As I got into my car to drive to the Rec Center I was a nervous wreck inside but knew I could never let it show. My Dad even asked me one last time as I was pulling out of the driveway if I still wanted to coach. Driving there I just prayed to god and asked him to lead me in the right direction.

As I pulled into the Rec Center parking lot I got out of my old rusty red Chevy Cavalier with the smashed in end, and took a deep breath. There was no turning back now. I was in it to win it from that point on.

When I walked into the room where the draft was being held I saw four grown men sitting around a large table. Almost in unison they stopped what they were doing and asked me if I was lost. I replied, "Is the room for the draft?" I was informed that it was the correct room so I replied, "No, I'm not lost." Fran then came in the room and asked me, "are you sure you still want to coach?" I said, "Yes." The four men sitting at the table began to laugh as Fran said, "Then take a seat." I had been there less than a minute and could already sense what my parents told me I would encounter.

I took a seat and introduced myself to the other coaches. The man sitting across from me was Tim Coyne. He seemed to be in his late forties and balding with a half shaven look. He had dark brown teeth and I could tell just by looking at him he smoked cigarettes and drank a lot of coffee. He did not say a word to me the entire time.

The next person I met was Jack Hill. Jack had to be in his late forties as well. He had gray hair and a look on his face that showed he was amused to see a young man in the room. He was shorter then I was and not all that well built.

Sitting next to Jack was a short dark man who resembled actor Gary Coleman. He looked so much like the actor that they could have been related. The man's name was Darryl Briggs. He seemed like a decent guy as he leaned over to shake my hand.

The final coach I met that day was Mike Molnar. Mike who was a friendly guy quickly engaged me in conversation. He asked me why I wanted to coach and if I knew anyone who would be playing. He generally seemed interested in why I was there and happy that I was helping out. Mike was a tall, skinny man in his early fifties.

Those four men had all coached the previous seasons. Fran explained that they each were allowed to keep eight players from their previous years rosters. The rest of the players would go into a live draft. We would draw numbers to determine the order of who got to pick first through fifth. Because their teams already had eight boys each on them, they would only have to pick five players each. The boys left after they had 13 players each and I had my first 5, would automatically go to me to fill my roster. There were not enough players to fill my roster of 13, which lead to me having to go out and find two more players.

After the coaches drew numbers it turned out that I would have the second pick in the draft. The first pick went to Darryl Briggs who took a boy by the name of Terry Beach. When it was my turn to pick I did not have a clue what I was doing and decided to go simply by feel. The following is the list of boys I chose to make my team with.

Pick 1 – Alex Uhlik
Pick 2 – Anthony Poli
Pick 3 – Mat Poli
Pick 4 –Billy Graves
Pick 5 – Dan Kitko
Pick 6 – Kyle Keller
Pick 7 – Mike Hach
Pick 8 – John Rehak
Pick 9 – Ryan Mackey
Pick 10 – Pat Morris

As I looked over my list of players one last time I couldn't help wonder what kind of team I was just handed. Fran had made a point of telling me that I was getting a group of players that no one else wanted. I hoped that perhaps there was a diamond in the rough on that sheet of paper. One thing was sure; I was going to do everything I could to find out.

Our first practice wasn't scheduled until mid-April, but I knew I couldn't wait that long. Now that I had my roster of players it would only be a matter of time before we began. I made a mental note to begin searching for available fields the next day in hopes of getting a head start on practices.

I needed to find two more players. I also needed to secure a team sponsor. As I sat down on my front porch to think about all this, I looked over at the yard next door. I saw a young boy who would change my life forever. He was tall and wide with arms like tree trunks. He and his family had moved in months earlier but I never bothered to spend any time getting to know him. On that day I formed a relationship that would change the course of a summer. It was then that I discovered the enigma known as Andy Barth.

Chapter 11
Building A Champion

"The world isn't all sunshine and rainbows. It's a very mean
and nasty place and I don't care how tough you are, it will
beat you to your knees and keep you there permanently if you
let it. You, me and nobody is going to hit as hard as life. But it
isn't about how hard you're hit. It is about how hard you can
get hit and keep moving forward. How much you can take and
keep moving forward. That's how winning is done!"
~ Rocky Balboa

I was now partially responsible for the summer of at least eleven
young boys. It was a huge responsibility but one I was eager to
accept. I looked over the roster numerous times thinking of how
much I needed to find at least one more player to put on the team. I
kept racking my brain about it when I looked over to the yard next
door and saw Andy Barth.

Andy was tall and wide with the arms of an ox. He was a
big kid, but from what I could tell by seeing him play in the yard
he seemed clumsy. Andy was also very much involved in
skateboarding. I never saw him pick up a baseball. He had the
perfect build to be a great power hitter though he was only ten
years old. I barely knew him and he never showed interest in
sports, I quickly dismissed the idea. He was lumbering around the
yard with his head down trying not to make eye contact. I cannot
blame him for this because in the year he had lived there I had
never given him much attention, and I was rather abrupt to the
boy in our few interactions. I was not usually unkind to children
but he always got on my nerves in the few exchanges we had so I
soured on him easily. It didn't help matters that his half step
brother Daniel was a big trouble maker and constantly setting
things on fire. I made the mistake of connecting Andy to Daniel's
torrid behavior. Not until Daniel moved out that I realized it was
he and not Andy who was causing trouble.

Andy came from a broken home and never even met his
real father. His mom Angie had married a man years later with two
children of his own. His mom and new dad decided to rent the
house next door to us. Andy also had a younger brother named
Mikey whom Angie had with an entirely different man. At the

time I knew nothing of all this and just thought he was an annoying boy who drove me crazy. After learning the details of his situation, I realized that Andy needed a friend.

Never having formed any bond with him in the year, he lived there I was extremely reluctant to go over and speak with him. However, something drew me to approach him to find out what was wrong. I walked across the yard and approached him as he cried on his front porch. I had seen him cry numerous times before so I didn't think the worst. When I asked him why he was crying he looked up and said, "My Grandpa just died." I sat with him for a few minutes in silence and just put my arm around him as he sobbed. I had nothing to say because I never had anyone close to me die. I wasn't even sure how to approach that kind of problem. The only thing that came to mind was asking him if he liked baseball". He promptly replied, "No." Not one to give up easily I asked him "if he ever had anyone teach him how to play?" Andy stated that no one had ever shown him how to play. It was at that point that I suddenly said, "I'll teach you."

Andy didn't have a glove, so I let him use one of my old ones. I explained to him a few basics about the game. He never took his attention away from what I was saying. In ten minutes I was throwing him ground balls and line drives. To my amazement he stopped every one. I started to throw the ball faster and harder but he let nothing get by him. I couldn't believe what I was seeing: the boy was a born natural at the sport. He ran after every ball full speed. He tried so hard that after our twenty minute session he was covered in sweat.

After the mini tryout I just put him through I sat him down and explained that I would be coaching a team of players his age that spring. Before I could even ask him he cut me off and said. "I want to play on it!" I explained that just because he lived next door to me that I wasn't going to go easy on him and would treat him just like everyone else on the team. He made it clear to me that he understood and asked me if I would continue to work with him in private sessions like the one we just had. I explained to him that what we just did was about to become a regular thing. I stated that we had just struck the tip of the iceberg when it came to teaching him about my beloved game.

We agreed that when he returned from the funeral in a couple of days we would pick up right where we left off. Three days later I got home from school to find Andy standing at my door with his glove in his hand, ready to play baseball. Despite the cold Cleveland spring weather, Andy let nothing stop him from wanting to play. I felt that after all these years I finally had a younger brother to teach baseball.

I put him through every physical drill in both fielding and throwing but also put him through numerous mental tests. I explained to him all the rules of the game and the situations of how he would have to handle them. I even gave him written tests on the ins and outs out the game to test his knowledge and how well he was learning. Andy was like a sponge as he picked up on everything I taught him. We even watched old Indian's games I had on tape just to further his knowledge of the game.

We had been practicing fielding for a week when I decided to let him have a chance to hit. I knew it wouldn't be long before I called my first team practice and I wanted to make sure Andy would be able to swing the bat well enough so he wouldn't be embarrassed in front of his new teammates. My lone worry was that he would forget everything I taught him once he had to do it in front of more than just me. I also knew that how he hit the ball would go a long way in giving him confidence before his peers.

Andy proved very interesting to watch at the plate. He didn't develop the natural swing I wanted for him to develop but rather that of a cave man swinging a club. I had to break him of that habit quickly, otherwise he would just pound everything into the ground. For as quickly as he picked up fielding he was suffering at hitting. The encouraging thing about it was that when he did swing level and kept his shoulder up, he drove the ball deep into the outfield. I knew it would be a battle to keep him positive while he learned this crucial part of the game. So every time he hit a ball deep I made it seem as if he just hit one out of a major league stadium. I tried very hard to boost his confidence as much as possible. I knew that his self-confidence would likely be his toughest battle all season.

I spent a week straight with Andy in order to prepare him for our first practice. I was not only worried about myself looking like I knew what I was doing, but also worried sick about Andy having a good showing so he wouldn't get discouraged and quit. It was the first time in my life that I felt responsible for anyone other than just myself. Andy didn't have a father or older brother like I did, so I knew that I was the only male role model in his life and I wanted him to know that I believed in him. I felt as though he was my pupil. I was proud of how far he had come in just a week's time but also hard on him as older brothers can often be.

In the midst of the one on one action with Andy I was also planning for our first practice. League rules forbid teams the use of field time and equipment earlier than April 15. Never being a stickler for rules or waiting, I called up each player and let them know that our first practice would be held at Little Clague Park on March 10, 2000. It was a full month before any other team would begin. I did this because we needed the extra time. I was a first year coach with zero coaching experience of any kind. Most of our players had no experience and I realized that we needed to get started right away if we were to have any chance. I also knew that we wouldn't have any batting helmets until mid-April, so I was focusing the early practices on fielding, running and fundamentals. I decided before our first practice that what we might lack in hitting that season, we would make up in defense, fundamentals and hustle.

I was incredibly nervous when I made the phone calls to the team to announce our first practice that I left the message with whoever picked up the phone. It didn't matter if it was the baby sitter or younger sibling. I just wanted to get off the phone as quickly as possible before anyone questioned my age. One mistake I made was to introduce myself as Vince instead of Mr. McKee. By doing that may have revealed my age to the few parents I spoke with.

The night before the first practice I spent over two hours working on a list of drills and things I wanted to accomplish. I wanted to test their ability to throw the ball and field both ground and fly balls. I also wished to tap into their knowledge of the game without completely overloading them with challenges and situations on the first night. I knew that the initial practice would go far in building an eventual championship team. It was important to set the tone early that I was coaching to win. I also knew it would be a challenge to incorporate this hunger to win without putting too much pressure on them. I wanted to make sure they had fun and that I didn't overwork them. With my age being such a huge factor against me, I knew that I had to impress them and the parents early on or it would be very easy to second guess everything I did.

The afternoon of the first practice I was having lunch sitting with Mike Bell talking over the things I wanted to do that night. He told me that he couldn't make it because his boss would not let him off work. I couldn't believe that I wouldn't have my assistant coach available the night of the first practice. I was livid and it required a couple of hours to calm down. I started racking my brain as to how I was going to run all the drills I had lined up with only Don and myself there. I saw Mike later in the day before school let out and apologized for yelling at him, but also asked him not to let it happen again.

By that point in the school year I had begun driving myself to school with the same beat up, old red Chevy Cavalier I learned to drive with years earlier. I didn't care how ugly the smashed up car looked, I was just pleased to have something to drive. On the way home I had the radio blasting and was singing the words to every song, because I was so nervous and excited I wanted to distract myself for a few moments.

When I arrived home I still had no idea as to who my assistant coach would be along with Don that evening. As luck would have it, his good friend Bill Meyers just happened to be at our house that day. Bill, who seemed to be over often, was a logical choice. I had known him my entire life and trusted him. With all the jokes we played on each other growing up aside, we got along well. I went over with Bill the same set of rules I had given Don and Mike. He had no problems with them.

After consulting with Don and Bill about what I wanted to achieve that night at practice, I went into my room and closed the door. I got down on one knee and quietly asked God to watch over me that season. I asked him to not let me quit no matter how bad it might get. My last experience with Little League baseball had been from playing for Mr. Jones. As hard as I tried to forget that ugly memory it never went away. I badly needed something good to happen in my life and hoped that this might be it.

I drove with my two fellow coaches to the field. We didn't bring anything except our gloves, because we didn't have anything else to bring. We didn't get our equipment until a month later so this practice would have to do without. When I called each house to inform them of the practice I made sure to mention that each player needed to bring a ball. I figured that if at least half of the players did then we would have enough. It turned out that every single player brought at least one ball if not two.

We arrived to the field thirty minutes before practice was scheduled to begin. I took the chance that no other league or form of sports team would be using the fields for any reason. I formed the idea that without the field being scheduled for use until mid-April, it was fair game until then. If the field was in use, I would have practiced in the parking lot, I was that determined to get things started. I walked to the middle of the diamond to soak in the beauty of the ball field before things got hectic.

I told Don and Bill to wait in the parking lot located about twenty yards from the field and greet the parents. I told them to send each player over to where I was standing and I would begin a game of catch with each one. I made it clear that I didn't want to speak with any parents until practice was over. I did this because I was so nervous that I worried about saying something foolish and a parent judging me before I even had a chance to coach their son. I wasn't showing it on the outside but on the inside I was shaking like a leaf.

As each player arrived Don and Bill sent him over to where I was standing in the middle of the diamond. The first player to show up was Brian Leciewksi. I played a game of catch with him until Alex Uhlik showed up, I then played a game of three way catch with both of them. The next player to show up was Danny Kitko and I partnered off with him and let Alex play with Brian. I was doing this with each boy who showed up in order to introduce myself to them, play catch with them for at least a minute and give them a one on one attention right away. Every player on that team can say that the first person they threw a ball to that year was their head coach. Those kinds of things are crucial in building trust in player's right from the start.

As more and more players showed up at the field I noticed that none of their parents were going home. Usually a parent will drop off their son and come back in two hours to pick them up. It was certainly a unique situation for the parents wanting to stick around. I don't blame them one bit for doing so, they were about to entrust an 18 year old with the lives of their children. Lucky for all of them, I was more than ready for the task.

I waited until the entire team showed up and then called a huddle to address them as team for the first time. I decided to huddle them up outside of the actual diamond, close to where the parents were sitting so everyone could hear what I was about to say. I introduced myself as the head coach and introduced both of my assistants. I explained to them that I was only eighteen years old but that would also be the last time all season that I would ever mention my age. I told them to call me Vince or Coach, whatever they felt more comfortable saying. I told them that I had played Little League baseball all my life and that I had been on some good teams in the past. I explained to them that I had been on three championship winning teams and that a championship was our goal that season. I quickly left the winning is "everything" routine to say that another goal that year was to have fun and learn the game. I told them that if they focused on what I was teaching them and practiced hard that winning and having fun would go hand in hand. The whole speech lasted less than a minute but I felt that I had gotten my points across and there was no need to continue.

We started practice with each player lined up at first base and the coaches taking turns throwing them ground balls. They lined up one by one and fielded ground balls in rapid succession. Once a player fielded the ball and threw it back to a coach, the next coach would fire one down to the next player in line and keep the chain going. We had extremely good speed going during the drill and it was nonstop movement. It succeeded in keeping the players attention and testing their skills in throwing, fielding and hustle all at once. The drill continued on for over five minutes until someone finally missed a ground ball.

I noticed Andy was moving along without any problems because we had repeatedly done the same thing in my yard. Each player attacked the ball and didn't shy away from it. I was impressed from what I saw right away. I moved them to each base after a few minutes of making the throws. While most players did good at first base and second, it was when we got to the shortstop throw that the big boys started to show their muscle.

Some of the smaller players like Munch and Billy struggled to make the throw from shortstop to home plate. I was not surprised because I was their size at their age and remember how tough it was to make that throw. While they struggled, it was Danny, Brian, Alex, and Anthony that thrived at launching rockets to the plate. As the baseballs were popping the gloves, it gave me goose bumps to think that this was my team. I knew it was only the first drill of the first practice but I became excited because of how well they were doing so quickly.

After they took several grounders from each position in the infield, I moved them to the outfield. I quickly realized that we might have a team of all infielders as they seemed to struggle at adapting to catching fly balls. I didn't panic because I knew it was only the first practice and we had plenty of time to improve. I also didn't panic because despite the struggles of some they were trying hard and doing everything we asked.

There were two players who did catch every fly ball we threw. Mike Hach and John Rehak seemed to be naturals at it. John, taller and lanky, moved gracefully when it came to running after fly balls. Mike had pure grit and determination unlike anyone I had seen in a long time. I almost looked past his ability to catch well because he kept joking around in line and I worried about his distracting other players. I decided to wait and see if he would stop acting up on his own before yelling at him. I didn't think it would have been the best of moves to scream at a player at the first practice with everyone watching.

We spent the rest of practice going over numerous other drills I had planned. Things seemed to be going smoothly the first night and I couldn't have been happier. I tried to be positive the few times I had to correct them. It was on the job training for me and my staff.

The biggest thing we drilled that night were the fundamentals and rules. I wanted to make sure they all knew how to play and what the game consisted of. This was important to go over because we had so many first year players. They learned quickly and didn't hesitate to ask questions.

I decided to end the two hour practice with the same way it began. I had them line up for a simple game of catch. It was during this game of catch that I partnered up with Brian. After a few soft tosses he had asked me if he could try pitching. I agreed and I gave him permission to toss a couple of hard ones. To my surprise he had a stronger arm than I realized and began to pepper fastballs into my glove. As he was pitching, the other players began to notice. They asked me if they could try to pitch also. I said, "Sure", and what was supposed to be a simple game of catch to cool everyone down became a mini tryout for everyone on the team that wanted to pitch.

When practice ended I told each player to go find their parents because I wanted to speak with them. As they pulled their parents over to where I was standing I had a chance to speak with Brian and ask him if he ever played before. He replied that the only playing experience he had was coach pitch in Cub Scout coed baseball. I found that extremely hard to believe due to his outstanding talents shown in merely the first practice. It wouldn't be until weeks later that Brian and his dad confessed that he had never even played the Cub Scout baseball. They only told me that because they didn't want me to know it was his first time playing baseball. Brian and his dad Ray didn't realize that he wasn't alone. It turned out that only Danny, Alex, The Poli Boy's, Mike and John were the only players on the team who had any experience. Half the team had no previous playing time at all!

I addressed parents and players at the end of practice because I wanted to formally introduce myself to the parents all at once. I was still too nervous to do it individually at that point. I explained that we had a long journey ahead of us because not many of the players were experienced. I also told them that we wouldn't have a set practice schedule until April 15th. In the mean time we would follow the weekly weather reports. I explained that not all practices would be at a baseball field. Some would be located in the massive field behind Maple School, because on the nights when the baseball fields were taken we still needed to practice. I told them that the odds would be stacked against us that year in every way possible, but that we would give it our best shot and only look forward. I finished by stating that the league only gave us the field time to have 10 practices before opening day, however, our goal was to have no less than 20. Eventually we had 23. While making the closing speech, I looked at each parent.

When the speech was over I handed them each a list I had typed up with what I considered our keys to victory. The list included tendencies and fundamentals we must learn to have any chance at winning. The list was as follows:

— Run on the field
— Run off the field
— Always pay attention out there
— Protect the plate with two strikes
— When batting keep your elbow up and step with your front foot while keeping your back foot planted.
— Keep your eye on the ball while swinging level and follow all the way though
— Runners, look at base coaches for all signals
— Talk it up out there, let your teammates know where the ball is going.

— Know the batting order, (who is up before you)
— PITCHERS COVER HOME ON PASSED BALLS!
— Run out every throw to first base.
— Slide on anything close.
— When applying a tag on the sliding runner, apply it on the feet or ankle.
— Shortstops cover the throw to second base on a steal
— OUTFIEDERS first step is always backward on a fly ball
— INFIELDERS call it, let the short stop take charge on anything close.
— Know the number of outs ALWAYS
— Listen to your coaches only, block out everything else.
— You play the ball, don't let the ball play you.
— Keep your mind on the game at all times. No daydreaming, no girl watching, no nothing. BASEBALL BASEBALL BASEBALL!
— If the bat is a little heavy choke up on it.
— If were facing a fast pitcher stand more towards the catcher in the batter's box.
— If the pitcher is slow then move up in the batter's box.
— Believe in yourselves and anything can happen.

Almost every parent came over to shake my hand and thanked me for taking the time to coach. A few of them never said a word. I knew that it was still going to take a while to warm everyone up to the Vince McKee way of thinking. One parent who did come over to me and thank me was Mr. Rehak. I told him that I was looking forward to coaching his son Johnny. He told me that he had been practicing long toss with his son in the yard for quite some time. It was only a minute long conversation, but one that I never will forget due to its thoughtfulness.

When I returned home I began looking over the roster and matching names with faces. I went over the roster one by one with Bill and Don and discussed who stood out among the rest. I got half way through the list before Andy came knocking on the door asking to play catch. I didn't hesitate to put down the list and meet him out front.

Later that night when I was trying to sleep and failing miserably to do so, I began thinking about our second practice and what I wanted to achieve. I knew that we had to do more than just field ground balls and fly balls. I developed a game plan in my head to bring them along slowly but make sure that each practice they learned something new and enjoyed doing it. I knew we still had much to cover, everything from base running to hitting. I also decided that I would have at least two separate practices for those who were interested in pitching.

I made a separate decision to let them decide on a team name, feeling that it would make them more excited about playing. I had a red and white hat from Wisconsin University with a Badger pictured on it. I knew that when we eventually received our uniforms they were supposed to be red and gray. I figured that it may be fun to have each player buy the hat and we could have called ourselves the Badgers. As it turned out, the league commission vetoed my idea. He said that we must wear the same North Olmsted Hot Stove hat the rest of the league wore. Despite the ruling I let my team choose a name. After much consideration they chose the Wildcats. It quickly made waves around the league and the other teams would no longer say, "we are playing McKee's team tonight", instead they would say, "we are playing the Wildcats." Knowing that I still had the red hat with the cat like creature on it, I was happy to name the team that. As coach I was not forced to wear the league mandated hat, but was free to wear whatever I wanted. It worked out perfectly and I would wear my hat for the rest of the season. To this day former players will mention that they remember my hat and how it was staple of who I was. It was much like the way I remember Mr. Wheeler for always wearing that hideous green jersey and bright orange hat.

Speaking of Mr. Wheeler, it became my goal when coaching to copy his way of teaching fundamentals and blend it in with Mr. Kubb's way of classy winning. I learned almost everything I know about coaching from those two men. I was blessed to have good coaching right from the start. Because of that I was more than willing to pass all my knowledge along to the youngsters I was now coaching. If I didn't have such great coaching as a youngster I don't believe I would have took to the role as quickly and as well as I did.

The next day at school when Mike asked me how good our team looked on a scale of 1-10, I calmly looked at him and proudly said, "8". I knew it was a bold claim but I was confident in what I saw. When hearing this news Mike's face lit up like a Christmas tree. I told him that because we didn't do any hitting that it may be a while before we got an accurate read on how much we need to work on.

After a couple more practices it was became more evident that we weren't going to be the league joke as the other coaches had   believed. It didn't matter where we held practice each player showed up and worked hard. After the initial practice where every parent stuck around, after the second practice only one parent stuck around. I had made a quick impression on the parents and it must have been a good one.

The parent who remained for each practice was Brian's dad, Ray. He did so because he wanted to help out. I was more than glad to have him. Ray was a good baseball man; he knew plenty about the game and never said "no" to anything I asked him to do. The players also seemed to like him. It was good having Ray around because he gave us the adult leadership that we needed. Technically I was considered an adult at the age of 18, but I was still learning how to act as one.

Ray was a well-built man who had actually claimed to have played Single A baseball earlier in his life. He said he used to pitch for the Houston Astros farm league. He had a huge knot on his right elbow that could be spotted a mile away. He said that he was an old pitching injury. I never looked into his story but chose to believe him. It would have been strange for someone to make up so I just accepted it.

Bringing Ray on board was the smartest thing I could have done. I say this because unfortunately as much as I love my brother Don, we learned quickly that we cannot coach together. Our styles just clashed far too much. We ended up having an argument one night before practice in my front yard. I was just about to leave for practice when Don approached me about some changes he wanted to make to the team. The conversation became heated and I disagreed with everything he wanted to do. This is not to say Don was wrong, but when it came to coaching we were completely different. Bill did not help matters by tackling me in the middle of the conversation and put me in a headlock as cars drove by honking. It was too much for me to take. When I got up I told them both that their help was no longer needed.

When I went to practice and told Mike and Ray what had happened, they understood. The practice went off without a hitch that night and I didn't second guess my decision. I did feel bad about it, however. The last thing I wanted to do was dismiss my brother when he was trying to help. I knew that his heart was in the right place. But I also knew that if I was going to earn any respect I would have to do this on my own. At a family get together earlier in the month, a few of my aunts and uncles asked Don about the baseball team "he" was coaching. Not a single one of them seemed to know that I was the coach and Don was helping me. I didn't bother correcting them but I felt it was something I would have had to deal with all season if Don stayed on board.

When I returned home from practice that night I spoke with Don and Bill. I told them both I was sorry for what happened earlier. They understood. Bill said that if I ever changed my mind to let him know and he would be happy to come back. Don understood that I was in a shadow when it came to our extended family. I was never angry at Don for this and realized it wasn't his fault, but we both knew I had to do this if I was to receive any respect.

In the midst of practices and trying to build a team I met a girl. It was on a Saturday night when I met Kathy Davis, she was the friend of Brad Russell's girlfriend Katie. I had met them at a fundraiser dance for the choir booster club. When I went up to her and asked her to dance, we hit it off right away. She was my height and very cute. She had pretty blue eyes and shoulder length Auburn hair. She was also extremely smart and finished as the number four student in her entire senior class a few years later. She was only in the tenth grade when I met her.

Later that night we went back to Brad's house and decided to take a walk around his development. Instead of talking to her about normal teenage things I talked about my team. As we walked along under the stars I proceeded to go on and on about my team and how eager I was for the season to start. I didn't even realize it but during the conversation she had grabbed my hand and began holding it.

It seemed as though my life was finally starting to come together. I had this cute girl hanging on my every word and I was talking about something I loved. I couldn't have met Kathy at a better time. It was right after I let my brother and Bill go and I needed something to keep my mind positive. I was excited about my team and it was nice to finally have someone to share my enthusiasm with. She had this soft sweet personality that went well with my tendency to be loud and energetic.

For some reason after I started coaching, I also started to lose my friends. I was spending the majority of my time with practices and very little time with them. It didn't help matters that once Dave Murphy started dating Julie I was somehow never asked to come around anymore. It was as if he took my spot in the group. Normally something like this would have driven me mad, but with the addition of coaching in my life and now meeting Kathy, nothing else seemed to matter. I had the choice of keeping my friends or focus on coaching; it was a very easy to choose the latter.

The most important thing to me at that point in my life was coaching my team. I decided to channel the anger of losing friends into focus on building a winner. I knew that the sweetest way to make the pain of that go away was winning. I had already begun to sacrifice my friendships; it was exactly what my parents had predicted. I never let on that I was losing friends because I didn't want them to get angry or second guess letting me coach.

About a month into practices we received another new player named Nate Dolesh. Nate was an extremely skinny boy with blond hair and glasses. Of medium height, he looked as though he was better suited for chess instead of baseball. It was no surprise when his father mentioned that this was the first time he would be playing. At this point it didn't matter due to the high volume of first year players we had on the team already. Nate was quiet but took instructions well and never talked back or got out of line.

The first time Nate swung the bat in batting practice, I realized not to judge a book by its cover. Despite Nate's small frame and mild look, he hit the ball a ton. He had a great swing for a first time player and regularly drove balls into the outfield. Nate may have had the look of a librarian but he had the bat of a major leaguer.

Soon after the addition of Nate I called a double practice one Saturday in early May. The original plan called for a practice both Saturday then Sunday. However, Kathy's birthday was that Sunday I and didn't want to miss it. Instead I called two practices for Saturday in which one would be held at Maple School in the morning and the other would be held at Clague Park later that night. To my surprise no one complained. Every single player showed up for both. The hunger to win and desire to learn the game was starting to build in them.

It was during the first practice that I started to show a giving side to the boys I had not yet done. Because I was asking them to work twice as hard in one day I decided to reward them. I brought popsicles and midway through the first practice I let them take a break to eat them. We had been practicing hard and it was nice to reward them with something simple. It went a long way in bonding with them. I was only eight years older and I knew what it took to get along with them.

It was also during this timeout that I began talking to them about my personal life. I didn't tell them too much because I wanted to keep their respect level up. But I did feel it necessary to show them I was just like them in certain ways. I told them that I had a new girlfriend that I really liked it and wasn't sure what to get her for her birthday. They were not short on ideas including video games and certain kinds of candy. It was funny to hear what the ten year old minds were thinking. A few of the players were teasing me that I could even like a girl, at their young age they had not yet discovered them. Then there was Andy Barth, who bragged that he had several girlfriends. It was just Andy being himself and it was good for team moral. Despite all the clowning around Andy and Mike Hach seemed to do, it never got in the way of practice or the games.

It was when practice resumed that a moment came I will never forget. I was tossing batting practice and Dan Kitko fouled a ball straight back that slammed into a glass window. To everyone's amazement the glass did not break. I had heard a story that elementary school's had unbreakable glass installed for safety reasons. I had never believed that notion until when the ball did not break the glass. As the team stood there in amazement of what just had taken place, I picked up the ball and threw it at the glass as hard as I could. I wanted to show them that the glass was unbreakable and for them to just have fun and not worry about breaking anything. When the ball shattered the glass window into a million pieces I soon realized that I was wrong and had just broken school property in front of my entire team. I still cannot figure out how the Kitko ball didn't break the glass, but I guess it doesn't even matter anymore. I told the players to never mention what they just saw to anyone because I didn't want to get in trouble. I felt terrible asking them to keep it quiet but knew it was important that they did.

Had one of my players went home and told his parents what happened and the parent would have called the league on me, I would have been done coaching that very minute. Luckily, not a single player told his parents about the incident and we relocated practice to the other side of the building until we were done.

When the first practice ended most of the players went home until the night practice at the park was ready to start. However, a few of the players decided to stick it out with me until the night time practice. The players hanging back with the coach were Mike, John, Brian and Andy. Each of their parents gave me a few bucks and said that if I wanted to take them to McDonald's for lunch that would be fine with them. Not only did I take them to lunch but afterward we still had time to kill so we went to Toys "R" Us. It was more bonding time for the players that began to make us feel more like a team. We each took turns boxing each other with these massive toy gloves that the store used to sell. It was a great chance to show them I could have fun and could not only be their coach but also their friend.

One thing that stands out most about the night time practice was my Dad walking to the park and watched it from the stands. I noticed he was there about half way through which made me really nervous. The whole time I was telling myself not to mess anything up while he was watching. I wanted to impress him and knew that if my team looked bad that I wouldn't achieve that. Dad had always supported me throughout the years and I wanted to let him see his faith was paying off.

Dad left at the end of practice so I didn't get a chance to talk to him until I returned home later that night. He had written out a list of things that stood out about practice. Most items on the list were good and he only made a few suggestions on how to improve. The suggestion that I remember most was the need to hustle more. He was right in his assessment because I felt the same thing. I knew I had a hungry group of players and I needed them to hustle more to get the most out of them. My father's watchful eye caught what could have become a major problem. I also factored in that it was their second three hour practice in the course of one day, and that they may have been slightly tired. Nevertheless I made a mental note to start the next practice with base running and chasing down fly balls to get their hearts and legs pumping.

The next day was Kathy's birthday and I was thrilled to spend it with her. We had been dating for over a month and things were going better than I thought they possibly could. A strange thing was occurring that up until that point had never happened, I was falling in love. Maybe it was the time in my life or maybe she was one of the very few people that believed in me at that time. There was just something about Kathy that I couldn't get enough of. If I wasn't thinking about the team I was thinking about her. My feelings became love.

I was worried about telling her that I loved her because it was so soon into our relationship. I decided not to mention how I felt unless I felt the time was perfect to do so. Later that night when I was kissing her goodnight in front of her house, she leaned in close and said, "I love you." I couldn't have heard three sweeter words that day and I quickly replied with, "I love you too." I truly meant what I said. There was not a doubt in my mind that I was in love and that things were shaping up for a huge summer.

The next day at school all I could think about was the night before in Kathy's driveway. I knew I had practice that night and tried to get back into the coaching mind frame. It was May 8 and school was basically over for seniors. We still had to show up to class but the workload was extremely light. I spent most of each day both thinking about Kathy and coaching. I filled up an entire notebook with baseball drills and potential starting line up's. It was a great way to round out my high school days.

That night at practice I was feeling so good about life that I sensed the need to share it with my team. I gave them a speech about how far they had come in such a short time and that I liked our chances for the regular season. I told them that I was thinking about coaching almost every second of every day. I made it clear that I liked the way things had gone so far but that we still had a long way to go. The team generally seemed pleased to hear this news and I thought that we would have an excellent practice.

A funny thing ended up happening that night, we had our worst practice all year. The boys seemed to do nothing right and didn't hustle at all. Every time I tried to teach them something I had to stop and yell at someone for goofing off. It was the first time I yelled in my coaching career and I didn't like it. They had lost all focus. It seemed as though they wanted to be anywhere but on the field. It could have been that I was over working them, or maybe just one of those days.

I cut practice short by twenty minutes and used that time to tell them how disappointed I was at their effort. It was totally different from the speech that I had given them just two hours earlier. I said that I would let them off the hook this time but I didn't want to see it happen again. I was angry and let them know. I blamed myself for letting things get too loose, and I vowed to not let it happen again.

There is a point when coaching children that it is crucial to have discipline without making it seem like tyranny. At the same time I wanted to make sure that things did not get too loose because I didn't want the children running all over me. It's a fine line to have a disciplined team without taking all the fun out of it for them. I was learning early on what it was going to take to have both.

After a couple of rainy days in a row it wasn't until that following weekend that we had our next practice. It was one that I called solely for the boys interested in pitching and catching. I did this in the hopes of settling on a pitching rotation and seeing what I had to work with at catcher. Those who showed up were Anthony Poli, Brian Leciewski, Kyle Keller, Alex Uhlik, Ryan Mackey, Dan Kitko and John Rehak.

Having a practice intended for just pitchers and catchers to attend proved to be a great idea. We could focus on those two things only for the entire time. I didn't even need to schedule field time for practice because we used the Maple School parking lot.

This practice went a long way in determining what we had in pitching and catching. Four players stood out above the rest when it came to pitching. Brian Leciewski seemed to have a knack for throwing hard but struggled at times with accuracy. I knew if I could get him under control that I would have a viable asset on my hands. A positive sign was that when he was missing the strike zone it was not by much.

Dan showed some pepper on his throws, but he also stood out because he had the accuracy that I was looking for in a pitcher. The biggest challenge with Dan was keeping him steady and not letting his nerves get the best of him. He had all the talent in the world it was just a matter of him keeping his poise.

Anthony Poli showed plenty of heart as well as arm speed. His problem was that he was too erratic. Unlike when Brian barely missed the strike zone, Anthony seemed to be all or nothing. This meant that either his pitches were right down the middle or nowhere close to the plate.

Alex Uhlik did everything I asked of him that night. He showed me he could play both catcher and pitcher very well. He had great speed in getting the ball down to second base out of the crouch. The best thing about Alex was that he was a total team player. Even though most of the glory goes to the pitcher, he was more than fine with anywhere I wanted to play him. Alex continued to amaze me in that despite his amazing talents he never believed he was bigger than the rest of the team. When one of your best players can lead by example and stay humble that is the greatest help to any coach.

Johnny Rehak showed good accuracy but not enough speed. I was worried that he was so accurate it would be like batting practice for the other team. I also knew that down the road as his body continued to grow his arm strength would eventually come. I just didn't see it happening until the next summer at the earliest. Johnny proved to be very coachable and took the tips from Ray with respect.

I didn't see much in Ryan Mackey when it came to pitching, but he really wanted to play pitcher. The boy was constantly talking about playing it, he never let it go. I promised him that because he showed up for practice that I would find an inning or two for him on the mound that season. I just worried that the promise would come back to haunt me.

I was struggling to find the right position for Kyle Keller, who showed heart and hustle. He was constantly busting his butt to do whatever the coaching staff asked of him. He lacked the speed that a typical pitcher was needed to do well, but he did have the heart that I knew he would be clutch in a tough situation. Because of his unreal hustle I decided to teach him how to play catcher. I realized his arm strength was going to be a concern but I also knew that his hustle would come in handy when it came to stopping passed balls. I knew Alex couldn't play every inning at the plate and that Kyle would be a suitable replacement when called upon.

When the pitching practice was over, I decided to drive to Clague Park. To my amusement there was a scrimmage game going on between Mr. Brrigg's team and Mr. Coyne's team. I happened to have a notebook on me so I sat down and started scouting. I was from the Mr. Kubb and Mr. Wheeler school of coaching that did not believe in scrimmaging so I knew this might be my only chance to get a sneak peak at the competition.

It wasn't before too long that the opposing coaches saw me sitting in the in the stands and said something to me.   They were not happy that I was scouting but they honestly couldn't stop me. I could tell it was annoying them greatly so I sat there and scouted them thoroughly.

The first thing I realized was that my team still needed work. The more I watched these two teams I charted things my own team needed to work on. I also noticed that my players did certain things better than these teams did. Sitting there not only annoyed the other coaches but also the parents of opposing players. It would become a sign of things to come later that summer.

A few days later Mike Bell and I drove to Jack Hill's house to pick up extra equipment and the year's schedule. Jack was one of the other coaches as well as the league coordinator for that age group. I considered it to be a conflict of interest for him to fill both roles but I made sure not to say anything about it. As the new guy on the block I didn't want to cause any trouble. I also figured that if things ever got out of hand I would just call up the league commissioner, Mr. Scarl, and voice my complaint.

I knew right away that Jack Hill had a big problem with my coaching. As we pulled up to his rather large house in one of the nicer communities of North Olmsted, I could instantly tell that he was upset because I was parking my rusty dented car in his driveway. It was as if the car reduced the value of his house by just being parked there. When I walked up to his front door he saw the size of Mike Bell and his eyes nearly leaped out of his head.

After he handed us the extra balls and equipment he made a point of telling me, "Don't expect to win any games this year." I couldn't believe what I heard so I just chose not to ignore it. When I looked over at Mike he had steam coming out of his gigantic frame. I could tell the comment angered him as much as it did me. I made sure to call Jack by his last name of Mr. Hill instead of calling him Jack. I did this to show him respect despite the level of ignorance he had shown. I also did this to make him feel old. He knew that he was older than me by twenty years and I wanted to remind him of that in case we did beat his team. No one likes losing. It becomes even worse when they lose to someone much younger and less experienced then them. As we drove away I didn't have to say a word because I was positive Mike was thinking the same thing I was. It was a silent car ride until arriving back at Mike's. He looked over at me and said, "We are going to kill them." I replied, "Count on it!"

I took that experience of extreme disrespect and decided to turn it to my advantage. I let his negative words motivate me into wanting to improve. I used his attitude to further enlarge the already growing chip on my shoulder. I knew coming into that season that every day was going to be a battle and that no matter what happened on the field that a mental battle would also be taking place in my head. In a mere forty eight hours I had felt strong hatred from people who barely knew me, I was feeling this because I had stepped on their turf and I wasn't backing down. The easiest thing I could have done was leave the field instead of scouting, and I stayed. It would have been easier to say something nasty back to Mr. Hill but I chose not to. I was determined to show these people that they were dealing with a young man and not a boy.

It was the most unique time of my entire life for many different reasons. On one hand I was about to graduate from high school and start life as an adult. I was falling in love with a beautiful girl whom I absolutely adored. I felt as though I had the world in the palm of my hands and I wasn't going to let anyone take it from me. It also put plenty of pressure on my shoulders not to screw any of it up.

I felt as though it was me against the world. I had just taken on a team of players no one else wanted. I was a first year coach with no experience and outside of my coaching staff and girlfriend, very few believed in us. I was facing extreme prejudice from the other coaches and parents before we played a single game. I was merely eighteen years old, taking on the pressures of being responsible for the summer of thirteen young boys. People have asked me why I took things so seriously when it came to coaching. I had no choice but to take things seriously. If I failed then everyone would have been proven right. All the critics and the naysayers would have gotten their way. I was bound and determined to prove them all wrong. I believed in each and every one of my players. They had all had heart and skill, and it would be up to me to show them that it could pay off in victories. For every reason someone would give me as to why I couldn't be a good coach, I gave myself ten reasons as to why I could. The second I let one negative thought cross my mind about my team I would have become a loser. I was not going to let that happen.

In the years I played for Mr. Wheeler and Mr. Kubb I learned to think like a winner. They taught me how to believe in myself and in my teammates. I knew that if my team was going to have any chance at success I needed to instill those same beliefs into them. When someone hears negative words against them it can have two effects. The first is letting those words get to them and they quickly become losers. The other is when they can turn those negative thoughts into motivation to win and prove people wrong. My mom has always said that I am at my best in life when someone tells me I can't achieve something. I just hoped that my team would react the same way.

As much as Mr. Hill's words angered me that day, I would thank him now if I ever saw him. I would thank him for lighting a fire under me that I truly needed to jumpstart that season and give me one more reason to succeed. I remember later that night telling Kathy as to what he said and she repeated the same thought that winning would be the best way to shut him up. One great thing about Kathy was that she always knew what to say to cheer me up and keep my head on the level. She didn't sugarcoat anything but instead always told me the truth on how she felt. It was exactly the type of honesty I needed.

With the start of the season quickly approaching I had to find a sponsor. I went around to numerous sports stores in the neighborhood but no owner was interested in sponsoring our team. Finding a sponsor was crucial because every team needed one or else the parents would have to pay extra money to have uniforms for the boys. If we didn't find a sponsor then the uniforms would be left blank and we would become the laughing stock of the league. It was something I already feared, and surely I did not need this additional problem to further enhance the image.

With a few days to spare I finally found a team sponsor. It was a locally owned store called "Play it Again Sports". It sold used sporting equipment and was located five minutes from my parents' home. I knew that I needed to do some sweet talking because the owner Jeff Snead would not budge at first. He said economic times were poor and he was losing out to major commercial brand stores. I decided to make him a deal he couldn't refuse. I guaranteed him a first place trophy and that all my players would only shop at his store for sporting goods for the next year. I had no way to provide either one of those things but it was the first thing that popped into my mind so I blurted it out. To my amazement he took me up on the offer and cut us a check for $500. At the very worst if our team was lousy then I would just never go back to the store and hope that I never bumped into him anywhere else.

The final practice before our first game I decided that the boys had been working very hard and that we would celebrate by having an inter-squad game. That is when a team divides itself into two teams and plays one another in a game that is strictly a scrimmage. It was tough to do with only thirteen players but I placed Mike Bell and Ray on each team as well to help out matters along with myself.

It was a sloppy game but the boys enjoyed and it was good to blow off some steam. One memorable thing I remember from that game was Mike Hach smashing a double ten feet over the center fielder's head. I looked at Mike as he looked back at me in pure amusement. Mike had been a great contact hitter in batting practice but that was the first time he showed some power. It was certainly a nice sign for the season.

We also used that last practice to hand out uniforms. Our jerseys looked great. They had red trim with a gray front and back. The numbers and team sponsorship were also in red. I still wore my Wildcat hat and the team wore their red hot stove hats. We looked and felt like a team.

At the end of the practice I addressed the team one last time. I told them that on scale of 1-50 I was excited about going to my senior prom that weekend on the level of a 30. I also told them that on a scale of 1-50 I was excited that we were less than one week away from our first game on a level of 50. I told them I was proud of how far they had come and that I expected big things from them that season. I told them that no matter how bleak things may look that we would stick it out and improve as the season went on. The main message delivered to the boys was that the following months were going to be a battle and I wouldn't want anyone else by my side fighting it. I had them all raise their hands together and meet in the middle, I said, "Boys, we have one goal this year: Win the championship!" Then on the count of three we all yelled, "Wildcats". There was not a doubt in my mind that this team was ready to play and win!

With the prom only a day away and graduation less than two weeks off, I had all but one of my classes done and over with. I had gotten such good grades my senior year with the exception of physics that I did not need to take finals because I already earned enough credits to graduate. I knew that despite how I did on my one and only exam that I would still graduate. It turned out that physics was not even the class that required me to take the final, but rather it was my film study teacher Mr. Oros.

I was not thrilled about having to go to school for one class in the middle of the day to take a final in a class in which I had already scored an A in. As I sat down to write my essay on the last movie we watched that year, Clockwork Orange, I decided not to write about it. Instead I produced a two page essay on my team. I gave an in depth player profile on each team member and what I thought our chances for that season were. I also wrote a few paragraphs on why I thought "Rocky" was the greatest movie of all time. That was the same class in which Cassie Kitko, who I had hoped was Dan Kitko's sister, was in. So as I walked out I placed a copy of our schedule on her desk while she was taking her test. I knew it was kind of an odd thing to do since I was dating Kathy, but I figured that if things didn't work out it would be a good idea to have a cute girl in the stands. I never found out what I got on that essay, but I'm willing to wager it wasn't good. I would have given anything to see Mr. Oros face when he read it.

As I left North Olmsted High School for the final time I made sure to stop by the choir room. All the underclassmen had to show up for two more weeks. I went in and said my goodbyes to everyone. It was an emotional moment as I exchanged hugs with many people I had become close with and shared memories with. I also took the opportunity to hand them schedules for my team that season in hopes that would come to some games and show support.

Before I walked out for good I made sure to give a hug to Mr. Chris Venesile. He was the best teacher I ever had. I wanted to make sure I paid him my utmost respect. I thanked him for including me in the choir despite my terrible singing voice. It was a great all around day and a perfect way to end my high school life.

Saturday May 20, 2000 was a day that went a long way in shaping the rest of my life. It was the day of my senior prom and also that morning was the opening day parade held in the streets of North Olmsted. I was very nervous about both and expected a lot out of each one. When I had played North Olmsted Hot Stove as a youth we did not have the opening day parade so that was something I looked forward to. I remembered them being fun when I played for Mr. Wheeler in the Cleveland league. It was nice to see that North Olmsted was finally doing something to make things more enjoyable for the children.

It was the night before this historic day that stands out in my memory because of the incredible nervousness I had running through my veins. Dad took me to a tuxedo shop at the mall to pick up my tuxedo. As we waited in line we talked more about my team than anything else. We didn't talk much about the prom the next night but more about the team. I was fine with that and didn't think too much about it. I later found out that my dad was trying to avoid the topic of prom because he didn't want me to be nervous. It all seemed pretty simple to me. I didn't think much about it because I considered it just another high school dance. The enormity of it being the last of my high school life hadn't sunk it yet.

I laid lying in bed all night and did not get a single minute of sleep. I couldn't keep my mind from racing about the parade and upcoming season. It was the first time that the weight of what I was about to take on started to sink in. I knew that despite my best efforts it might not be good enough. I also knew that I was going to give it my full attention, and utilize everything I had been taught from Mr. Wheeler and Mr. Kubb.

After tossing and turning all night I decided to give up on sleep all together and crawl out of bed around 5 a.m. I took a note pad with me and walked up to Little Clague Park. I remember watching the sun come up as I was charting different line ups and game plans for our first game that Tuesday. As most students were sleeping the night before the biggest days of their lives, I was up and working on something that had nothing to do with school or prom, and everything to do with fulfilling a dream.

I knew we had both the talent and the heart. I knew we had all the makings of a winner. I just did not know if and when I could put it all together into a championship team. I thought about how easy Mr. Wheeler and Mr. Kubb made it look all those years ago. Sitting on the bench in the dugout I knew that the next three months of my life would be the most important.

I eventually walked home from the park before anyone else in my house was up and out of bed. I never breathed a word to anyone as to what I did that morning. I have learned that sometimes the most special things I experienced in life were the ones I kept all to myself.

As I drove with Andy Barth to the parade I was running on no sleep for over twenty four hours and hoped that the excitement of the morning was enough to keep me alert. When I arrived at the meeting spot by North Olmsted Police Station my entire team was there waiting for me. Cleary they were every bit as excited as I was. I looked at my team in their uniforms and brimmed with pride. It was much like when parents looked at their child on the first day of school. No matter what the season held for us, I knew we would take it head on as a team and not back down.

The parade turned out to be a blast as my dad showed up and the team had made signs to put all over his pickup truck. Most of the signs said simple things like "Go, Wildcats", and things of that nature. A few of the boys rode in the back of the flat bed while the rest of us ran alongside the truck. I could tell that the children on the other teams were jealous of the cool looking pickup truck when they looked on with mouths wide open and pointed fingers at us. We over-heard numerous children say that it looked really cool. It was another way to make my team feel special. The other coaches hated it. Mr. Briggs even said, "This isn't that big of a deal, you guys overdid it." I saw that a few of his players overheard what he said and looked sad by it. To the children the parade was a big deal and for them to hear their coach say that it wasn't, ruined it for them.

As the parade passed through the streets of North Olmsted many of the parents of my players said some very kind things to me. Numerous parents pulled me aside along the walk and wished me good luck this season. They showed so much positive enthusiasm towards me that I felt really good. Other parents such as Mrs. Hach made sure to tell me good luck that night at the senior prom. I could tell that Mike Bell was getting a kick out of things as well.

When I returned home I knew I had several hours before I had to get ready for the prom so I decided to take a long nap. Just when I went to do so Andy Barth showed up at my door asking to play catch. He still had his uniform on from the parade and I didn't have the heart to say no. As I was playing catch with Andy I made sure to tell him that I was proud of him and that now that the season was just around the corner it was time to apply everything I had been teaching him.

I ended up sleeping all day, the best thing that I could have done. By the time I woke up to go to the prom I was well rested and had much enthusiasm for that night's events.

That night Kathy looked more beautiful than ever. She had on a purple and black dress that made her look incredible. The dark tones in her dress matched perfectly with the black tuxedo that I was wearing. As we took pictures with family members I leaned over and whispered in her ear, "This will be the best night of our lives." I truly meant what I said and was determined that it would be so.

The prom was held at the BP building in downtown Cleveland. It was the same place where the prom was held four years earlier when Don took Abbie. I saw that as a good sign. I drove my busted up red Chevy Cavalier that had already seen numerous good times. I was never thrilled about riding in a limo and didn't think twice about taking the Cavalier. The great thing about Kathy was that she didn't care what we drove in as long as we went together.

The prom itself was a fun time but not nearly as big as the hype that people surround it with. It felt like going to a wedding without the bride and groom. I liked the prom but it wasn't the event that people made it out to be. I spent most of the evening dancing with Kathy but also talking baseball with Joe Ghramn and Mike Bell. Kathy didn't seem to mind and I was never short on the topic of my beloved team. Joe was one of the few friends who stuck by me in my decision to coach. I talked for numerous minutes with Mike on the line up and a few ideas we shared. Mike showed as much enthusiasm as I did towards things with the team. Kathy didn't seem to mind at all that the team was dominating so much of our conversation that night.

The after prom party ended early the next morning about 6.a.m. Instead of taking Kathy straight home we stopped off in the valley and watched the sun come up. It was the most romantic thing of my young life. I felt as though it was the right thing to do with the girl I loved. We just sat back and held hands and eventually she fell asleep on my shoulder. It was a pretty amazing 24 hours that I will always cherish.

Our first game was slated for that following Tuesday night and I had a few days off from work before hand to relax and prepare for it. The Monday before that game I went with Bill to Cedar Point. It is a large rollercoaster theme park in Northwest Ohio that people travel from all over America to visit. I remember it being cold that day for May but still a fun time. We talked mainly about the team and how things were going. He made sure to mention that if I ever wanted him to come back and help coach that he would be glad to do so. I remember thanking him for the offer and telling him that it was a possibility. He also mentioned that he had gotten into a fight with his Dad and that my parents had given him permission to live in our basement until things cooled off. So I knew where to find him if I ever needed him.

I was pleased to have Bill living with us because we got along well. He had been my brother's best friend for so long he was like one of the family. Dave Murphy had always been perceived in the same way when it came to family. As luck would have it, Bill moving in helped out in numerous ways that summer. It was a long day packed with fun but I was anxious to get home and game plan some more.

After I called Kathy to say goodnight I said my nightly prayers and tried to go to sleep. I reflected one last time on how far my boys had come in a short time and knew that no matter the outcome of the season we had already earned people's respect. I knew that as I went to bed that night Monday May 22, 2000 as Vince McKee high school senior, the next morning I would awake Vince McKee the adult.

The time for talk was over. The time for wondering and hoping had come to an end. I woke up on Tuesday, May 23, 2000, with one purpose and that was to win! It was time to play ball!

Chapter 12

Game Time

"Get a dream, hold onto it and reach for the sky!"
~ Dusty Rhodes

It began as a normal spring afternoon with the sun shining and birds chirping. This day was anything but normal for me as I paced around my room waiting to leave for our first game. It was a moment I had been waiting months to arrive. I had set my expectations high on the kind of season the team might have. I knew we had the talent to win the championship but it takes more than talent to win. I hoped for a fair shot at winning and playing hard despite the early cards we had seemingly been dealt. It was during this time of getting ready for the game that I wondered if Mr. Wheeler and Mr. Kubb had these feelings before every game.

My thoughts turned to the other coaches I would battle all season. I wondered if they were as nervous or excited as I was. I could tell by early interaction with them they seemed to be cold towards me as well as something new. I felt as though I had stepped on their turf and was very unwelcome to be there. To them the season was just another excuse to get out of the house and feed their enlarged egos. It made me stop and think about an age old question that I had often pondered. The question of what separates good from evil had been something I wondered about my whole life.

I believed that God creates human beings with the full intent that they will do the right things in life. He creates man with the hope that they will choose to be a kind person and not intentionally hurt others in what they do or say. I realized that no matter what kind of hatred I might face that season, I should do my best to realize that these people are good on the inside. As the season progressed I founder it hard to remember that fact.

During this relaxation period is when I started to prepare myself mentally and physically for that night's game. In my playing days I had developed numerous habits and routines and it quickly seemed that my coaching days would be no different. Before every game I made sure to listen to songs that I loved such as "Higher," a song by a group I liked called Creed. It helped to prepare me mentally for each game. I made sure to put in their CD for that one particular song while getting ready.

The other tradition was to always put my chain with my crucifix on last. I made a point of kissing the cross every time and saying, "Let's bring home a victory tonight". I never believed in praying for a win in any sport no matter what the reason, however, I didn't see this as full blown prayer but rather another way of letting God I felt His presence with me. It was also a way to show God that regardless of the outcome we would face it together.

The traditions continued into the car ride to the games. As I drove to pick up Mike Bell I decided to play country music on my car's stereo. I had never listened to country music before in my life, but I felt as though it might be fun to try something new. Not only did I end up loving country music but it also served its purpose in helping me to relax. Though I wasn't thrilled about driving across town to pick up Mike, the music at least gave me good company.

A few weeks before the season started Mike decided to go drag racing in his Dad's car and got in serious trouble. Police took his license away and I became his designated driver to and from practice and games. I was nice enough to do it because he had driven me to school many times the prior school year. I did keep hope that he would get his license back sooner rather than later.

A very bizarre thing happened on the way to pick up Mike. As I was driving the sky opened up and an enormous rain storm broke. It started raining so hard that I thought the game would certainly be cancelled. By the time Mike got into my car the sky had grown pitch black, as if a tornado was about to touch down. As we pulled into the parking lot of North Olmsted Middle School the rain magically stopped. It was only a five minute spring shower, I was happy to see it end. Having our first game getting rained out would have been a lousy way to start the season.

Earlier in the day my mother had asked if I wanted her and my father to attend the game. I explained it wasn't a good idea until we played a few games. I wanted to make sure I knew what I was doing before I felt comfortable with them being there. I also mentioned how I was nervous to begin with and their attendance might make me even more so. I cannot explain why, but for some reason I was more nervous about them seeing me perform as an adult then I ever was as a boy. When I was a child I wasn't worried about letting them down or my losses upsetting them. However, as an adult I was much more nervous that if my team lost and looked horrible than they might feel worse about letting me coach.

Don had been coaching basketball for years at that point. He had seen his share of wins and losses. Every time I would go to a game with my parents that Don coached I saw the look of sadness and pain in their eyes whenever his team lost. They cared so much about their son's that it hurt them to see us in any pain or sadness. With that lying heavily on my mind I didn't want them to see my team on the field until I knew we had a chance at winning. Without having coached a single game I still had no definite idea as to how competitive my team might be.

Kathy appeared at the field wearing a homemade tee shirt with the word "Wildcats" on the front and "Coach's Girl" on the back. It was really inspirational to see my girlfriend showing so much support. I knew that with her by my side I stood a fighting chance against anyone. There is an old saying," Behind every great man there is a great woman." In my case this saying served to be true. I could have never made it through those early times without Kathy by my side every step of the way.

Don and Abbie also attended opening night. It was encouraging to have my brother sitting only ten feet behind me. After we agreed that we couldn't coach together no friction existed between us. Although we had talked numerous times about the team and it never lead to an argument. Don understood that I needed to do this by myself if I was to get any respect. This was one of those times when I needed to prove to myself I could do it on my own. Having looked up to Don my whole life, I now had my first chance to follow in his footsteps. I was determined to make him proud of me.

Before I looked over the lineup for a final time I looked over the crowd filling in. I didn't see a single one of my friends at the game, even though they all knew how important it was for me. I hoped that a few would trickle in once the game started. I was wrong as not a single one showed up. It is something I will never forget. I didn't expect all of them but I had hoped for a couple. My heart was so incredibly involved in coaching I made the mistake of thinking other people were too.

Immediately I had to make adjustments in the lineup. My original plan was to start Dan Kitko at pitcher because he had looked best in the practices. The night before the game I received a call from his father saying Dan had a school band concert and wouldn't be at the game. I would have to imagine that they knew about the concert for weeks and was not thrilled they waited until the night before to tell me about it. My thoughts raced back to what my parents had told me of when I first talked to them about coaching.

After that phone call I decided to go with my heart and let Ryan Mackey pitch because he had worked so hard for it. I also believed that he might actually be decent that night because we were playing against his former team. He had played for Ohio Envelope, which was coached by Mike Molnar the previous year and didn't like many of the players. I was hoping to catch lighting in a bottle with Mackey. Something happened that changed my mind five minutes before the first pitch. Ryan Mackey's pitching debut suddenly looked like it would be delayed.

I hadn't posted the lineup card and still had time to change it when I walked over and saw Brian Leciewski throwing rockets into Ray's glove. Ray turned to me and said, "He's nailing the corners all night if the ump is going to call them." It was at that point that I made coaching mistake number one of my coaching career. I decided to go with his suggestion of starting Brian and rewrote my lineup for the third time in 24 hours. The final lineup card for our first game ended up looking like this.

(In order of which they batted)
CF Matt Poli
SS Anthony Poli
3B Alex Uhlik
P Brian Leciewski
LF Mike Hach
2B Billy Graves
1B Pat Morris
C Kyle Keller
LC Andy Barth
RF Nate Dolesh
Reserves – John Rehak and Ryan Mackey

We took the field first as the home team. I was proud of my players as they ran onto the field for the first time. I wasn't too nervous at that point because I was relieved to finally get the season started. It wouldn't take long to second guess my decision of starting Brain at pitcher. As good as he was in practice it became clear that the nerves of playing in an actual game were just too much for him to handle. I had not considered that he had never been in a real game before, because of his talents in practice it was easy to forget. I remembered back to my first real game against John Hancock and how I struck out three times. It doesn't matter how talented someone is if they can't fight off the nerves.

My worst fear came true when Brian walked the first nine batters he faced and we were quickly down 6-0 without a single ball being put into play. I was partly at fault for starting a rookie in the first game. The other part belongs to Mike Molnar who instructed his players not to swing the bat until they had two strikes on them. It was a wise strategy but also one that should not be used in Little League. I fully understand letting one strike happen before instructing the player to swing away, but telling your team to wait for two is not correct. The entire point of Little League is to put the ball in play so the children can learn how to hit and field. Brian was able to get the first two strikes on numerous players but could never get that elusive third strike.

As I stood there watching nine consecutive players draw walks without swinging at a single pitch the only thing I could think of was the movie "Major League". The same thing happened to the star of the movie in his first chance at pitching. Before anyone on Ohio Envelope had a chance to hit a grand slam I decided to pull Brian from the mound. It was brutal having to go out and pull player who was trying his heart out to get an out. I told Brian that he was very talented but this didn't seem like the night he would get to show it. I patted him on the back and switched him with shortstop Anthony Poli. I told Anthony not to worry about anything but throwing strikes and having fun. I could tell that Anthony was a nervous wreck. I couldn't blame him and didn't know anyone who would have felt comfortable coming into that situation. Anthony battled through it and showed a good deal of heart as he got us out of the inning trailing 9-0.

The Ohio Envelope team wore medium green Jerseys with blue pants. They had a weird looking uniform color combo, but for what they lacked in fashion they made up in ball playing. This team was led by the excellent pitching of Anthony Marflak. Anthony was a bigger child but he had an arm like a rocket. He had a stocky built but was very athletic, moving gracefully on the mound. Other players on their team stood out as well, but it was Anthony who opposing batters feared.

When I thought things couldn't get any worse they quickly did as Marflak struck out the first three batters he faced. When my team took the field for the second inning I told them to relax a little and not play so tensely. They must have heard me because they proceeded to field three straight ground balls and shut down their opponent's offense. Billy Graves looked great during this stretch making two very impressive plays at second base.

Still down 9-0 I made a decision to call for a hit and run with Morris at the plate with Hach flying home to try and score. Sadly, Morris missed the sign and Mike was tagged out at home plate. We eventually scored later that inning when John Rehak came in the game and hit a double to score our first two runs of the season. Nate Dolesh followed it up with a RBI double and we cut the lead to 9-3. That would be the closest we came to getting back in the game.

As the game progressed on it was more of the same from the Molnar bunch, very little swinging the bat and forcing our pitchers to throw perfect strikes. Danny Molnar crushed a ball in the fourth inning to deep right center field where Andy Barth was standing flat footed. Unfortunately he did not use two hands so the ball popped right out of his glove. As I jumped onto the fence in the dugout to yell out at Andy to use two hands, my jersey got caught on the fence and ripped a tiny quarter sized hole in it. I never bothered getting it sewn up and no one ever mentioned it. The whole remained for the rest of the season.

The dropped fly ball was only the beginning of Andy's problems as he went 0-3 at the plate with three strikeouts. I couldn't believe how badly he was playing. It was as if a different human being was occupied Andy's body. He showed no confidence and didn't do a single thing that we had taught him. I was starting to become worried and feared that he might quit. The agonizing part was that I knew he could play so much better than the way he was.

The players did show improvement as the game continued but not nearly enough to make it competitive again. I had to give them credit for not quitting after the nightmare first inning. As bad as the game went I still didn't abandon all hope that things would eventually improve.

When the game was called for darkness in the bottom of the sixth inning, we trailed 14-5. A part of me was disappointed that we couldn't finish the game and have a chance at coming back; however, with the way things were going it may have been a blessing to call the game early. Games were normally scheduled for seven innings but could be stopped by the umpire if he felt that the sky was getting too dark. Darkness would make it too dangerous for the boys to be out there. Adequate light is needed to see line drives and fly balls, without that it could lead to a player getting hurt.

As the team gathered up for my post game talk I noticed that all three other coaches in the league were at the game. Jack Hill, Darryl Briggs, and Tim Coyne had just enjoyed watching my team lose. In a weird sort of way I took it as a positive that they were there because I felt that we didn't show nearly how well we could play, which would lead them to underestimate us. It didn't feel good to lose but I have always learned to try and find some positive in losing, as much as I hate when it happens.

I couldn't blame the boys for being upset one bit. Having worked very hard in pre-season through all those practices, they expected better from themselves. I told them a baseball season is like a marathon and not a sprint. It doesn't matter how quickly they start but how they finish. Inside my head I was trying to tell myself the same thing. I repeated to them that I was proud and to rest up because we had a game on Thursday and we shouldn't expect anything less than improvement. They huddled up and Brian and Anthony led the team in a "1-2-3 Wildcats" cheer, it was nice to see them have some fun despite the thrashing we just took.

Driving home was brutal; I had to take Mike all the way to East Cleveland where his dad lived. After a tough loss the last thing I wanted was to be around anyone. I was not taking the loss very well. I just didn't believe that Molnar had the better team. I felt that when we faced his team again it would be a different story. We had a few bright spots to look at but we still knew how much we had ahead of ourselves.

The ride home also sparked another tradition. I decided that every time we lost a game I would only listen to alternative rock stations on the radio. It served a more mellow purpose, something that reflected the depressed mood I was in. It also had a higher frequency of playing Smashing Pumpkin songs which would help cheer me up.

When I returned home that night I called Kathy, spoke with her about the game and thanked her for coming. It was pleasant to hear her soft voice on the other end. As painful as it was to lose, it was comforting to know I still had her. No matter the outcome of the season she would stand by me.

Dad came into my room and sat on my bed to talk to me. When I told him how bad things had gone he was very supportive as usual. He was quick to remind me of the summer when I played for Mr. Hurley. We had a bad start, but bounced back and had one of the best summers of my childhood. It meant everything having a father who was always there for me. I don't know what I would have done without him.

Don and Abbie also came to give me a hug, telling me not to worry about it because losing is a part of the game. Don also joked saying that whenever I won my first game I would have twice as many as Mr. Chambers did in his entire coaching career. I laughed and started to get my mind off things.

Not too long after I got home Andy came knocking on my door with his glove in hand. He seemed to be fighting back tears and asked me to play catch. I felt as though it was what we both needed to get over the loss. We spent the next several hours playing catch with a tennis ball in my back yard with the garage light on. We played with a tennis ball because it was dark and didn't want to run the risk of hurting each other with a hard ball.

Afterward we went inside and watched movies all night with Bill. It was the perfect way to blow off steam after a hard night. It never dawned upon Bill or me that Andy had to get up for school the next day until about 2 a.m. when his mom came looking for him.

The next day I slept in until it was time to go to work. With school over and games only a couple times a week, I had more hours available for work. To help cope with the hours of boredom that come with my cashiers' job, I decided to make mental notes on how the team could improve after the game one debacle. I never told my team how angry I was because I didn't want to shatter their confidence so early in the season. However, deep down inside I remained angry. From that point forward I expected better from them and myself.

I spent the evening at Kathy's house helping her study for final exams. The underclassmen still had class for two more days and I needed something to take my mind off baseball. As I was quizzing her on the different things she needed to know, I couldn't help but bring up my team. I wanted to stay off the topic and help her study but I couldn't take my mind off the first night loss no matter how hard I tried. I asked her who I should start at pitcher between Dan and Alex. She refused to answer because she didn't want to take the heat if the player did not do well. I decided to give her a kiss goodnight and headed back home still undecided. It wasn't fair for her to have to listen to baseball talk when she was trying to study.

The next day was graduation practice at the high school. I sat and listened to the principal ramble on about how important the following Sunday was. As I began to day dream about that night's game I realized who was sitting next me. It was my old friend Paul Hut.

Paul and I had broken apart our friendship sophomore year and never really patched it up. It wasn't as if we were mean to each other, we just ran with different crowds. Paul started hanging out with people more into the drinking scene and that wasn't my cup of tea. He had let his hair grow long while trying too hard to fit in with the high school mentality some students had. I couldn't help but look at Paul and flashback to his dad and the drunken tirades I was once privy to. It was a shame because during the forty five minute practice we barely said two words to each other. We had changed as people but I was fine with it. I chose to remember Paul for the great friend that he was.

Not talking with Paul at practice gave me more time to think about beating Jack Hill. If we were going to get our first win it couldn't have come against a better person than Jack. I thought about those words he spewed weeks earlier in his driveway and knew that this would be our first chance to throw them back at him. It was also the same reason I decided to start Alex Uhlik at pitcher because of the mean things he had to say about Alex. I figured that if Alex did well against him it would be the perfect way to stick it to him. I thought so much about my team that I wore my jersey to graduation practice. It was my way to keep myself focused on the team and let people know that I was proud to coach.

When practice ended, each student received $20 worth of free tokens for the Swings and Things batting cages up the street from school. As I raced to my car to get to the batting cages first I had the brainstorm to stop at home and pick up Andy. He was home from school and I thought it would be a good way to boost his confidence.

When I reached my car there was a note on the windshield from Kathy reminding me that she loved me and not to worry about the game because she promised we would win. She must have snuck out after one of her finals and spotted my car. It was a nice thing for her to do, something I will treasure always.

Andy was thrilled when I took him to the cages. It also gave him the chance to hang out with some high school kids for a few minutes. He later said that he would enjoy high school someday because of the girl's; I reminded him that he barely passed the fourth grade. He took the chance to impress some of the students watching him and crushed the ball on almost every pitch in the cage. I needed to find a way to make Andy feel as comfortable in the real game as he did in the cage and as he did when I pitched to him.

I enjoyed the country music alone on the way to the game because Mike actually got his own ride. No offense to Mike, but I get extremely nervous before games and it's better for everyone if I remain alone. The last thing I want to do before a game is speak with anyone because it is my time to mentally prepare.

As I pulled into the middle school parking lot for game two, I felt this time might be different. If we lost that game to Jack Hill I honestly didn't know how I would react. I wanted to win so much more as a coach then I ever did as a player. It's one of those indescribable feelings I can't put into words. At that moment, I wanted to win more than I wanted to breathe.

As I paced the dugout waiting not only for my team to arrive but also the other team I noticed that my friend Joe Ghramn had showed up. It was nice to see Joe. He walked over to me, asking, "Why are you the only one at the field", I told him that "I liked to get there early", and promised him that a game would take place. Shortly after Joe's arrival both teams starting to appear.

My team looked nervous and I knew that a motivating pre - game speech was needed. I just hoped that I didn't disappoint. Before Alex had a chance to look at the line-up card I wanted to tell him personally that he was pitching. I always liked to tell my pitcher personally and not wait for him to find out from someone else. I did it to instill confidence in the player and let him know I was behind him. I made sure to tell him to relax and just throw strikes. I was confident in our defense's ability to field and wanted the ball to be put in play as much as possible.

Alex showed how composed he was and thanked me for the opportunity to show his stuff. He was such a smooth player on and off the field. If Alex ever got rattled he never let anyone see it. After that two minute talk with Alex I knew he had what it took to be a winner.

After posting the line-up I took one last look over the crowd and saw that Lianna Early had come to the game and was sitting next to Kathy. I hadn't spoken to her in weeks and was surprised to see her. She was one of the group members to stop talking with me after Dave started dating Julie. I was happy to see her and was also happy to notice Brad Russell and Katie in the crowd sitting next to her. Not only did I have the support of my girlfriend, but Brad had brought his. It was the extra mental support I needed at the time.

Our line-up that night had a few changes in it but was still as potent as ever. I looked across at the opposing team dressed in red tops with white lettering and solid gray pants. They had a classy looking jersey but that was the only nice thing they had working for them that night. The following was our lineup for game two.

CF Matt Poli
SS Anthony Poli
P Alex Uhlik
C Brian Leciewski
3B Dan Kitko
RC Andy Barth
LF Mike Hach
LC Nate Dolesh
IB Kyle Keller
2B Billy Graves
Reserves – Pat Morris, Ryan Mackey, John Rehak

I felt bad about having to start the game with three boys sitting on the bench, but the simple fact was that there were 13 players yet only 10 spots in the starting line-up. If it wasn't for the Little League rule of allowing one extra outfielder it would have been even harder. A coach never likes having to bench anyone but unfortunately it is part of the game.

In the pre-game speech I let them know that this game was about them learning and having fun. I told them the reason they played poorly last game was because they were trying much too hard which sometimes can be a bad thing. I wanted them to continue to try hard but also relax enough to have fun and stay light on their feet. I explained that it was all right to make mistakes because that is how learning is done. I concluded by telling them to win for themselves and not me. I had been told by several parents and players how much they wanted to win for me, and I wanted them to win for themselves every bit as badly.

Umpiring the game was a young man named Tom Grodek. Tom had been a classmate of mine in school that year. North Olmsted Hot Stove had a way of hiring mainly teenagers to umpire the games. Tom and I had lunch study hall together that year so it wasn't as if we were friends, but we did know of each other. He was also a freshman so I never actually spoke with him. Before the game started he came over to the dugouts and explained the rules to each manager. It was standard procedure, however, when he left my dugout he said, "Good luck Vince." Jack overheard him and scowled.

Alex struck out the Hall line up in order to start the game and our team steamrolled from there. We jumped out to a 7-0 lead in the first and never looked back. Unlike our first game when nothing seemed to go right, this time the team played with the same intensity but didn't make as many errors. It helped matters that Alex was looking sharp and caused several batters to strike out swinging. He was in such control that our outfield only saw one fly ball which Mike Hach fielded cleanly.

Billy Graves continued to shine at second base, fielding every ball that came his way cleanly. He was off to a slow start at the plate but his glove was one of the stronger on the team. He had a good chemistry working with shortstop Anthony Poli. They communicated well as to who was going to cover the bag at second when there was a play there.

I also continued to be impressed by the hitting of Nate Dolesh. He had a pure swing and excellent pop in his shoulders when he swung at the pitch and drove the ball. In his first at bat Jack shouted out to his outfield to scoot up to the edge of the infield. He must have taken one look at Nate and thought he had no pop in his bat. Jack couldn't have been more wrong as Nate smashed the first pitch into deep right for a triple.

Despite the blowout we had going against Sedmack, the game did not lack some small drama. I was not trying to run up the score but I wasn't going to tell my team to stop hitting. Late in the game with us up 17-3, Alex Uhlik managed to steal home on a passed ball. Mike sent him from third to be aggressive and I had no problems with it. Since it was only the second game of the season, we wanted to teach them that they needed to run on a passed ball. Jack took it the wrong way as the next pitch was thrown from his own son David's hands, directly at the head of Mike Hach.

Mike ducked out of the way, but I could tell that he was angry. Mike shouted something out to David and Jack was quick to respond. He yelled over to my dugout saying "I needed to control my team." I didn't show him the courtesy of responding. I would learn in the coming months that this was typical Jack Hill behavior.

The other bit of drama came in the fourth inning when I pulled Alex from the game and inserted Dan Kitko to pitch. Dan was cruising along as usual but his dad kept yelling things at him on the mound. Not only was he making Dan nervous but I could tell it was affecting the other players. Mr. Kitko was a good guy who seemed like a caring parent so it was tough to get angry at him. Dan went the next two innings and made it clear that he would be one of our aces on the mound that year. Despite what anyone was yelling at him from the stands, he seemed to have all the natural abilities to be a dynamite pitcher.

The game was not all good news. Andy Barth continued to struggle at the plate and went a brutal 0-4 with three more strikeouts. He had showed so much promise in practice but seemed to get unfocused and shaky in the actual games. It was hard to watch him struggle.

In the bottom of the fifth inning with an 18-4 lead, the umpire called the game do to the mercy rule. With a 14 run lead late in the game I think he knew the boys in red had no chance at a comeback. Surprisingly there was no rebuttal from Jack concerning to the early stoppage.

I tried hard to control my team's enthusiasm as they celebrated in the dugout, I didn't want it to seem as if we were showing off, but there was no doubt that it felt amazing to get that first win. The last time I felt that good about a win came nine years earlier when we won the championship with Mr. Wheeler.

I was looking forward to the post game hand shake with Jack Hill but it never happened. As both teams walked down the line and slapped hands saying, "Good game", Jack was nowhere to be found. I searched around to find him standing in his dugout scowling. I had a hard time believing a grown man would be acting so badly but I didn't let it spoil the excitement of our first win.

The team huddled up behind the dugout alongside their parents. I gave out a couple game balls to Alex and Billy. I also made a point of saying, "it was a total team effort and that we couldn't have done it without everyone's help." I was so proud of them and I made sure to let them know it. I asked them to hold onto the feeling of winning for as long as they could. I explained the importance of how good it felt and that it would make them want to play that well every game so they could keep feeling it. I saw a few players close their eyes and soak it in. I knew I had gotten my point across when I saw that.

I have always felt that to experience how good winning feels you have to lose first. Then a person can feel the pain that comes with it. The joy of winning can overshadow the pain of losing and make a person work ten times harder to feel it again. It was extremely important for my team to get a win early in the season so they would know how it felt and want to keep working hard to achieve that feeling time and time again.

I was walking to my car smiling about the victory when I was stopped by Mr. Dolesh in the parking lot. He shook my hand and told me that Nate really enjoyed playing and was happy to be on the team. It was nice to hear such things that made me feel that I was doing actually meant something. It was what he told me next that I couldn't believe. Nate's family had planned a cross country trip that summer. They planned to travel the country for over a month. This caused Nate to miss the next sixteen games.

I was rather angry about this at the time because I wanted his bat in the line-up and felt that he was getting robbed of a chance to develop a skill. After I had time to think about it I calmed down. The child was going to have the chance to see the country and that is something amazing in itself. In the long run I was happy for him and his family. I also knew he would back in time for the playoffs and state tournament if we advanced that far.

The sound of hip hop music was blaring on the car stereo that night. I had decided that after every win I would put on stations that only played hip hop music. I wanted the feeling of excitement and electricity to carryover with me on the drive. This became yet another tradition as every win resulted in hip hop music afterwards in the car.

I went straight to Kathy's house after the win and celebrated with her. I was happy to get all the stress and worrying about winning a game over with so soon. Kathy was excited for me and kept telling me how good a game it was to watch. I explained to her that we still had considerable work to do but it was enjoyable to let this soak in until our next game. The win was one of my happiest moments and I was thankful to share it with the girl I loved.

We had the weekend off and weren't scheduled to play again until the following Tuesday night. I was not happy about having so much time in between games but the break came at the right time because that weekend I had something important planned. The Sunday afternoon following the big win was my high school graduation ceremony.

Instead of the ceremony being held at the school, graduation took place in downtown Cleveland at the State Theatre. It was a classy establishment that usually hosted plays and concerts. It was good to see all my classmates dressed up and looking all grown up. I was able to feel like an adult in my suit and tie.

I remember Mom taking a good amount of pictures to cherish the occasion. I felt as though the day meant the most to her because she had gone through so much that she thought she may never be alive to see me graduate. All the years I was in school it was Mom who took the extra time to help me study. I was proud to make her proud of me. I still felt bad about not making honor roll in high school, but I did manage to make merit role a few times.

I was only allowed to give away six tickets to my graduation ceremony. The State Theatre was not intended for graduations and it needed to limit how many people were allowed in at one time. With the first five tickets going to my parents, Don, and my grandparents, it presented a problem with who would get the last ticket. Don made a strong case for Abbie to be there. As much as I loved her I decided to give the final ticket to Kathy. I was so incredibly in love with her that I thought it was the best thing to do. I feel bad about not getting a ticket for Abbie, it was one of things in my life that I wish I would have done differently. Abbie was part of our family for years at that point and deserved to be there, I had only been with Kathy a few months, it shows how wrapped up into Kathy I was. If my biggest obsession was coaching, then my second biggest was Kathy.

Kathy bought me the latest Smashing Pumpkins CD as a graduation gift. That night Dave came over and we listened to it. After listening to our favorite band we decided to walk up to Maple School for one of our famous chats about life. Dave had graduated from St. Ignatius earlier that day so Kathy understood why it was important for me to celebrate the night with my best friend.

Dave would be leaving that fall for college in Cincinnati. He had been accepted into Xavier, a prestigious private school. I was happy for Dave because he worked very hard to get there. We talked about how weird it would be to no longer live around the block from each other but four hours away. As we puffed on our cigars we talked about how the last four years had just made our friendship stronger so that this would be no different.

The interesting thing about our lives is that they always seemed to mirror each other in so many ways. We both met our girlfriends around the same time. We both went to prom on the same day as well as graduated from high school on the same day. A few years earlier we even got our driver's license on the same day. My mom often joked that we would even get married on the same day.

Sitting there that night on those monkey bars, we had no clue that our childhoods had disappeared and that being an adult loomed. I felt as if I had been an adult since spring when I took over the team, I just may have not believed it yet.

I had a hard time sleeping that evening because my mind was flooded with thoughts. They were mostly good thoughts and also a few concerns. I had just gone through an incredible two weeks and I knew that the best maybe yet to come. I was trying to soak it all in but sometimes that is easier said than done.

At eighteen I was taking on so much and I had to cling to hope that I was ready for it. Above all else was coaching, it seemed to top whatever else was going on in my life. I was in love with Kathy. I had a job, friends and more responsibility than ever before. I was naïve as to what life had in store for me and I knew that as long as I stayed true to my values and worked hard that everything would somehow work out. The scariest thing in life is uncertainty about the future. I loved coaching but I had no idea was in store for me next. At only eighteen years old, I was fearless about many things, but the thought of failure was not one of them. I feared failure, wanting to do whatever was required for it not to happen. It was a fear I never let go of.

I learned quickly that I could only protect my players when they were around me. I could watch over them and guide them to the best of my ability. I could be as strict or as fun as I wanted to with them but the second they left the field they were in someone else's care. It didn't matter how much thought I gave into our team improving. If the boys weren't thinking about it on their own, then it didn't matter how much effort I put in.

One thing I never thought about in coaching was a child getting hurt. I had seen players get hurt in my playing days but I had never been hurt myself. It never dawned on me that one of my players could possibly be injured outside practice or a game. It was the Monday afternoon after graduation when the phone rang forcing me to realize this first hand.

Dad called me into the living room with a look of great concern showing on his face. I had not seen him wear this look in many years. It was one that symbolized that something was seriously wrong. After hanging up the phone he told me, "Sit down." The phone call came from a parent of a player. Tragedy had just struck.

Chapter 13
Paying Dues

"Prosperity isn't without many fears and disasters, and adversity isn't without comforts and hopes."
~ Francis Bacon

Playing baseball, growing up, getting hurt was the last thing I ever thought about. I was taught from a young age to play with reckless abandon. At home I developed the same attitude and never worried about injury. I felt invincible like most children seem to do. When I decided to coach it never dawned on me that one of my players could get seriously hurt. It would become an everyday thought soon after a phone call from Mr. Graves.

Dad took the call and relayed the message that Billy was hurt badly on the playground that day. He had been playing with some buddies and happened to walk past the swing as his friend was swinging backward on it. Billy, who was not paying attention, got smacked hard on his back. This caused Billy to fly backwards and rupture his spleen. A ruptured spleen if not treated right away can be fatal. His friends rushed to a nearby house where the owners called 911. Billy was rushed to Fairview hospital to receive immediate care for his injury. If his friends hadn't reacted as quickly as they did Billy would not have survived.

After hearing this news from my dad I was in a state of mild shock. My initial thought was wondering how to tell the team. I needed to figure out the long term magnitude of how they might react. I didn't want to scare them with a horror story but I also didn't want to conceal the truth. The saddest part was that Billy's entire summer had ended in a day. When he got out of the hospital weeks later he was told that he couldn't even ride a bike for at least a year. The slightest bump would cause him to rupture again, this time it could be fatal.

Looking at things in strictly baseball terms it took my roster down to eleven players until the end of the summer when Nate would return. It wasn't the worst thing to have eleven players to fill ten spots because it meant I would only have to bench one player each game. I hated to see any boy have to sit the bench so it was helpful to know that only one player would have to do so each game. I spent the rest of the day reshaping my lineup for that night's game.

When I was about to leave to pick up Mike Bell the phone rang. Mrs. Morris was calling to tell me that Pat would miss that night's game because they received Indians tickets for that night. I wasn't exactly happy that he was going to miss the game but I wouldn't let it get me down. Missing a baseball game to go watch the Indians was not an excuse I dealt with kindly. There are 81 home games a year when their child could be taken to see the Indians play. There are only a handful of Little League games each summer a child has a chance to play in. When a parent signed their son up to play on a team it was their responsibility to get him to each game.

As I drove to pick up Mike Bell I was listening to the great sounds of Kenny Chesney when I noticed a chill in the air. I rolled up my window because the air was getting cold and it didn't seem as if summer had arrived. It was the first week of June; however, this was the typical weather of Northeast Ohio. I assumed this meant that runs would not be easy to come by that night. It is much harder to get good swings on the ball when the air is cold.

I wanted Brian to pitch but I hesitated because he did so poorly in the opening game against Molnar's team. I knew he had the talent to be good but I wanted to get a few wins under our belt before I went back to him. I decided that I would pitch Alex the first three innings then go to Dan for the final four. I knew I was stretching it a bit with Dan going four but I wasn't ready to try Brian again so I went with my gut.

Mike made a comment on the way about the country music, I could tell it was getting to him because he loved heavy metal and this was far from it. I backed my decision of country music and told him, "Until he found his own way to the games that he would have to deal with it."

I gathered the team before the game knowing that I would have to tell them about Billy. I explained that he was going to be all right, but unable to play again this season. I passed around a baseball and had the entire team sign it along with the coaches. I thought that this would be a good way to show our support for Billy as well as a sign of team unity. I wasn't sure when I would see Billy next but knew that when I did I needed to make him feel that he was still part of the team.

I sensed that when I spoke about Billy and how lucky they were able to play that my words were sinking in. The boys had looks on their faces of serious focus. They were upset to lose a teammate but also inspired to win it for him. This gave them one more reason to prove everyone wrong and finish on top.

Before posting the starting line-up I looked over the crowd as I normally did before each game. I saw that my parents were sitting in the stands. My heart skipped a few beats making me want to win even more. It was tough for them to miss the first two games because they hated missing anything that I did. I knew from now on there was no way to keep them at home for any more games. For the rest of the season they came to every game. I was happy to see them in the crowd but it did make me extra nervous that first time. I didn't want to let them down the same way the children didn't want to let me down.

It was good having some support in the crowd because Kathy could not make it that night. She worked part time at the drive in theater. She missed many games that season, which was not to my liking, but I understood. Her work consisted of all nights so it was rare that she could make games once the summer started.

Our opponents were dressed in dark purple tops and solid white pants. The jersey tops had white block lettering across the chest. I'm not sure how he managed to do it, but Mr. Brigg's had each player's names on the back of the jersey as well.

I walked to home plate where I handed over our line up to the opposing manager Darryl Briggs. He was a short, dark- skinned man of generous proportions. He looked just like actor Gary Coleman but was a foot or so taller. He wasn't the nicest man but was not overly mean. He had a look in his face that clearly showed he was unhappy about coaching against someone my age. This was becoming a common trend. I was starting to realize some of the same prejudice that Mr. Wheeler and Mr. Kubb faced years ago. The lineup for that night is as follows:

CF Matt Poli
SS Anthony Poli
P Alex Uhlik

C Brian Leciewski
3B Dan Kitko
LF Mike Hach
RF John Rehak
2B Kyle Keller
1B Ryan Mackey
RC Andy Barth

We did not have anyone coming off the bench so it was important to get off to a fast start so as not have to make any major switches early on. I felt confident with Alex on the mound with the defense I put behind him. I was nervous about removing our best glove from the infield by putting Brian Leciewski behind the plate. But I knew he had the strong arm and Briggs had fast players. I wanted to keep them honest with Brian's arm strong enough to throw out anyone trying to steal second base. Kyle Keller had been showing improvement with the glove so I wanted him to try him at second base to replace Billy.

A mere five minutes passed before I grasped the coaching technique of Darryl Spriggs. For a man so short in stature he had a loud mouth. He didn't hesitate to constantly correct the umpire, Scott Pogros. Darryl seemed to have a problem with every call Pogros made.

It was not only Darryl but also his wife Kelly sitting behind the backstop barking away. She was a huge woman with skin whiter then snow and jet black hair. She weighed over 300 pounds and wasn't hard to miss. I felt bad for the umpire but also worried about her yelling distracting my players.

I could tell the constant jabbering was getting to my players so when it was our turn to pitch I asked Pogros to move her away from behind the backstop. The rulebook clearly states that no one is allowed directly behind the backstop during game play because it distracts the pitcher. They thought that since I was new that they could get away with breaking the rules. They were not counting on the fact that I had played Little League for several years growing up. I knew the rulebook like the back of my hand.

This sparked a negative reaction from Kelly. She asked how I knew the umpire's first name was Scott. I made the mistake of addressing him by his first name and not the standard "Blue", which is protocol when speaking to the umpire. Although I didn't know him personally, we did attend the same school so I knew him. He was two years younger than I so I didn't see it as a big deal to call him by his first name. It was a mistake I never let happen again.

Darryl appeared to be angry that I stuck up for my team. He and his wife must have thought that my age made me easier to push around. They did not understand that I lived and breathed coaching my team. It was the biggest thing in my life so I wasn't going to let anyone disturb my players.

During this game I developed the habit of pacing around the dugout all game long. I was consumed by nervous energy such that I couldn't allow myself to sit and relax. It didn't matter what inning or the score I paced around. I felt I needed to be on my feet at all times in case I needed to change something about the game. There were games when I would get home and be soaked in sweat just from pacing. I returned home some nights with more sweat and dirt on me then I had done in my playing days. I didn't want to miss a single pitch or swing. To me being a good coach meant not missing anything that happened. I wanted the ability to communicate with my players no matter where they stood on the field. It didn't matter if it was hand signs or shouting instructions when needed, I made sure my players knew that I was there if they needed me. Assistant coaches Ray and Mike also did a good job of this.

The weather caused the game to be crisp and fast paced. Both teams sensed the urgency to score as many runs as possible. The runs proved minimal that evening much the way I figured they would be. Alex did a good job of pitching strikes and letting the boys in purple put the ball in play. Kyle Keller was doing a good job as the new second baseman. He managed to field everything hit his way on the ground or in the air. Despite the good defense we trailed 3-2 after three innings.

In the top half of the fourth with two men out and two men in scoring position I put on a hit and run with Brian Leciewski at the plate. Matt had great speed on third base and Alex was every bit as fast at second base. Brian swung at the first pitch, crushing a two-run double and putting us ahead 4-3. A minute later Dan hit a soft line drive that dropped in for a base hit. We had overcome a deficit and turned it into a two-run lead with Brian scoring on the line drive. It was an exciting turn in the game to see my boys battle back from an early deficit and take the lead.

We would not hold onto the lead long because in the bottom of the fourth Briggs team scored four runs and retook the lead 7-5. The three runs came off of a Terry Beach three run homerun on what looked like a fastball from Dan Kitko.

Terry Beach was considered the best player in the league by many that season. I totally disagreed as I felt that I had at least five or six players better than he. He was a big boy with long hair which drew him much attention. He could hit the ball a mile when it was placed directly over the plate, however, he never got around quickly enough on the inside fastball. I went over the scouting report with Dan and Alex before the game started when it came to Beach. Dan knew that he was to stick with the inside corner. It wasn't as if he meant to put the ball right down the middle. I could tell the mistake was annoying Dan so I walked to the mound for a visit.

I tried to calm him down and reassure him that we still had at bats left with plenty of time to get back in the game. Since it was only a two run lead I needed him to keep it close. I knew that I didn't have a back-up plan if Dan couldn't pitch the 4th through 7th innings. It was essential that he settle down and brush off the mistake. True to form Dan handled it like a winner, striking out the next seven batters he faced in the fourth, fifth and sixth innings.

Still down 7-5 in the top of the seventh we were down to our last three outs and needed some magic quickly. Uhlik lead off the inning with a double while Brian drew a walk. With two men on and nobody out Dan worked the count full. Adam Sedgmer who up until that point had pitched a beautiful game threw the next pitch right down the middle and Dan crushed it. He drove in both runs as he slid into second with the tying double. Our bench was electric with enthusiasm as it breathed new life into our team. I could hear Mr. Kitko screaming at the top of his lungs, "That a boy kid, that a boy!" It was a good moment making me realize how much I had missed the last couple of summers. No amount of money could match the feeling of watching my boys succeed. Some moments in life are too good to be bought and this was one of them.

Mike Hach clipped a perfect bunt down the first base line to sacrifice Dan over to third. Having the go ahead run on third base with only one out in the top of the last inning, I could sense victory. After Rehak was intentionally walked to put a man on first base and open up the double-play possibility. The next two batters struck out so the rally ended before we could take the lead.

With the game all tied up in the bottom of the seventh, I knew we couldn't let up a run or the game would be over. Dan had pitched three innings and I decided to let him pitch his fourth. In Little League a pitcher can only go four innings at that level. I hoped Dan could get the game into extra innings and then I could go with Anthony Poli in the 8th if need be. Dan proved to be untouchable for the third straight inning as he set down the lineup in order. He last struck out Corey Benkowski with a wicked curveball. I did not know how Corey didn't realize it was coming as Mr. Kitko screamed, "Throw the curve kid, show me the curve."

Sedgmer had one inning left in him which would be all he needed as he set down the line up in order in the top half of the eighth. As the away team extra innings meant sudden death if the opposition scored. I was nervous as my team took the field for the bottom half of the inning but I made sure not to let it show. I didn't want to make the boys any more nervous than they already were.

I pitched Anthony Poli partly because I had no one else left. I was still hesitant about pitching Brian. Even if I wasn't I couldn't pitch him because he had played three innings at catcher when Alex was pitching and I was sure his arm was tired. Alex had caught the last four innings for Dan so I knew I couldn't use him, despite his one inning left of eligibility. My choices were Anthony Poli and Ryan Mackey. I trusted my gut and went with Anthony.

It looked as if I made the right choice when Anthony forced the first two batters he faced to ground out to Brian at third. When he had to face Terry Beach things became dicey. Beach crushed the first pitch to deep right field and over the head of Andy Barth. I had been screaming at Andy earlier in the at bat to back up but he didn't listen. As good as Andy was at practice, he was playing terrible in the first three games. I constantly found myself asking him, "Andy Barth, what are you doing?" It became so regular that it developed into a catch phrase for the poor boy. I felt bad about it but it didn't stop me from repeating it time and time again.

Terry Beach continued to be a cocky as ever when it came to showing off. For a ten year old to show so much bravado angered me. He cupped his hand to his ear and pointed at Anthony. I fully expected reprimand to come from his coaches but that never occurred. They as well as his parents applauded his every move. It was driving me crazy to see a ten year old with such cockiness. If he would have actually hustled around the bases he could have easily had a triple. Instead he decided to showboat which almost cost his team the game.

Anthony was shaken up and proceeded to walk the next two batters on eight straight pitches. The bases were loaded but we still had two outs. I went to the mound to settle my team down. They had fought so hard all game I did not want to see them go out this way. I told them to "calm down". Despite my pleading that they relax and stay loose, I could tell that they were extremely tight after the double and back to back walks.

Anthony tried so hard but it didn't seem to matter. The first pitch to the next batter landed right on his leg. It was a hit batsman and our second loss of the season. Adding insult to injury was Beach walking home down third base line backwards as he crossed home plate to win the game. I looked over at Ray and could tell he was every bit as angry with Beach as I was. The player showed no respect for the game. Even worse his coaching staff and group of parents encouraged it.

As angry as I was with Terry Beach, I was every bit as proud of my team. They had come back twice from deficits in the game and forced extra innings when other teams would have just given up. I made sure in the post-game speech to let them know that losses like this one built character. I told them that the next time we got in a game this close we would be more prepared and battle tested. As bright and positive as I played on the outside, I was dying on the inside.

As the players were packing up and heading back to the cars, I stopped Ryan Mackey and told him he would be our starting pitcher for Friday night's game. His eyes lit up with excitement. I felt like doing something encouraging because he had a rough game and I wanted to end the night on a positive note.

Any thoughts I had of the night ending positively note quickly disappeared when I was driving home on the freeway after dropping off Mike Bell when a North Olmsted police officer pulled me over for speeding. I didn't realize it but I was going 69 miles per hour in a 60 mile per hour zone. I was so incredibly sick over the close loss that I didn't realize I was speeding. When most people speed they know they are going too fast. I truthfully wasn't paying attention. It didn't change the fact that I was in the wrong and the officer didn't hesitate to write me a ticket.

When I finally returned home I wasn't sure what to be more upset about. I had just gotten my first ever speeding ticket and had no clue how I was going to tell my parents about it. I was also sick to my stomach over the loss. It was the worst I felt about losing a game since the summer of 1990 when the first Mr. Wheeler team I was on lost the championship. I had to face the music with my parents over the ticket but I hoped they would go easy on me because of the heartbreaking loss.

Mom and Dad made it clear that I needed to watch my speed. They also made a point of telling me that I would pay the fine. Otherwise they did not give me any grief over it. As for the game my Dad knew how disturbed I was about it. He advised me to try and beat them the rest of the season when we played them and this loss wouldn't seem too bad. Dad always knew what to say to cheer me up.

Cell phones did exist but not nearly as popular as they are today. I didn't have one and most people knew didn't. Consequently I had to wait until after midnight if I wanted to speak with Kathy to say goodnight. She never got home from her job any earlier than midnight and it would have been too late for her to call my house and wake up my parents. I devised a plan to call the weather line repeatedly until she called in on the other line so I could click over and receive her call.

Some nights it would seem as if I was on the line for an hour listening to the weather before Kathy clicked in. This night seemed like an eternity because I was so sad over the loss. Talking to her helped a little, but it was what my dad told me about beating them the rest of the season that helped me sleep.

Dad was correct in his idea of turning this loss into motivation to win, it was the best possible solution on how to get over it. When I was a player I would let a loss eat away at me for days, this time I focused on Friday night's game against Mr. Coyne's team and tried to quickly forget about the heartbreaking defeat. Learn from it and use it as determination to win the next time around is the best way to get over a tough loss. It was my father who taught me this valuable life lesson.

I didn't have to wait long until we had the chance to get back on the winning track. Friday arrived before I could blink my eyes. The game wasn't until 6:15 p.m. so I had plenty of time to think about it at work. The great thing about coaching was the distraction it gave me while I was at work. No matter how busy or slow the day was I made sure to think about the team and ways we could improve. It was nice to have something to take my mind off the endless stream of weird customers that came in.

The game following a tough loss is a vital time for any team. It is crucial that it bounce back and fight hard to put it behind them. Our team was still stung by the loss of Graves as well as the heartbreak resulting from the extra-inning loss. I knew the next game would be crucial in the development of us as a team. It was our first true test on dealing with adversity. I was eager to see the results and be able to truly gauge what kind of players I had. I had never questioned their heart in the past; this was a chance for them to prove my faith correct.

I kept everything about my pre game ritual the same. I stayed with "Creed" as my music of choice while putting on my uniform. Country music remained on the radio during the drive. I began to get very comfortable with my pre game rituals. Straying away from them wasn't an option.

This game as did the first three took place at Middle School Park. I was eager to start playing games at Little Clague Park which was closer to my house. The schedule slated the first four at the Middle School field so I dealt with it. The main difference in the Middle School field was the grass infield. It was a nice field with the back drop of the middle school in deep left field. I had teased some of my heavy hitters, telling them that they might hit a ball to the school one day.

In center and right field there was the yard lines marked for football the following fall. The high school team had used the field for practice during the summer. This part of the field upset me because it detracted from the baseball atmosphere that I so coveted. I also worried that it might distract my players who looked at the field and thought about football instead. The attention span of a ten year old is not always the greatest.

Mike let me know that he no longer needed a ride to and from games because he arranged with one of his friends to help him out. I didn't know who but I wasn't about to ask questions. Mike knew when the games were, I counted on him to be there.

I was getting worried about Mike because the players never seemed to gravitate towards him. They were beginning to follow me around. But I worried that Mike was starting to lose his spirit for coaching. I remained confident his knowledge of the game and hunger to win would pull him through.

Ray became loved by both the players and me. He was not only my first base coach but also my right-hand man. He brought the equipment to and from each game while storing it in his shed between games. He also set the bases into the ground before each game and took them out afterward. He never refused anything I asked him to do. He was a great assistant coach; I couldn't have made it through that season without him.

An essential part to have when coaching is a solid assistant coach. Even the greatest coach in the world will need some help. The most successful coach in college history is Joe Paterno; even the legendary "Joe Pa" needs a staff working under him. If there was something I lacked, Ray made up for it. It didn't even have to be an area in which I lacked but just one I didn't have time for. The biggest example of that came between innings when it came time to warm up the pitchers. I had to go over the line up with any switches or adjustments between innings which didn't allow me time to warm up the pitchers. Ray had no problems with grabbing a catcher's glove and getting behind the plate until whoever was ready to come out and catch.

This game would mark the long-awaited pitching debut of Ryan Mackey. I never questioned Ryan's heart for pitching because he talked about doing it non-stop. What I questioned was his talent for the position. I realize I was not the greatest pitcher in my few attempts at it; however; I honestly didn't think that Ryan was cut out to pitch. I if I pitched him and he got crushed it would kill his spirit to play another position. I also worried that if I never let him pitch that he would not want to play any other position until he got his turn. I decided to roll the dice and see what Ryan had.

I had both Anthony and Dan ready to come in if necessary. I wasn't sure how long Ryan was going to last and I wanted to stay prepared. My thoughts drifted back to the first game when Brian was shelled and knew it was important to always have a back-up plan. In my heart I wanted to pitch Brian again but I just couldn't get past the image of him walking in all those runs the first night. I promised myself that the first chance I had to pitch Brian in a no pressure situation I would. Meanwhile it was Mackey's turn to show what he could do.

The opponent for the Wildcats this evening was Pat's Cleaners coached by Tim Coyne. They were a third year team that included a few really good ballplayers. Their best was also their smallest. A young man named Chris Gore was one of the top pitchers in the league for several seasons. He had great command of his pitches, knowing how to mix them up. Despite his small size he possessed a strong arm. Not only could Chris throw a variety of pitches, but he was also left handed. A left handed pitcher in Little League is unusual. Let alone one with the skill set of Chris Gore.

Chris Gore was one of the finest pitchers we faced that season, but he was also a great person off the field as well. Before and after each game we played against him that season he came up to me and said, "Hello, Mr. McKee". It was special to have the opposing team show me respect. I received none from the opposing coaches so it was nice to get it from one of their players. Chris had mentioned to me several times that season that he wished he were on my team.

Chris wasn't the only all-star on their team that season. Pat's Cleaners had a player on the roster named Tyler Counts. Tyler was a stocky young man who reminded me in many ways of Steve Pecatis. If Steve ever had a younger brother it would have been Tyler. He was quick for his size; he had short chunky legs but could move really fast. The other great thing I liked about Tyler was how hard he hustled. No matter the score of a game he would give it one hundred percent. Sometimes young children who are overweight get a bad label for being lazy. This was not the case with Tyler who was one of the hardest working players we faced.

As I went to home plate to exchange line-up cards with Mr. Coyne I noticed that Don and Abbie were in the crowd. I was happy to see them there with my parents. Once again Kathy was unable to make the game due to her work schedule. It was always encouraging to have support of my family, especially for a Friday night game when so many people are out on the town. The Line Up for that night's game is as all follows:

CF Matt Poli
SS Anthony Poli
C Alex Uhlik
2B Brian Leciewski
3B Dan Kitko
LF Mike Hach
RF John Rehak
1B Kyle Keller
RC Andy Barth
P Ryan Mackey

It was important to score as many runs as possible early in the game because we did not know what kind of performance we would get from Ryan Mackey. To his credit he started off well by only giving up two runs in the bottom of the first. But in the bottom of the second he gave up six more. After two innings we trailed 8-2. When Ryan walked into the dugout he quietly asked me to take him out of the game. I told him he did an excellent job and to be proud of his efforts. I was going to take him out in the third inning anyway, but at least this way aloud both of us to save face.

Being down six runs in Little League is normally not that big of a deficit. In this case I knew it wouldn't last long because Chris Gore had already pitched two innings, I told my team to keep it close until Gore was taken out of the game in the fifth. Rules prohibited a pitcher to throw any more than four innings in a game. I had scouted Coyne's team well, knowing that they had no one nearly as good as Chris to come in and pitch.

Going into the fifth inning we cut the lead to 8-6 and had full confidence that an explosion of runs was on the way. My belief that the next pitcher would falter against our line-up came true quickly. We pelted the pitcher with timely hits after the bases were loaded with walks. The hitters were patient at the plate and took walks in order to put men on. Every time we had the bases loaded a player would get up and knock in a couple runs. Matt Poli also stole home in the sixth inning, further showcasing his speed.

In the bottom of the seventh, the Wildcats led 16-10. I had used Anthony Poli in relief for four innings and was forced to make a switch. Alex had caught all game and I didn't want to turn to him because I knew his arm had to be tired. I was still hesitant about using Brian until the timing was right. In a risky move I opted to pitch Ryan Mackey for the last three outs instead of going to my ace Dan Kitko. It was a strange move to make but I had this gut feeling that Ryan could finish what he started. With only two innings of pitching I knew his arm would still be fresh as well.

When I rattled off the lineup for the seventh and final inning, Ryan looked shocked. I tapped him on the bill of his cap and said, "Three more outs." It was simple and to the point without putting a world of pressure on the young boy. Ryan had sat on the bench the previous four innings so I knew he was eager to get back in the game. He didn't see it coming and I knew the opposition would not either. I had Dan Kitko sit out, staying ready in case of a Mackey meltdown. I told Dan quietly so only he could hear me say, "If anyone gets on base I want you to start warming up."

As Ryan began to take his warm up tosses I looked over to his mom who mouthed the words, "Are you sure?" I just gave her a smile and nodded my head to put her at ease. I couldn't explain it but I just had a gut feeling that Ryan would be okay.

It didn't take long for him to shoot down my theory, or at least make me a little nervous about it when he walked the first batter. What happened next was a thing of beauty. It had been years since I saw a double play turned in Little League but on this night I saw one of the prettiest one's ever. Tyler Counts smashed a ground ball near the hole at short that Brian dived to grab and flip to Anthony covering the bag. Anthony turned to pivot and launched a rocket to get Tyler out at first base. It was the first double play we had turned all season. It came at a crucial time in the game.

The drama was not yet over as Ryan walked the next three batters. Just as I was about to call time and pull Ryan for Dan, he was able to force the next batter to pop up to Kyle Keller at first base ending the game. This win pushed our record to 2-2 and gave new hope for the season.

As I went through the line of parents after the game to shake hands with them Mrs. Mackey gave me a huge hug. She thanked me for playing her son but jokingly asked me not to do that again. I could tell that the drama had gotten the best of her nerves. It was good to see that the parents were starting to like me. Maybe not all of them at once, but slowly most of them began to warm up to me.

Sadly that night Andy Barth turned in another 0-4 performance at the plate. With a few days before our next game, I was determined to get him on track. I told him to "Take the night off when he got home and not even think about baseball." The next morning we would get up early and head straight to the field for batting practice.

Driving home I was ecstatic after the big come from behind victory. I was shouting out the words to every song that played on the radio. I was on cloud nine the entire trip until I returned home where I realized that I had no one to celebrate it with. None of my friends had called in days. Kathy was working until well after midnight so seeing her was out of the question. It was a beautiful Friday night at the start of summer yet I had no one to spend it with. This was another cruel reminder of what I was sacrificing to coach.

I was tempted to call Dave or another friend but none of them had cell phones so it wasn't easy to track anyone down. I sat in my room the rest of the night going over game stats and smoking my dad's cigarettes. It was in the middle of doing this that I realized a strange thing; I was happy. As disappointing as it was not having anyone to hang out with, I began to realize that the solidarity was not the worst thing either. All my friends were doing teen age things while I had just accomplished something most men twice my age couldn't.

It was moments like these that increased my desire to win more than I thought possible. It would have been sad to lose all my friends and time with my girlfriend to fail at coaching. I knew that if I was going to sacrifice everything that I held dear I needed to make it worth it. My biggest fear was losing everything, not just coaching but all I cared about. If the sacrifice didn't pay off with winning a championship then none of it would be worth it. I was gambling everything by spending my summer coaching. As big of a sacrifice as it was, I knew that the payoff would be worth it.

It may seem selfish for me to put coaching ahead of everything else but it was my chance to show what I could do as an adult. Because it might have been my only chance I had to do everything I could to make it count. One thing I have learned is that the future is never 100% certain. Living every day to the fullest is important. I'm not saying to do crazy things, but if life gives someone a chance at pursuing a dream then they should never let go. I hated to lose my friends but it was a small price to pay if my dream of coaching a championship team would come true. I also learned one extremely important thing: "Loneliness drives winning!"

Between looking over statistics I made sure to call Ryan Mackey at home that night. I wanted to thank him for trying so hard as our pitcher. I told him that he played well enough to earn another chance at pitching further on down the season. I remembered a few times that Mr. Kubb had called me after games making me feel better about what happened on the field. Ryan did a good job even though it wasn't good enough to consider him as a full time pitcher.

We enjoyed a few days off before our next game. This gave me much needed time to spend with Kathy. It didn't matter what we were doing I would somehow start talking about the team. I felt bad about this but I couldn't help it. The team was starting to consume my every thought and I was letting it show. I could tell Kathy was beginning to get annoyed by this.

To smooth things over I took her to dinner at the Ground Round restaurant a few minutes from my house. I did a good job of not talking about the team through the entire dinner. It was when we came back to my home that things went wrong. We had just sat down for a movie in my basement when Andy Barth knocked at the door. He wanted to play catch and I didn't have the heart to say "no". Ignoring my girlfriend was clearly the wrong thing to do as it showed my immaturity. It also showed my willingness to help Andy improve. The night ended early because when I was done with Andy, Kathy asked me to take her home. It was our first little argument and I could tell that it might not be the last. She supported my coaching but this was too much. Kathy had every right to be angry about it. I wish I could say it was the last time I chose coaching over her, but sadly it wasn't. This one incident started to become a regular thing.

Our next game was also against Mr. Coyne's team. We had just beaten his team a few days earlier and I was convinced that should have given us the mental edge. I intended to tell my players this in the pre-game huddle. If we could beat the same team twice in a couple of days, it would set the tone for the rest of the season whenever we met them. I knew it was crucial to drive that point into every players head. Unfortunately my mental edge was thrown off upon arriving at the field.

I was ecstatic that the game was being played at Little Clague Park. It was the field where I played most of my games as a boy. It was second to only Terminal Field in Cleveland as my favorite ballpark. Located only minutes from my home I told all my players to call me early if they needed a ride. With the exception of Andy Barth the whole team lived on the opposite side of North Olmsted. I needed plenty of notice to drive across town to pick them up and come back. Whatever the reason, Mrs. Poli managed not to listen.

Denise Poli was a strong-willed woman with the drive and determination to do anything she wanted. She went on to own a tanning salon in the years following that season. The one thing she was unable to do because of a medical condition no fault of her own was drive a car. As a result, Mr. Poli had to drive the boys everywhere. To the Poli's credit they managed to get their sons to every game and practice until that point. That is why I was amazed to learn about two minutes before game time they wouldn't be there.

The story told to me was that Mr. Poli got called into work earlier in the day leaving Denise with no way to get the boys to the game. Instead of calling the coach she had Anthony call Brian telling him that they wouldn't be at the game. Why they would tell a ten year old boy instead of their coach I never understood. Ray would have had no problem with picking them up. When I asked Ray about it he stated that he didn't know about it either. He was even angrier then I was. I never truly got the full story and it was something that bugged me for weeks following.

Missing the Poli boys threw off the entire chemistry of the lineup. I had Anthony penciled in as the starting pitcher. Matt "Munch" Poli, our leadoff hitter, started at center fielder all season. This was a bad way to begin the night before a single pitch was tossed. Team chemistry is an important thing, for two key players not to be there threw everything off.

Without Graves and Dolesh we already missed a few key players. Now without the Poli boys it was going to be twice as hard to form a decent lineup. I fully believed in the rest of my players, but it was so important to have chemistry in the lineup.

Matt was an incredible leadoff hitter because of his ability to get on base. His small size made it easy for him to draw walks and create havoc at the top of the order. When he wasn't drawing walks he was still hitting his way on base. The driving force for any line-up is the leadoff hitter. Any team needs that player to get hot and set the table for the heart of the order. I was furious about this because of the timing and complete disrespect shown to me by the Poli parents. There is no excuse other than a family emergency for not calling the coach to let him know a player won't be there. In this case it was twice as bad because it involved two players. I was so angry it altered my attitude for the rest of the night. This was a drawback of being a new coach. As the season continued I became much better at not letting things rattle me. With that being said, this was the line-up we fielded:

CF Ryan Mackey
LF Mike Hach
P Alex Uhlik
C Brian Leciewski
3B Dan Kitko
2B Kyle Keller
1B Pat Morris
RF Andy Barth
SS John Rehak

The decision to place Mackey first in the order was based upon his ability to make solid contact with the ball whenever he connected. He hadn't struck out very often and had a good eye at the plate. I was counting on Mackey to fill the role of Munch as best as he could.

A strong sense of urgency hung in the air that evening because of the gloomy weather. I urged my team in the pre-game huddle to get off to a fast start because it would break the opposition. We had just beaten them days earlier so they still stung from the loss. Coupling that with the bad weather it didn't look as if we would play all seven innings. We had a team of slow starters but falling behind early was not an option.

I started Alex on the hill, intending him to pitch the first three. Then Kitko would pitch the final four. My only fear was that Alex had incredible accuracy allowing other teams to put the ball in play against him often. Normally I encouraged this because of our strong defense. I wasn't as sure of our fielding this night because of the shakeup in the line-up. Though I had faith in my back ups, I naturally had doubts.

I also knew that Mr. Coyne would be starting Chris Gore again so if we could keep it close while he pitched then we would be able score against whoever they put in next. Looking at the sky darken I hoped for a fast-paced game so we could get ahead before the rain came thundering down. With Chris Gore on the mound it seemed like that might be possible as long as our defense held up its end of the bargain. The one thing I didn't expect was bad umpiring.

Tim Hirz, an eighth grader, was the youngest umpire in the league. While most umpires weren't elder statesman, they at least had some experience. Tim was about to umpire his first game and it couldn't have come at a worse time. As hard as he tried he couldn't seem to get anything right. His strike zone moved repeatedly, creating havoc for both pitchers. Because of his inconsistent strike zone both pitchers could not find a solid groove leading to many walks. A pitch thrown belt high down the middle was called a ball; the next pitch in the dirt was called a strike.

I knew the young man was trying his hardest but I couldn't contain my anger. It didn't help matters that Mr. Coyne was also screaming at Hirz for every blown call. I was trying hard not to be too tough on the youngster but it wasn't easy. By letting myself get so angry it didn't help ease my team. This common mistake is seen even in professional sports. Too many times bad officiating will cause a coach to lose his calm, when this occurs it rattles the players. The last thing a coach wants to do is have his actions cause distraction and put doubts in his own player's minds.

Tim Hirz called both coaches to the plate after the third inning. He explained it was his first game and actually admitting to blowing calls. I felt bad for the young man because he had tears in his eyes when he admitted to blowing calls. He assured us that he was trying his best and asked for patience. I was willing to give him the benefit of the doubt but Mr. Coyne wasn't. He continued to scream at the poor boy throughout the rest of the game.

It was very hard to find a good flow to the game due to erratic umpiring. After four innings we trailed 6-5 as Chris Gore finished pitching. I felt good about only being behind by a run at that point. Their best pitcher was done for the night and mine had three innings left. Before our team could take advantage, the rain began.

As the sky opened rain poured in. Little Clague had a pavilion about twenty feet from the field where everyone ran. I stood next to my Dad and told him that if we kept going that a win was inevitable. I was so angry about the rain that I didn't even notice that people were flocking to their cars. My team stood by my side not wanting to go anywhere. Mr. Coyne's team packed up their cars and prepared to leave. I begged the umpire to re start the game but he was looking for a quick way out of a horrible night. After only a few minutes he called the game awarding it to the opposing team. I was livid!

Our team record dropped beneath .500 at 2-3. To say I was not happy would be a gross understatement. I was so incredibly angry that I refused to leave the pavilion until it stopped raining because I was convinced that it was a mere rain cloud. Kathy was not in the mood to stick around while I played weathercaster so Ray was nice enough to take her home. Despite the rain not stopping for another two hours I stayed and sulked alone. It wasn't even the rain that was causing the most anger but the fact that nothing had gone right from start to finish.

When I finally drove home I was soaking wet. My Mom had a towel waiting for me on my bed and never asked where I was. My parents knew I was angry, choosing to stay out of my way. There is a famous line in Rocky, "You're going to eat lightning and crap thunder." Rocky's trainer Mickey tells him this to motivate him. I was so incredibly angry that I honestly felt like I could crap thunder. The only saving grace to the night was staying up all night watching "Ultimate Fighting" tapes in the basement with Bill. There was something about watching men destroy each other that helped me feel a little better about my own pain.

It rained for two more days causing the cancellation of the next game against Mr. Briggs team. Nothing makes a loss worse than too much time to think about it until the next game. With the rainout five days passed until we took the field again. This time would be a rematch against Mr. Molnar's team. We were still angry about the loss to them and wanted revenge. I truly believed that we had the better team so this would be our chance to prove it.

I was tempted to call a practice between the games but I was unable to find a decent field. I also wanted to let the boys have a few days off to enjoy the summer without thinking about anything too serious. I was hoping that a few days off would let them rest and come back strong. I couldn't have been more wrong.

The game was set for Middle School Park. It was the same location where we had lost to them the first time. I tossed around several ideas about whom I wanted to pitch. I thought about starting Dan because Molnar's team had not yet faced him. I was also tempted to give Brian a second chance at pitching in the hope that this might be his time to break out. Ryan Mackey also crossed my mind in the thoughts of letting him face his former team. I was still kicking myself for not letting him pitch the first time. My final decision was to start Dan and use Poli out of the bullpen. The starting lineup is as follows:

CF Matt Poli
SS Anthony Poli
C Alex Uhlik
3B Brian Leciewski
P Dan Kitko
LF Mike Hach
1B Pat Morris
2B Kyle Keller
RC John Rehak
RF Andy Barth

I was comfortable with playing Keller at second base because he was improving rapidly at fielding ground balls. It was early in the season but I still felt as though I had many options for Kyle. He showed the ability to play both infield positions on the right side and catcher when needed. It was clear that his heart was in everything that he tried. I never questioned his intensity and hustle.

It was also good to have players whom I could lock in at permanent positions such as Hach in left and Munch in center. The biggest positive we had working our way was the incredible amount of options I enjoyed. I was more than happy to have the group of players that no one else wanted.

All the players arrived in plenty of time, but my assistant coach didn't. Only five minutes before game time did Mike finally arrive at the field. I was just about to lash into him for being tardy when I noticed his bloodshot eyes. I was very naïve about drugs and alcohol and didn't realize that Mike was impaired. I told him to sit on the bench and let me handle coaching third base. I knew something wasn't right as I smelled smoke on him that was clearly not from cigarettes. I couldn't overreact in front of the boys so I just chose to ignore it until I had a chance to do something.

Mike's condition caused me to be extremely distracted. I spent more time watching him than my own players. My first reaction was to send him home right away. What stopped me was worrying that it would even further distract my players by losing a coach in the middle of the game. I was nervous about this even more with Don and Abbie, my parents and Kathy were all in the stands. That last thing I wanted was to have something embarrassing happen.

The game started off well enough with Dan cruising through two innings putting us on top 3-1. Molnar countered with his son who pitched well. It looked for a while that it might become a solid pitcher's duel. Any thoughts of that ended when Dan had to leave the game with a sore elbow in the middle of the third.

It was a big blow to lose Dan so early in the contest. His Dad insisted that he keep pitching but I could tell Dan was in bad shape. I had him sit the rest of the game with ice on his elbow. He could have gone back in but I didn't think it was worth further injury. I wanted to win as much as anyone but my first concert was Dan's health.

The second I inserted Anthony into the game our team forgot how to play defense. It was like the first game all over again. I felt bad for Anthony because it didn't matter how he threw the ball, they managed to hit it to someone who couldn't field it. By the time the third inning was over we trailed 7-3.

A four-run deficit wasn't much to overcome and I was more than confident my team would make up those runs right away. I was not counting on their totally losing focus as they began to do. I gathered them up before the start of the fourth to rally them with a speech but they were joking around during it. It was as if they suddenly had no clue how to act. Weeks earlier a few of the boys overheard Mike and me talking about wrestling and chose this night to bring it up again. I tried to keep them focused on the game but constant chatter between innings seemed to be about everything else. Furthermore I wasn't on the bench during at bats because I had to coach third base. Third base was close to our dugout so I didn't hesitate to walk over and shout at them when I saw them goofing around. The game was slipping away fast yet no one besides me and a few others seemed to care.

The worst part was I truly thought our ball club was much better than Mr. Molnar's team. I thought they were the worst team in the league yet we were about to lose to them for a second time. I could tell this was angering Ray as much as it was infuriating me. The problem was that I couldn't yell at children for having fun, but this was certainly not the way I wanted to run things. I was not happy with the way things went that night. I told myself to never allow it to happen again.

The second the game was over I walked over to Mike and told him, "You're fired!" He didn't even seem to care as he walked away laughing. I couldn't believe that someone would spend time showing up to practice then not care about things when it actually mattered. Unlike the gut wrenching decision to let my brother go, this was an easy one to make.

The toughest part was lying to my players about it. I had never lied to them before and I didn't think I would be forced to this time. I knew, however, that I would have to because if they knew the truth then it would crush them. I also believed that most of them wouldn't have understood why I let Mike go. At their age I didn't believe they needed to know such things. I made up the excuse that Mike had found a new job and needed to start right away. I told everyone including my own parents that he had to work nights making it impossible to be there. I never told a single soul the real reason I let Mike go.

When I addressed the team after the game I told them, "Good news, guys The Wildcat's just won the game, they beat The Wildcats." I could tell they were confused about what I meant so I explained how their own errors and lack of focus caused the loss. It was nothing that the opposition did but mistakes we made on our own. I made it clear to them that this was not to happen again. I felt as though I got my point across without losing my temper.

Our next game would take place the following Saturday against Mr. Hill's team. I knew that to get back on the winning track we needed to make some changes. I told Brian to get his arm ready because he was starting on the mound for Saturday's game. As for the other changes, they would be big and small in the hopes that they would be enough. One thing was for sure, the season was about to get very event full as our team was about to go for broke.

Don & I at a very young age at Grandparents house. September, 1987.

Uncle Pete & I at Confirmation Mass/Party. December, 1996.

The team showing up at my Graduation Party.

I let them dye my hair after the win streak.

National Anthem before Championship Game.

Final pitch of Championship Game.

Celebrating the win of the Championship Game. The team dumped water on me.

Final speech to team following the Championship Game.

M.L. Photography

Little Clague Park, North Olmsted, Ohio. Photo by Molly Lamb.

Terminal Field, Cleveland, Ohio. Photo by Molly Lamb.

Chapter 14
Desire

"Desire! That's the one secret of every man's career. Not education. Not being born with hidden talents. Desire.
~ Bobby Unser

A few weeks into the season the last thing I wanted was a total overhaul of my team. I knew a few minor changes would be in order to turn around our early fortunes. I felt it was time to give Brian Leciewski another chance at pitching because he had done so well in practice numerous times. I also believed that a change in the batting order was needed. Matt Poli would remain at leadoff with Brian staying in the clean-up role. Alex Uhlik would continue to hit third because that is the best spot for a team's best on base hitter. The change would come by switching Dan Kitko and Anthony Polis spots in the lineup. Dan had showed early consistency at the plate causing the move to be made. With Dan's ability to put the ball in play it created scoring opportunities for Matt. Dan and Alex showed the most consistency at the plate which allowed more opportunities for Brian to hit them in. It wasn't a criticism of Anthony's ability but just a change that needed to be made to spark the order.

I also hoped that the move would take pressure off Anthony who no longer had to follow his brother in the lineup. I was worried that Anthony felt pressure to match and succeed whatever his brother did because of the older brother's competiveness. I had full confidence in him at the plate and wanted to give him the chance to hit with runners on base and start driving in runs. I don't know if batting after his brother made him nervous but he seemed to blossom after I dropped him to fifth in the lineup. Anthony proved he was a great team player because he never complained about being dropped in the batting order.

There was also an opening at base coach after the abrupt dismissal of Mike Bell. Mr. Rehak and Mr. Hach had both showed interest in helping out so I decided to let them do so until I could find a suitable full time replacement. Ray was scheduled to attend a meeting for the state tournament on Saturday morning in Spencer Ohio. This meant I would be down two assistant coaches.

I knew I could count on Mr. Rehak and Mr. Hach to step in on short notice.

The following day, after the embarrassing loss to Mr. Molnar's team I was worried I may have been too tough on the team. We needed something to lift team moral after the 2-4 start. After hours of searching for an idea I asked my parents if I could throw a team party at our house on Friday night. It was an out of the ordinary request to fill up their house with a group of 10-year- olds but I asked them anyway. Luckily enough my parents agreed to it. I was banking that a team party would lift their spirits and help them play better. I felt that losing focus was the main reason for our painful loss. I also worried that a few more losses would crush their spirits for the rest of the season. The next weekend of games was going to be pivotal for the rest of the season.

Despite my calling the players on short notice almost every one of them arrived at my house that night. The only player not there was Alex Uhlik whose parents took him to Niagara Falls for the weekend. He would not return until Monday afternoon. It was a big blow to lose Alex for three games but there wasn't much I could do to change it. His parents had informed me of the trip weeks before we played our first game so I had no grounds to be upset. I knew family time was important; I didn't make a huge deal about it. It did annoy me that he had to leave in the middle of the season but knowing that it would only be for three days helped ease the blow.

Some of the parents were as excited for the party as their children. It may have been because they had a free baby sitter for the night. Most likely the parents were enthusiastic because they saw their children having a great time. It also made me feel good to know that the parents trusted me. Mrs. Rehak even went as far to bake cookies for everyone.

The party was another great way for them to bond with each other as well as with me. It was good for us to see each other out of our normal element. I had been tough on them early on so I wanted to remind them I was a fun guy with deep desire to win. Sometimes the toughest job of a coach can be installing confidence into his players without putting so much pressure on them they can never live up to his expectations. It was important that I let my players know that I believed in them. I wanted them to understand that mistakes were common but that they needed to learn from them.

The party was scheduled from 6p.m. to 9pm but lasted until midnight. When it became too dark to play whiffle ball outside, we took the party into the basement. Some of the boys played with my action figures while others gathered around to watch wrestling videos. Everyone got along so that there wasn't a single altercation or argument all night. It was incredible to see them bond tightly as a team. During the party I made sure to pull each player aside and discuss some things I had noticed about his playing they needed to improve on. Because I was coaching while they were having so much fun it stuck in their heads. Children tend to remember things better when related to good times. I didn't miss a chance to go over improvements they needed to make.

At the end of the night as we sat around waiting for each player to be picked up, the team and I came to a pact. We had four games scheduled for the next three days. A game Saturday afternoon against Mr. Hill's team, a double header against Mr. Briggs team on Sunday, with the last game coming Monday night against Mr. Coyne's team. We came to the agreement that if they could win all four games I would let them bleach my hair blond. Being an Italian I had very dark features including dark brown hair. Earlier in the year 2000 the bleached blond craze had overtaken people of my age group so it wouldn't be that uncommon for me to do it as well. However, having t brown hair and brown eyes, it wasn't something I wanted to do. I was willing to risk looking different if that meant they would start winnings games. Every player was ecstatic at the thought of dying my hair blond.

I drifted off to sleep that night hoping that the changes I had in mind would pay off. I knew that the next few days could determine the direction that the rest of the season would take. Bleaching my hair blond was not nearly as embarrassing as the thought of my coaching a losing team. I believed in my heart that I needed to coach a winner to vindicate everything Mr. Wheeler and Mr. Kubb had taught me years before. I owed it to them to carry on the winning tradition that they had taught me.

Driving to Little Clague Park the next afternoon I hoped that the winds of change would bring victory. The desire burning inside of me had grown ever since the first day I became a coach. I could tell that the players had the same desire. Despite the four early losses I still believed in our team. It was important that the players had confidence in their own abilities to turn things around.

With Alex Uhlik out for three games I had to adapt the lineup before he returned and I could execute the one I had planned. Before his return I decided to still switch Dan and Anthony in the batting order but move Mike Hach into the third spot. Mike had good ability to make contact so as to help Matt and Dan moving along in front of him if they reach base.

This game would mark the return of Brian Leciewski to the mound. I was nervous about pitching Brian after the implosion he had in game one. He had been so dominant in practice every time he pitched I couldn't resist letting him pitch again. His work ethic was incredible as well as his desire to win and achieve success unmatched for a player of his skill. Some times when a boy of that young age is extremely talented he doesn't try as hard because it comes so easy. This was never a worry with Brian because he never gave less than full effort. Ray confided in me that Brian had practiced pitching every night since the opener. If Brian was looking for a chance at vindication, I was willing to give it to him.

I penciled in the lineup to allow Brian to pitch the first two innings then have Dan take over in the third. It didn't matter how well he performed I was going to let Brian pitch two full innings. Without Alex I was forced to do more shuffling then I would have liked. If the game went seven innings I was prepared to let Anthony pitch the last two. Normally I would have let Alex pitch the end of the game but in this case I didn't have that luxury.

Coaching for the first time without Ray and Mike by my side was going to be challenging. I had grown accustomed to having Ray as my right hand man whenever I needed him. He would not be at the game because I had to send him to a meeting that the state commission was calling for all teams who might be playing in the state tournament. I let Anthony and Brian decide what signals we would be using that game. I changed them every game because we were being scouted and I didn't want other teams to catch on. I had the two boys show Mr. Rehak and Mr. Hach the new signs so they would be ready for the game as well. I was proud of both boys for never shying away from the chance to show leadership.

In my pre-game speech I explained to the team that this was a fresh start. I wanted them to start over without thinking about our prior defeats. Instead of focusing on the negative things that happen in the games I wanted them to turn them into positives. The key to winning was letting the desire they had in them to produce good play. The biggest thing was to keep focused at all times without ever letting their minds wander away from what was taking place on the field. It was one play at a time from that point forward with only worrying about the next second in time.

It was important that I was able to get my message across because we needed to start winning. Each loss made the mountain we had to climb a little taller. Even without Alex playing for the weekend games, I still had plenty of confidence in the lineup.

CF Matt Poli
3B Dan Kitko
LF Mike Hach
P Brian Leciewski
SS Anthony Poli
1B Pat Morris
C Kyle Keller
RF Andy Barth
2B Ryan Mackey
OF John Rehak

The team quickly erased any doubts about the effectiveness of my pre-game speech when they scored seven runs in the top of the first inning. With a combination of speed on the bases and timely hitting, we began scoring runs at a good pace. They were making smart choices on the bases and at the plate. I could tell their level of focus had increased dramatically. Despite their ability to hustle on every play they made sure not to run themselves into any outs by being over aggressive. The inning was capped off by Andy Barth getting his first hit of the season.

It was an incredible feeling too see Andy finally succeed at the plate after so much hard work. I knew how much potential he had, which made it even more important for him to succeed so that he wouldn't get discouraged. Watching Andy get his first hit gave me the same excitement as it would for any of my players. But I couldn't help but to pull for Andy because of how far we had come together in such a short period of time. So when he did well I felt a little extra special at times. I made sure not to show favoritism but with Andy it was hard not to. Just as in the same way I was harder on Andy than any other player I ever coached. When he failed at something I felt as though I had failed him. When he succeeded at something, I felt as though I played a big role in it.

Andy's hit was the highlight of what was an all-around solid inning. Brian wasted no time plowing through the top of Mr. Hill's order and getting out of the first inning scoreless. It was great to see Brian regain his confidence on the mound by throwing the ball hard and accurately. He became a little wild in the second inning but by that time we held a 10-2 lead.

After two innings on the hill Brian looked one hundred times better than his first performance. This gave me confidence I could have him pitch the rest of the season. When I pulled him from the mound I made sure to tell him how proud I was of his play. I also made sure to let him know he would be pitching much more during the rest of the season. He was happy to get both bits of news. Brian was extremely competitive and I could tell he has been waiting a long time to show me what he could do after the early debacle.

The game went on to be a blowout and was called for mercy rule after the fifth inning with our winning 15-3. Mr. Hill was fuming yet again because his team lost when we didn't have one of our best players. Before the game had even started he made a point of asking me where Alex Uhlik was? His team had only lost two games so far and it infuriated him that both losses came against us. His team's record was 3-2 while we held a record of 3-4. As the season progressed his team would never again see an above .500 winning percentage. By that same token, we never dipped below .500 again. The win marked a new era in Little League for that season, I was happy to see it arrive.

In the post-game speech I gave a game ball to Brian for his dominant performance on the mound. Dan had gone more innings allowing one less run, but I felt Brian deserved it because he had improved so much. I also gave a game ball to Mike Hach for getting three clutch hits throughout the game. I let them know that I was proud of them but also that this was only the start of what had to become something much bigger. The key was to learn from the win and be ready for the double header the next day against Mr. Briggs team. We owed them payback for the heartbreaking loss of weeks earlier. When I asked who was angry that we lost to them each player raised their hand. When I asked how badly they wanted revenge the entire team shouted, "Badly!" I concluded the post-game speech by asking, "Who are we?" Every player screamed at the top of his lungs "Wildcats!"

With the post-game celebration of fruit snacks and drink boxes well under way Mrs. Hach gave me a hug and reminded that it was only three more wins until I had blond hair like her. I laughed it off with a smile but was still just taking things one day at a time. If dying my hair motivated them to win then I was more than willing to go along with it.

The game between Mr. Coyne's team and Mr. Molnar's team immediately followed our game so I stuck around to scout. We had played both teams but I felt we still needed to learn more about their strengths and weaknesses. It was a great feeling to have a few players stay to watch with me. Both Poli boys and Mike Hach stuck around. Andy went home to grab his skateboard then came back.

Parents and coaches of the other teams noticed us having fun in the stands which angered them greatly. We could tell that it was getting to them but it didn't discourage us from remaining for the entire game. I am not sure how much scouting the players did but I kept track of several things that both teams were doing. There was nothing about the Molnar team that I felt was better than my group. It caused me so much confusion about why we had already lost to them twice.

When the game was over I went straight to Dave Murphy's graduation party. I felt bad being late to it but knew that it would probably go on all night. When I got to the party all I could think about was our big win. I was also consumed with the two games we had to play the next day. I made sure not to brag about my team to anyone because the day wasn't about me, it was about Dave.

The party turned out to be a very good time with many activities going on at once. It was a mixture of basketball and volley ball in the front yard with poker games in the house and garage. The one thing I could say about a Murphy party was that it was always a good time.

Despite all the good times going on around me I left early. It was another form of sacrifice that I needed to make. With the double header the next day I had to plan for it. There was much more planning that went into getting ready for a double header than just one game. In addition I was eager to get home so I could sit on the porch and go over stats. As much I hated leaving my best friend's party I knew that there was still work to be done. There was no party that could entice to me pass up on work I could do to improve my team.

As I went around saying my goodbyes to his numerous family members and neighbors that I had gotten to know well over the years, I ran into his girlfriend Julie. I had been close to Julie and her sisters before Dave had started dating them but they had grown cold since. It seemed as though when my best friend started dating one of them I was shown the door. That combined with my coaching seemed to be a sore subject with many inside the once tight group that I was no longer a part of. I didn't understand why my friends stopped calling me when I became a coach and started dating Kathy. It is a question that always haunted me but if given the choice over again I still would have chosen coaching.

While sitting on the porch going over game plans and stats Bill Meyers approached me. He knew that I had gotten rid of Mike Bell thereby creating an opening at assistant coach. Before he could talk me into letting him come back I cut him off in mid-sentence. I said, "Bill I would love it if you came back starting tomorrow." He accepted my offer. I was glad to have Bill back in the fold.

Ray Leciewski stopped over with Brian to drop off the state tournament papers from the meeting. There was a still some moonlight so we grabbed Andy to play whiffle ball. It was 10 p.m. and three grown men were playing against two children with a plastic bat and ball. I couldn't have been happier. It was in times such as those that let me forget all the sacrifice by enjoying the moment. It was the simplest moments that brought me the most pleasure. It was also the perfect way to cap off what had been a great day.

A few minutes after the goodnight call with Kathy I was fast asleep with dreams of not one but two wins the following morning. It would be a big day with the chance to improve our winning percentage to over 500. I knew the day would be action packed but not nearly as pivotal is it became.

June 25, 2000 began with a wake-up call at 6:00 a.m. from Ray. I stumbled out of bed to grab the phone before it could wake anyone up. It would be a few hours before my parents would leave for church so they were still asleep. It should have been an early indicator that this day was going to be unique. Ray informed me that he had been called into work for an emergency in the plant he worked at in Mentor, Ohio. He didn't go into details but I assured him I could pick up Brian for the games. He didn't know how long he would be gone but said he would try to make it back in time for the second game.

I had to drive to his side of town that morning to pick up Kathy so it wasn't a problem to make an extra stop. They both lived on the complete opposite town as me so it gave me the chance to develop a game plan in my head on the way to pick them up. I was not alone in the car ride because Bill decided to join me on the trip. This would be his first day back into coaching with the team so I felt it was important he drive with me.

While I drove to pick them up rain fell extremely hard just as it did throughout the prior night. From the time we came into the house from playing whiffle ball until the time I woke up it had been raining. It finally stopped a few minutes after I picked up Kathy. From there we picked up Brian and headed towards Little Clague Park.

We arrived at the field with forty-five minutes to spare before the start of the first game. The field was a giant pool of mud, however. Bill and I instantly began raking the mud to try and make solid dirt to play on. It rained so hard and so long that it seemed to be an impossible task. The entire area around home plate was flooded. When I stood near the plate my foot sank into the mud all the way up to my ankle. The chances of a game being played were slim to none, let alone two games.

When players of both teams started showing up we had them warm up on the side lines and grass outfield. We wanted as few people tracking through the mud as possible. I was determined that the game to be played as I was sick of rainouts. The last thing I wanted was for two more games to have to be made up. Most coaches would have jumped at the chance to post pone games in which one of their best players wouldn't be there. I looked at it differently because I believed that my team was better despite the absence of Alex and wanted to prove it.

The umpire Scott Pogros decided to let the coaches make the decision whether a game or games could be played. I talked it over with Darryl Briggs for a few moments in the hopes that he would still want to play. He noticed that we were missing Alex and asked if he would show up. When he learned that Alex would not appear he suggested that we do everything possible to play the games.

After talking it over with both coaches and Scott, we decided to postpone the game until 4 p.m. Bill and I stuck around to rake the field for as long as it took to get it playable; meanwhile the team went home and rested. The other team went home including their coaches, none of which stuck around to help.

The entire ordeal showed plenty about Bill's character. It was his first day back with the team and he showed that he was an ultimate team player. We groomed the field for hours to make it playable with Bill never complaining a single time. Bill worked so hard that when we were done he had blisters on both hands. It meant a lot to me that Bill remained to help when everyone else left. From that day on I never once questioned Bill Meyer's heart.

I sent Brian back to my house with Kathy to rest up for the games we expected to play. When Bill and I stopped home for a quick lunch break, Kathy was fast asleep while Brian was playing with all of my action figures. It was a really heartwarming feeling to see that he felt comfortable enough to play with his coach's toys. My Mom had taken them out of the attic days earlier for the party. They had been hidden away since I started dating Kathy. Brian was having so much fun that he asked, "Can I live here?"

By 4.p.m. we had the field in playable condition. I use the term "playable" loosely because there were still huge puddles of muddy water behind home plate as well as second base. Scott insisted that if the ball landed in either one of the massive puddles that play would stop for a dead ball. That meant that if the ball got past the catcher then the runner would have to return to the base if he was trying to steal. It also meant that if the ball landed in the massive puddle behind second base that it counted as a single and the base runners would get to move up one base. It had the feel of a backyard game but it didn't matter to me because I just wanted to play. The field itself looked dark brown with dust covered by mud. With the sun beginning to set on what became an extremely hot afternoon it looked as though we were baking one giant mud pie. I can best describe it as a neatly- kept pig pen with baseball lines drawn onto it. Sometimes in sports a bad playing field can be the great equalizer; this appeared to be one of those times.

Not wanting to change something that was working, I decided to use the exact same lineup from the night before to start the first game. Giving Brian the chance to pitch in back to back games was a big step up from being afraid to use him. I told him that if he did well again I would let him pitch three innings instead of only two. I liked what I had seen the night before from Brian which caused me to be eager for more. Having numerous solid pitchers would put us up a step above the rest of the league. The other teams only had one solid pitcher they could count on.

Ray showed up two minutes before the game was going to start. He thought that it was the end of the second game, when he found out that the first game hadn't even started he was shocked. I was glad to have him there because I felt it improved our chances. Ray took his normal spot at first base while Bill trotted out to coach third. I took one look at Bill and saw that he was every bit as happy as I was that the games would be played.

Brian went on to perform as well as he did the night before. He was finding the strike zone as well as nipping the corners of the plate. He was not only accurate but also throwing some serious heat. It was clear that Brian had the strongest arm in the league. It got to the point that some opposing batters were literally shaking in fear when they stepped to the plate to face him. The biggest sign of fear at the plate shows when the batter moves his back foot out of the box, a common habit among Little Leaguers. With Brian's ability to throw smoke this became the trend of most batters he faced. He pitched our team to an 8-4 lead through three innings.

If facing Brian was bad for opposing batters then having to oppose Dan Kitko was a nightmare for them. Dan came into the game in the fourth inning and picked up where Brian left off. Dan was also throwing smoke on the mound as well as keeping everything up and in. If the batters got around on the pitch quick enough they would just pound it into the mud making for an easy out. Dan would go on to pitch four scoreless innings and preserve the 13-4 win.

The game couldn't have gone any better than it did because our team showed fight with a hunger to win. They played through bad field conditions making it work for them. We set a team record of 16 stolen bases while scoring five runs on their best pitcher, Adam Sedgmer. We earned our revenge from the earlier heart breaking loss. The one thing better than one win, is two, which is exactly what we planned on achieving. Because the game moved at such a quick pace it ended a few minutes after 6 p.m. This allowed us plenty of time to play the second half of the double header.

Twenty minutes between the two games allowed both teams to rest. I used that opportunity to give the boys an inspiring speech that I thought of at that moment. I didn't have anything prepared so I decided to speak from the heart. I explained to them how far they had come in such a short period of time. We had the chance to win our third game in 24 hours which is almost impossible to do. I told them that this was their chance to have a winning record. We had battled from being down two wins to match our record of losses with four apiece. This was a golden opportunity to move our record to 5-4 putting ourselves right back into the race for first place. I asked them to forget about being tired after a long day and to focus solely on winning one more game that day. I knew that if we could beat Mr. Briggs team twice in one day, it would demoralize them for the rest of the season.

As I spoke I began to look into each of their eyes which were all filled with intensity. They had the look of desire in them which is so incredibly important in building anything successful. At that moment the entire team was focused on winning. After the speech they didn't even joke around or relax but began warming up. There was something in the air that day that brought everything together. It was only a matter of time before we broke through and came together as a team, I believed that moment was about to occur.

That night's game was also the debut of "The Bell". Years prior James Steele's mom had brought a large wooden handled Bell to our games when I played for Mr. Kubb. Every time we scored a run one of the parents would ring the Bell. It became a familiar tradition that our team was known for. Earlier that summer my mom had found a large Bell similar to the one used years earlier. Without thinking twice I took the Bell to the games that day and left in my car. I remembered it was in there after the first game so I took it out. I handed the Bell over to Mrs. Hach while asking her to ring it every time we scored. She had no issues with doing so and promised to share it with other parents who wanted to have fun as well.

Because already played two games as well as the two games yet to be played that weekend, I had to be very careful about who I put on the mound. Dan and Brain had already both pitched quite a bit so I decided to give Anthony Poli the nod. The following is the complete lineup used that evening.

CF Matt Poli
3B Dan Kitko
LF Mike Hach
SS Brian Leciewski
P Anthony Poli
C Kyle Keller
2B Ryan Mackey
RF Andy Barth
OF John Rehak
IB Pat Morris

I decided to go with Anthony because he was better than our second option, Ryan Mackey. That gave us the better chance at starting off the game strong. I was not sure about who else would pitch because of the 7 innings already pitched by Dan Kitko. Brian had only pitched 5 so far that weekend but I didn't want to overload him. I had confidence in Anthony because he showed much desire to play hard but I still worried about his mental toughness at times. I just needed him to soak up some innings that game and was willing to gamble.

Any worries I had about Anthony's mental toughness came to the forefront as soon as the game started. The last time he faced Mr. Briggs team he ended the game with walks and a hit batsman that cost us the game. I was hoping that he would have shaken that off by then but I was sadly mistaken. Anthony promptly walked the first three batters he faced leaving them loaded for Terry Beach. As I calmly walked to the mound to settle down my pitcher something happened that would change my life forever, I was heavily booed. It was the first time in my life that I received such a loud negative reaction. I couldn't believe what I was hearing and had to make sure it was me that they were booing before I could believe it.

The entire set of parents on the sidelines for Wilsons Bike Shop stood up and booed in unison directly at me. It was the single most painful moment of my entire life. They continued booing the entire time I was on the mound talking with my team. Brian leaned over my shoulder and said, "Shake it off, coach, we still love ya." It was a touching moment that I will never forget. I looked over to the stands where I saw my Mom and Kathy both trying to hold back tears. I could tell that the booing had upset them both.

Some moments in life I don't remember. No one remembers their first words or steps. I don't even remember the first time I rode a bike. But I will never be able to forget those two minutes in which I was shown such hatred so strongly by a bunch of strangers. When I was jogging back into the dugout I grabbed my cap and tipped it in their direction. In baseball terms the tip of the cap is the ultimate sign of respect. I wanted to show kindness to the same people showing hatred because I knew that would be the best way to show I was the bigger person. It was sad that I was twenty plus years younger than most of them and showed more class.

Happily my Dad had left by that point to go home and do more yard work. He hadn't had the chance all weekend to do so and wanted to make the most of it. If he had been there when that happened it would have broken his heart. I knew how supportive he was of both his sons so I was glad this was one of the very few times he wasn't around.

It was life-changing moment I needed to have. Until that point I was naïve to think that no one had a problem with my coaching. Whatever the reason, these people truly hated the fact that my team was not only good but also having fun. They saw a young energetic man doing things that they never could and it drove them insane. It was the negative reaction that I received which gave me even more desire to keep coaching.

Anthony continued to falter and give up six runs that inning. I felt bad for leaving him in the game but I had no choice. I needed more out of him because of the lack of depth we had. It was brutal to hear Antony ask to come out of the game between innings. The six runs had wrecked his confidence leaving me with a choice to make. For a player with the heart of Anthony to want to stop pitching made me realize that the smartest thing I could do was remove him from the mound. I didn't want to damage his confidence further than it was so I told him, "No problem". I was racking my brain to find a solution when I decided upon Kyle Keller.

Kyle had done everything asked of him so far that season. He never complained and just kept looking for ways to improve. No matter what position I gave him to play, he worked hard until he was able to become good at it. With all of the hard work he put into improving and his willingness to do anything to help the team, I gave him the chance to pitch.

I moved Anthony to shortstop by placing Brian behind the plate. I told Kyle to just try his hardest and aim for the Brian's glove. What happened next was better than anything I could have asked for. Kyle went to on to pitch four scoreless innings only giving up two hits. It was the most incredible clutch performance I have ever seen a Little Leaguer have. Here was a boy who never pitched a day in his life coming into a 6-0 deficit and didn't allow a single run. Kyle didn't have much speed behind his pitches but because he was accurate the defense behind him kept fielding balls to get the outs. It was incredible to watch. The entire time he was on the mound I held my breath waiting for something to go wrong but it never did. Meanwhile our offense came alive and we tied the game heading into the sixth.

Kyle was never the flashiest of players but I always said that if I had nine players with Kyle Keller's heart that we would be the best team in the world. I was proud of him in that moment not only because of the results he produced, but the poise and humility that he did it with. After every inning he asked for pointers on how to get better. It was Kyle's hard work that personified how the entire team performed.

In the midst of the comeback to tie the game along with Kyle's clutch performance the crowd became loud. With every run we scored the cheers got louder from our parents and drowned out the boos from the opponents' side. The team responded well with the overwhelming crowd noise that it began to pump them up even more. The Bell was a big hit as it began to be passed around to each parent throughout the game.

On the field Brian was leading the team in repetitive chants of "Wildcats". The mixture of chants from players and parents became so loud that Dad later said he was able to hear it down the street. I have to give my Mom credit: she became as vocal as any of the parents out there. Mom had gone from being against my coaching to one of my most vocal supporters. After the long day in the sun with constant raking of mud something finally snapped inside of me. I stopped caring about what anyone else thought and began chanting "Wildcats" with everyone else. It got to the point that between every pitch I would scream, "1-2-3" followed by the entire team and set of parents yelling, "Wildcats!" It was the ultimate show of unity on our part that no one could take from us.

Not only was the chanting a motivation but it also became fun for the players. It pumped them up and made them play better. It was making the opposition fans even angrier that their boos were being drowned out by our fans. I looked over at Darrly Briggs to see his dark skin becoming red with anger. I knew that it upset them but I didn't stop my team from having fun. It was a long day of irritation that this change of events helped to bring about.

When Dan Kitko came into pitch he easily followed Kyle's brilliance with two shutout innings of his own. I hated to have pitch Dan again because he already gone numerous innings to that point. After those two innings it brought his total to nine in just over 24 hours. The league rule was 10 in a 48 hour time period which meant I could only use him the next night for one inning.

As Dan Kitko was mowing down opposing hitters our lineup came alive and scored four runs to lead us to a 10-6 victory. It was our third win in 24 hours and without a doubt the biggest win of the season.

During the postgame speech I noticed that every player was covered in mud from head to toe. I couldn't have been happier with how they played in both games. It was the first time all season that we had a winning record. I told them to rest up because we had one more win planned for the next night. I pointed out that it was a total team effort that they all took part in. I did give out a few game balls including one to Kyle Keller for an amazing night on the mound.

It had been an incredible day of baseball but it did not come without sacrifice. My good friend Joe Graham's graduation party was that day. I was unable to attend because I had been at the ball field all day. I felt bad about this because Joe was a great friend who had always stuck by me. I knew he would understand why I wasn't there but it still did not make me feel any better about missing it. It was just another sacrifice I had to make to coach. No amount of wins can make up for the things a coach has to sacrifice when it comes to friends and family.

It was past 9 p.m. by the time the last inning had been played. A big wrestling show was on that night that I had planned to watch. I had already missed Joe's party so I decided to at least catch the wrestling event. Bill and I took both Poli boys with us to a local sports restaurant to watch the matches that evening. I remember not caring who won the matches because my whole attention had been focused on the three previous wins along with the game the next day. I looked over at Kathy and could tell she was every bit as exhausted as I was. As soon as the wrestling event was over we took the Poli boys home. A few minutes later I took Kathy home as well. When I walked her to the front door of her house I thanked her for putting up with the marathon day. She hugged me for several minutes while telling me not to let the boo's get to me because there would probably be more to come. As sad as it was, Kathy was right: there would be more boo's to come.

It was early the next morning when I received a rather interesting phone call from Mrs. Kelly Briggs. I was getting ready to go to work as I was scheduled 8 a.m. to 4p.m. that day when my Mom handed me the phone. Kelly was highly upset with the behavior of me and my team's actions the day before. She insisted that we had acted highly inappropriate by cheering for one another. She explained that we didn't show any class and that I was teaching the children how to be bad sportsmen. She went on to say that she was calling the commissioner to make a report on my coaching. Her husband told his entire team that we were a group of bad sportsmen and to be thankful they didn't play for me.

After listening to her insult me for a few more minutes I decided to just hang up on her. I had been taught to never disrespect my elders so it was for the best that I just hung up before I said what I was really thinking. I was extremely angry with the call and told my mom that if she called back not to answer. We had caller ID on the phone so we could tell who was calling. My first reaction to her call was that she was going to apologize for the rude behavior of her player's parents. When it turned out she was calling to yell I felt no need to listen to it. The bottom line was we beat them twice the previous day and she could do nothing to take it from us.

If I was surprised by the phone call then I was stunned when she showed up at my job a few hours later. She came in with her young son Frankie to buy some groceries. She insisted that she did not know I worked there. She mentioned the phone call again and seemed to be looking for another argument. I couldn't get in an argument at work so I just told her we would work on it and proceeded to walk away. I was learning a valuable lesson in that sometimes it is better to walk away than to let anger get the best of me. As crazy as it was I liked working there so I didn't want to do anything to jeopardize my job. I made up my mind that every time we played them from now on that I would tell my players and their parents to be as loud as they possibly could. This woman had angered the wrong young man.

I was even more excited for that night's game against Mr. Coyne's Pat's Cleaners than usual because with Alex coming back it allowed me to finally use the new lineup I wanted to try. Because I was low on pitchers I thought it was for the best to let Alex start on the mound that evening. I was hoping he would be good enough to soak up a few innings. Before leaving home to head to the field I looked over the lineup one last time and smiled. The lineup for that evening is as follows:

CF Matt Poli
3B Dan Kitko
P Alex Uhlik
2B Brian Leciewski
SS Anthony Poli
LF Mike Hach
C Kyle Keller
RF Andy Barth
OF John Rehak
1B Patrick Morris

The game was to be held at the Middle School field. We had a less than stellar record there thus far that season; I hoped everything would turn around that evening. I couldn't figure out why we played better at Clague Park, maybe because we held most of the practices there. It didn't matter to me because I was confident that my team was finally complete and that the momentum would be on our side. The location of the ballpark was only a small concern.

I did make one costly mistake in the pregame that I never did before or after. It was the first time that I didn't give any kind of pregame speech. Instead I let them use their entire warm up time to have Bill throw them high fly balls deep in the outfield. I wanted to let them have fun before the game to take off the nerves of trying to win four in a row. I couldn't have made a bigger mistake. While it is important to have players stay loose before a game, they also need to stay focused. It wasn't the biggest mistake I made but it came very close. One of my greatest coaching talents was my incredible ability to motivate my players. Good motivation by a head coach can turn a mediocre team into a great one. After winning three in a row I missed the perfect opportunity to use that winning streak as motivation. It wouldn't be much longer until I was paying dearly for my mistake.

The first two innings turned into a nightmare as they made numerous costly mistakes. Alex was pitching good but almost too well. The boys from Mr. Coyne's team were focusing in on his pitches that seemed to be coming right over the plate. Alex wasn't walking anybody but he wasn't striking anybody out either. The biggest problem was that the balls they were hitting were being muffed by my players. This was a case when it wasn't the pitcher's fault. Our normal sure-handed defense was looking as if it never played before. After two innings with countless errors we trailed 0-11.

While the defense was faltering so was the batting order that I had taken many hours to design. After two innings we had not yet reached base. Chris Gore was on fire on the mound, setting down batter after batter with the greatest of ease. The worst part was that my team looked shell shocked with no signs of improvement visible.

I switched Alex for Brian in the third inning to change at pitcher. Brian was able to settle down early focusing on the strike zone to get batters out. It was the third time in three days I had called upon Brian to pitch but I had no choice. I was worried he might get tired but he never did as he pitched two strong innings only giving up three more runs. Meanwhile our lineup had been shut out as we entered the bottom of the fifth down 0-14.

The good news was that Chris Gore had used all four innings causing him to be done for the game. The bad news was that if we didn't score at least five runs to cut the lead to 9 then the game would end due to the mercy rule. As their new pitcher Tim

Kelly began to take his warm up tosses a stranger thing occurred. The sky went from being sunny to pitch black in a matter of minutes. It looked as though we were headed for a typical summer Cleveland thunderstorm. I will never forget Mr. Coyne screaming at umpire Tom Grodek to call the game. The problem was that not a single drop of rain or bolt of lightning had appeared. I remembered how we had lost to them earlier in the season when the game was called for rain when we were about to come back. I urged Tom not to stop the game while pleading with him to let us have our last at bats. Tom saw that the score was lopsided but insisted that we get the chance to play on. Perhaps he figured that there was no chance that we could come back so he would let the game end after the inning by mercy rule. Whatever his reasoning was I was just happy we had the chance to attempt a comeback.

What happened next was something that no one who was present would ever forget. The lineup in which I had spent countless hours working on finally came together. It became a perfect combination of hitting and base running that inspired a massive comeback. Before anyone could blink we had cut the lead down to seven runs with only one out. It seemed as though we had caught Coyne's team at the perfect time with their guard down. Every single player was hitting with reckless abandon. The chemistry of the order was working brilliantly. We had the right amount of speed on the bases when the right power hitters would come up to knock them in. With two outs in the inning we had comeback to trail only 11-14.

With Mike Hach at the plate and the bases loaded we had a chance to tie the game or even take the lead. Mike swung at the second pitch he saw and drove it over the right fielders head for a base clearing game tying double. The crowd went wild and it was even louder than the previous night's celebration. The Bell was ringing loudly as the chants of "Wildcats" echoed across the field. Mr. Rehak even got up and gave Kathy a big hug lifting her off the ground. I looked over at my brother and voiced the words, "Can you believe this?" The feeling was unreal as tying the game seemed almost impossible just a few short minutes earlier.

While our sidelines were roaring with excitement, Mr. Coyne's was letting his team have it by screaming at them nonstop. I felt bad for his team because they didn't deserve that kind of treatment. He was acting as if his team had already lost when in fact the game was only tied with a long way to go. During the fourteen run explosion the skies overheard had cleared up with the threat of a storm no longer looming.

The batter following Mike grounded out but the damage had been done. Heading into the top of the sixth it was a whole new ballgame. I was desperate to keep the game tied trying not to allow Mr. Coyne's team to regain momentum. I put Dan into pitch one more inning because I was confident he could keep the game tied despite how much I had used him the last three games. I knew I could only use him for one inning but it didn't stop me from putting him in.

Sure enough Dan had no problems in recording three straight outs to keep things tied up going into the bottom half of the inning. We had the bottom of the order coming up which untimely led to zero runs being scored and keeping the game tied. Andy Barth hit one solidly but right at Tyler Counts, I was hoping that despite it being an out it might get Andy out of what seemed to be a season long slump.

With the game still knotted up heading into the final inning I had a big problem on my hands. I could no longer use my best pitcher Dan Kitko because he had pitched the maximum amount of innings for the 48 hour span. Mr. Kitko had told me between innings to go ahead and play Dan one more inning on the mound because he felt that no one would have noticed he went over the limit. As badly I was I wanted to win I knew I couldn't cheat so I decided against it. Instead of going back to Alex or Brian I rolled the dice one more time on Kyle Keller.

Kyle performed brilliantly the day before so I hoped to catch lighting in a bottle twice. What I didn't consider was that Kyle had played catcher the entire game with his arm extremely tired. Take into effect he had pitched four innings the day before after never pitching before it was a recipe for disaster. As hard as my team played that game it was my horrible coaching mistakes that kept them from winning. Both before and during the game I made a couple moves that cost us the game. I couldn't blame Kyle when he was unable to get a single batter out. He walked five straight batters before I took him out. I went to Ryan Mackey who managed of get us out of the inning only down by two runs.

We didn't have enough fire power to come back one more time on the bottom of the seventh causing us to lose the game 14-16. In the post-game speech I let the team know that I felt responsible for the loss. I didn't have them ready to play and it showed in the early innings. I told them that I was proud of them for fighting hard all game and making an incredible comeback. After the slow start our new lineup performed great and that would become our regular batting order. I let them know that if we could play as a team the way we did in the later innings that would be our last loss for a long time. Some of the players had tears in their eyes as they had worked so hard and come so close. In closing I let them know that despite the loss I would still let them dye my hair. I made the deal in which they could highlight blonde only and not bleach my entire head. It was a fair trade because they didn't win four in a row like originally asked. They were happy to get the news which helped soften the blow of the gut wrenching defeat.

As I was packing up my car with the equipment my parents drove up to me in their Ford Ranger to console me. I was feeling horrible because I felt as though I had let the team down with some terrible decisions. Of the five losses that season I felt that was the only one I could blame solely on my coaching. Dad said that even know we had a .500 record at 5-5 that there was no reason why we couldn't win the championship. My parents made a point in telling me not to give up and that I was on to something big with this team. They were right as I felt the same way about things, but it didn't change the fact I felt horrible about the loss. One thing was for sure, that night's loss became our last one for a very long time, things were about to turn around for the better in a way no one saw coming!

Chapter 15
Winning Time

"It really doesn't matter if I lose this fight. It really doesn't matter if this guy opens my head. All I want to do is go the distance. Nobody's ever gone the distance with Creed. If I can go that distance, if that bell rings and I'm still standing. I will know for the first time in my life that I wasn't just another bum from the neighborhood."
~ Rocky Balboa—1976

As the baseball season went on I realized that surviving the tough times without letting them discourage me or my team may be the toughest test. It seemed that every couple of games it was a new roadblock that presented itself. I often thought about how the odds were stacked against us many times but the best way to overcome them was to believe in ourselves without giving up. I looked to the movie character Rocky Balboa for inspiration. I believed our team had many of the workman qualities that Balboa possessed in his movies. When no one gave him a chance fighting the invincible Apollo Creed, he stood up to the challenge with heart and determination. It became my new goal for the team to get through the season as best we could without letting anyone's negativity bring us down. Like Rocky, the goal was to get through the entire battle still standing with every ounce of heart and soul left on the field.

The night following our epic heartbreaking loss to Mr. Coyne's team I kept my word by allowing the team to dye my hair. We agreed that because the team only won three in a row that it would get to highlight it with blond streaks without completely dying it blond. It didn't bother me much because Kathy had been asking me to try highlights in my hair for a while. So it was a way to please both parties.

The entire team came over my house to celebrate putting in the highlights. Each player took turns ripping stands of hair through the skullcap I had to wear. It was a cap that is used to pull hair through when getting highlights. It has many holes in it to pull the selected pieces of hair to be dyed. The boys wasted no time yanking in each strand while laughing hysterically as they did it. It wasn't extremely painful but it certainly didn't feel good either.

My mom who had been doing peoples hair for ten years was grand marshal of the festivities. She directed each player on exactly what to do and I could tell mom was having every bit as much fun as the boys.

It took about fifteen minutes to complete the process which left plenty of time for the rest of the team to have their hair dyed also. It wasn't part of the original plan but Mom was given permission from most of the mothers the night before to do so. There were only a few parents who objected to this process. I hadn't a clue that the boys were planning to dye their hair completely blond, but I wasn't against it because it created more team unity. As foolish as I felt it was for a grown man to dye his hair blond, these were little boys and I didn't want to spoil their fun time.

As the night went on we ended up outside in the front yard playing catch while the boys waited to be picked up. It worked well because I wanted to schedule a practice for after the Fourth of July holiday later that week. It was easier to tell the parents as they arrived instead of making twelve separate phone calls. I told the players to enjoy the holiday but be ready to work their butts off the next day at practice. I was determined that the previous loss would not happen again.

I ended up having to work on Fourth of July which was another lesson in what manhood meant for me. I thought back on the years of being a child and running around my Aunt Josephine's backyard while waiting for the fireworks to begin. I enjoyed having a job and making some extra cash, but I never felt good working on a holiday.

The store was slow that afternoon because of the holiday which gave me time to work on some new plays I wanted to teach the team at practice. I took a foot long sheet of register tape and began to draw up several plays. If anyone saw me using company material for personal use I am sure I would have been reprimanded but it never crossed my mind. I couldn't help that my every thought turned into coaching my players. Every spare minute I had went into thinking of ways for us to improve. It became clear to everyone around me that coaching was my number one priority.

I was lucky enough to leave work at 8 p.m. leaving me plenty of time to pick up Kathy for the evenings fireworks. We drove to Big Clague Park located in Westlake. It was the same park that had the swimming pool where we walked with Steve Pecatis years ago. Not one of my friends had contacted me about meeting up with them to watch the show, not even Dave Murphy. I don't fully blame him because I had been exiled from their little clique a long time before. At the same time, I never called any of them to hang out because my free time was spent coaching and being with Kathy. Never the less, I will not forget how I was shunned that summer by people I spent so much time with before I began coaching. Despite being continually shunned by people I thought were my friends, I refused to feel bad about my decision to coach.

It was pleasant to watch the fireworks with Kathy because it was one of the few times that summer that we did something together that had nothing to do with baseball. The season had been hard on her with the recent booing I received was taking its toll. I tried promising her that things would improve and all the sacrifice I was making would be worth it. I promised my parents months ago that coaching would not affect my life in major ways. This left me determined not to let it. However, as the season went on it began to do exactly that. Years later I'm glad that I decided to coach despite the rifts it caused with Kathy and my friends. There is no doubt in my mind that it was worth every bit of it. If people didn't love me for who I was and what I believed in then they weren't worth it.

The next day practice was held at Maple School in the early evening. I wanted to simulate our practicing around the same time and under conditions that we would be playing in the next day. The Maple School field was basically one giant parking lot alongside a massive field of grass. There wasn't dirt anywhere to be found; meaning that any ground ball practice would be coming off the tough cement. I thought that if they could field hard ground balls bouncing off cement then fielding them coming off dirt would seem easier.

When ground ball practice was done I knew it was time to install the new plays I desperately wanted them to learn. They weren't plays I created but plays that Mr. Kubb had taught me years earlier. I knew that if the boys could master these strategies they would give us a huge edge on the competition.

The first play was one that Little League teams have been using for years but I had not seen used yet that season. It was also a play made famous in the movie "Little Big League" that came out years before. The play was designed for a batter to be involved in a count with three balls and with a runner also on third base. The number of outs didn't matter but it was always better to try it with fewer than two. It was also essential that second base was open with no base runner on it. When the batter received ball four his job was to drop the bat and sprint down to first base at full speed. When the batter arrived at first base he must not stop, instead he makes the turn towards second base. The key is to distract the opposing player with the ball whether it is the catcher or pitcher it didn't matter. When the opposing player turned his full attention to the base runner heading towards second, then the base runner on third would make a dash for the plate. This type of play would almost never work in the Majors, but in Little League it has a chance every time. The goal is to have the runner from third base score while the pitcher or catcher concentrates on the batter sprinting towards second. It is used in tight games when every run counts. It's also great to use if the coach thinks the batter on deck will not be able to hit in the runner from third, thus not wanting to take the chance of stranding the runner. In close games it is important to score every run possible. I knew that if we waited for the right time that we could catch a team off guard often enough to use it.

The next play I taught my team has been around since the game was invented. It is called the "Suicide Squeeze". It takes place when a fast runner is on third in a tight game. The object is for the runner on third base to take off for home plate the second the pitcher releases the ball. Meanwhile it's the batters job to lay down a bunt towards first base line. It is crucial that the batter gets the bunt down or the runner from third will surely be nailed at the plate. In most situations opposing players will get to the ball thinking they have a chance to throw out the runner at that plate. That is why it must only be tried when one of the fastest players on the team is on third base. It is too risky to try in any other situation. When teaching my team this play, I looked over at both Anthony and Alex with the full intent of having them use it one day. I didn't know it at the time, but those two players ended up performing the play to perfection at one of the most crucial times in my coaching career. I explained that this play is performed at great risk but the reward is incredible if performed correctly.

I could tell that everything I was teaching them was sinking in their minds. It was important that they could grasp these scenarios. I took my pitchers with the catchers aside for the next play to be taught. I gave the rest of the boys a ten minute water break while allowing them to play on the swings that Maple School provided. I knew I was overloading them with new information so I wanted to make sure I inject a little fun. The pitchers and catchers were taken aside to learn the pitchout play. It's a simple procedure of having the catcher call for a pitch outside of the strike zone high and away. The pitcher throws it as the catcher gets out of his stance while getting his body ready to throw out the opposing runner at second base. It is done most times with the first pitch at bat if the opposing team has a speedy runner on first base is sure to try to steal second base. The variation on the play comes when the opposing team has a runner on first base with a lazy lead and not paying attention. Again, this is very common for young children playing ball presenting itself to be taken advantage of numerous times in a game. The catcher will call for a normal pitch and if not hit will then launch the ball down to the first baseman in an effort to get the absent minded runner out before he gets back to the bag.

When doing these types of plays it is vital for the manager not to tip off the opposing team. We created code words to further insure that they would not catch on. If I wanted my catcher to call for a pitchout to second base I would say the words "nip two". I chose "nip" stemming from the word catnip. Because our team name was named the Wildcats, it only made sense. If we wanted to use the play more than once in a game I would change the word to something similar. Most times it was something that rhymed with nip. It was my job to vocalize the word nip to the catcher while Ray would follow it up with one or two. "One" meant to throw it to first base in an effort to get a leaning runner off the base. As simple as this code was no one ever cracked it. I truly feel that most times the opposition did not even hear us. I would only say it loud enough for my catcher to hear. The catcher would then quickly flash the number one or two across his chest for the pitcher, first baseman and shortstop to spot. It was about as subtle as a team can get, but it worked frequently.

I concluded the new plays with one right out of the Mr. Kubb playbook for double steal killers. It was taught to me when I played for him six summers earlier in 1994. It was the simple strategy of having the catcher get up looking as if he is about to throw the ball down to second base to get the runner out, meanwhile the second baseman comes charging in for the catcher's throw. When the second baseman cuts off the throw half way to the bag at second and throws it back to the catcher in enough time to tag out the runner trying to score from third. This play has to move quickly with little error to be effective. With our talent on the field, these plays all had a strong chance of working.

I concluded practice with a lengthy speech to the team about starting fresh one more time. I explained to them that they had come a long way since the 2-4 start. I mentioned that 5-5 wasn't a horrible record but that I felt we could have done much better. The first loss had much to do with us being nervous causing simple mistakes to happen. The second loss was in extra innings with us battling Mr. Briggs team all the way. The third loss took place in a game that was cut short due to rain. The fourth defeat came at the hands of Mr. Molnar's team in a game we had the lead until completely losing focus. As for the most recent loss, I blamed that one solely on myself for not having them mentally ready as well as making bad pitching moves late in the game. Instead of dwelling on the five defeats we had to focus on the things we did right in all ten games. I told them we had to learn from our mistakes but also build off the things we did well. As much as it hurt to be 5-5, it was much better than the 0-10 start the rest of the league had expected.

Earlier that day I had went to the local library and typed up a short letter to all the players and parents in an effort to make a state of the team address. I felt it was important to recap what happened in the first part of the season as well as point out our mission for the rest of the season. The following is a copy of the exact letter that was written word for word.

On March 23 we had our first practice. 104 days later we have a record of five wins and five losses. Not bad for a first year team with a kid for a coach. Let's face it guys, we are good. But we can be so much better. It is up to only you guys now on how good this team will be. In my eyes the only team that can beat us is us. Four of our losses never should have happened. Two games we lost to Mr. Molnar were sloppily played ballgames, you guys played dumb baseball and that's why we lost. There is no way that team should beat us. You guys have worked harder and are just flat out better. We have two left with them, let's make up for it. The two losses against Coyne's team were both very weird games. The first time we could have come back but it started to rain. The last time you guys just came out too flat and a little too tired. It was a good comeback but they never should have gotten up by that much. We have it all guys, pitching, hitting and fielding. We are the only team where everybody gets along. We might be a first year team but you guys are tight with each other and that is what I like to see. It is so important that everybody gets along. People play better when they are with the guys they want to win for. Remember it's a team game, no one person can be the hero. Nobody gave us the chance at the beginning of the season. Let's prove we can do it. No first year team has ever won the championship. I know we can do it! Wouldn't it be sweet to go back to school in the fall and be the envy of all your friends because your team won the championship? Start believing boys because it can happen. It is all up to you guys now. HOW BAD DO YOU WANT IT? Remember all those trophies you saw in my basement, nobody bought those for me, I earned them. So can you! Six wins in a row and a championship in our first year together. Go out there and take it Wildcats!

It was the first long passionate thing that I had written outside of normal schoolwork. I poured my heart into the letter because I truly believed it was best for the team to understand where we had been and where we needed to go.

Getting dressed the next night for the game I kept all the same traditions intact. I thought about how nervous I was for the first game just over a month before. I reflected on how scared I was that my team may not be any good. I took a deep breath while thinking of how fortunate I was to coach. Ten games had already passed in a sixteen game season with many of those feelings of nervousness replaced with feelings of hunger and desire to win. I no longer hoped our team was going to win ballgames, but I expected they would. It was easy to tell from the looks of the players they no longer hoped but also expected to win. I knew if I could build a team with the skill level of the Mr. Kubb teams mixed with the heart of Mr. Wheeler teams, no one who could stop us. There was no doubt in my mind that my team possessed all those qualities.

It didn't matter whether people supported us or were against us, we were in it to win it. Every player on the team believed that there was no room to take a backseat to anyone. I did my best to instill the same mentality I believed in the hearts and minds of my players. After ten games everyone realized that we had the hungriest team in the league.

As the music group Creed sang their famous tune "Higher", I thought about just how high my team was set to ascend. The song had a way of getting my heart pumping before every game, unlike any other one that could have possibly played.

Heading into that night's game at Middle School field against Mr. Hill's team the league standings were as follows:

Mr. Coyne – Pat's Cleaners 7 wins 3 losses
Mr. Molnar – Ohio Envelope 6 wins 4 losses
Mr. Mckee – Play it again Sports 5 wins 5 losses
Mr. Briggs – Wilsons Bike Shop 4 wins 6 losses
Mr. Hill – Sedmack Insurance 3 wins 7 losses

Despite the mediocre record our team still had a chance because no other squad had pulled away from the pack. It was crucial that we not lose again to give us the chance at finishing with the best record in the league. The best record also earned a bye in the first round of the postseason tournament.

Brian had been on a roll in his last few outings so I stuck with him. I told him to do all the things he had been doing. I also told him not to worry about walking a batter or two because it just meant we would have a chance to pick them off base. Of course I didn't want him to walk anyone but it was a way to put his mind at ease. His shaky outing from game one was a distant memory with his many good performances since then. I always let Brian feel that I had full confidence in him because he performed at a greater level when he knew we believed in him. He had all the talent in the world but it wasn't until he proved it to the coaches that he finally believed it in himself.

I handed the lineup card to Mr. Hill with full confidence that another win was on the way. The lineup used that day looked as follows:

CF Mat Poli
3B Dan Kitko
C Alex Uhlik
P Brian Leciewski

SS Anthony Poli
LF Mike Hach
1B Kyle Keller
RF Andy Barth
2B Ryan Mackey
OF John Rehak

I continued to use the same seven starters at the top of the order for the remainder of the season. Their talents complimented each other's in the lineup so well that I couldn't abandon it. After I posted our copy of the lineup on the dugout fence I decided to make one more crucial move.

Until that point in the season Mr. Kitko had been extremely overbearing any time his son was on the mound pitching or at the plate hitting. It wasn't that he was being too hard on Dan. The problem was that his constant coaching from the sidelines was starting to annoy some of the other players. I didn't seem to notice it as much but I constantly had players and parents of mine complaining to me about it. The more I paid attention to it I noticed that it was making Dan nervous at times, so I was in need of a solution. My answer was to hand Mr. Kitko the score keeper's book that I kept. It didn't matter who kept the official score as long as someone on each side did. I didn't particular liking doing it so it was a perfect solution to turn over the job to Mr. Kitko. This way it freed me up to do other things, while giving Mr. Kitko a slight distraction from yelling to his son.

I don't condemn how Mr. Kitko acted because he was just showing compassion for his son. He coached Dan from the sidelines because he truly cared how his son performed. I prefer a parent like that over one who never showed up or supported their son. The problem was that it became such a distraction that I felt I needed to do something before it got out of hand. My other main concern was that the team listened strictly to the coaching staff during the game without feeling any need to turn their attention anywhere else.

It was a typical mid-summer night in North East Cleveland with just a slight chill in the air. I counted on the hot streak our batting order got on late in the last game to carry over. I didn't have to wait long as the boys grabbed a quick 6-0 lead heading into the bottom of the first inning. It also provided Brian a nice cushion going into pitch in the bottom of the first inning.

In the pregame huddle we went over the new plays a few times with the intent that we would use them the first chance we saw. With a runner on first base and no one out I called for "Nip 1". Alex flashed one finger down which signaled to Keller at first base to expect a throw over. Sure enough after the next pitch Alex was able to launch the ball down to first and catch Miles Morgan napping for the out. As the umpire called "out", our entire team exploded into cheers. Normally we would not erupt with such emotion if it wasn't for the fact that a play we practiced so hard actually worked on the first try. It just felt incredible to see the hard work in practice payoff. Mr. Hill took it as an insult because of the score and the fact we would play that way. I saw nothing wrong with our using the play because it was all part of teaching the boys.

As the game progressed we continued to blow them out. I inserted Dan at pitcher in the bottom of the fourth inning with a 14 -2 lead. Every time the Bell rang with run after run scoring I could see Mr. Hill's face become redder than the jersey he was wearing. He was short and stocky with a bright red jersey, if he had a mustache with a tail I would have been sure he was the Devil.

After Dan mowed down all three batters he faced I called a team huddle in the dugout. I reminded them of the base running play we worked on during practice, telling them if we got the chance in the top of the fifth we would use it. I knew it could have been looked on as a lousy thing to do being up by so many runs but it didn't stop me calling for it when the chance presented itself. Mike Hach walked than proceeded to steal second base as well as third. After Kyle took ball three, both he and Mike looked to the dugout for a sign. I softly touched my bottom lip which was the signal for the trick play. The next pitch was out of the strike zone so Kyle took off like a rocket down the first base line and made the turn for second. Just as planned the catcher let his full attention focus on Kyle by tossing the ball five feet over the pitchers head. While the opposition scrambled to recover the ball Mike was easily able to come sprinting home.

If the first two plays set Mr. Hill into a rage of anger then the third most certainly sent him over the top. With us leading 18-2 in the fifth inning the game was just about over. They had a runner on first base with two outs. With nothing to lose I was sure Mr. Hill would likely signal his player to steal second base. I'm not sure if it was the excitement of wanting to use another new play or simply the desire to stop anything they tried. Whatever the case, I did not hesitate to signal "Nip 2" to Alex behind the plate. Dan proceeded to throw the ball high and wide as Alex got out of his crouch and threw the runner out at second base by at least two feet. It was the perfect way to end the game. I regretted that we didn't use the squeeze play but was happy that the three we did try worked to perfection.

The win put us above .500 with a 6-5 record. It was the third time that season we had beaten Mr. Hill's team. It was a far cry from what he expected when I met him in his front yard months earlier. The 18-2 win was also the largest win of the season, making me feel great about the new batting order I installed. Every man in the order was starting to hit the ball. Andy had not yet come along as well as I hoped but he was showing slow signs of improvement. The important thing was to keep his confidence up so he would not give up.

During the post-game hand shake ritual something happened that set off a chain of events that increased our hunger to win 100 times over. Mr. Hill went through our entire lineup shaking hands with each one of my players and assistant coaches until it came time for him to shake my hand. When I stuck out my hand to say the traditional, "Good game", he chose not to shake it. He then grabbed me by my arm to motion me over by home plate.

It was at home plate that Mr. Hill began to verbally insult me for over five minutes. He took the opportunity to explain to me that he thought I was the worst coach in the league. He went on to proclaim that he was going to make sure I never coached again. He said I had no respect for the game and that I taught my players how to play dirty. He then repeated himself by stating that he would do everything in his power to make sure that I never coached again.

I was so stunned by what I heard it left me barely able to walk towards the dugout where my team was waiting. Mr. Hill spoke quietly enough that no one had heard what just happened. It wasn't what he said about me that irritated me, it was the threat of my never coaching again that sent a chill down my spine. Some moments in life are polarizing, this event certainly one of them. I was in such a state of shock that I became speechless for the first time all year. I was trying so hard to hold back tears that I didn't even give my traditional post game speech. After every game I always gave a solid motivational talk followed by handing out a few game balls. This time I simply said, "Good game and I will see everyone Saturday".

The scariest thing was that I didn't know if Mr. Hill actually had the power to prevent me from coaching. I was aware that he was our league coordinator but also knew that there were many people above him. I was thankful that my parents had already left because I knew it would have been impossible to lie to them if they asked if anything was wrong.

I was starting to pack up my gear when Mrs. Uhlik came over to me and asked, "If everything was okay"? Until that point I had not yet looked anyone in the eyes, including Kathy. I didn't want anyone to see me tear up, which is exactly what happened when I went to answer Mrs. Uhlik. I was lucky enough that everyone else had left with the exception of the Uhliks and my good friend Joe Graham. I couldn't hold in the emotion any longer, I began to cry as Mrs. Uhlik gave me a long hug. I felt terrible crying in front of my girlfriend, my close friend as well as Alex. But there was nothing I could do to hold it in, I was extremely upset. Mrs. Uhlik promised that she would do whatever she could to make sure his words didn't come true. I have to hand it to Joe Graham who was extremely supportive as well. He put his arm around me as well and swore at Jack Hill's car when he drove away.

On my way home from dropping Kathy off, I was searching my mind for something to tell my parents if they asked what was wrong. They were standing by the dugout when I gave my postgame speech that led me to believe they certainly would know something was wrong. My plan was to go right into my bedroom when I got home so that I wouldn't have to face them.

When I finally arrived home my parents were pulling into the driveway right behind me. They had stopped somewhere for ice cream. I thought my plan was going to work because if I got in the house before them I could just hide in my room until I felt better. I was sitting in my room about two minutes later when Dad played the answering machine out loud for everyone to hear. There was a message on it from Mr. Kubb. I can't recall his exact words but I can relay most of them.

"Don and Maria this is Carl Kubb. I just received a phone call from Joanne Uhlik, her son Alex plays for Vince. She explained to me what happened and that Vince was in no

kind of mood! I want you to rest assure that I am still on the league committee and will personally address this issue with Jack myself."

There may have been more to the message but those were the lines that I recall. It was incredible to have the support of Mr. Kubb because he exerted such a powerful influence for the entire league. I also had but no choice to tell my parents exactly what happened after the post-game hand shake. I wasn't even halfway done with my story when our phone began to ring off the hook.

Mr. Rehak was the first parent to call and ask if I was okay. He said he didn't notice Jack yelling at me but could tell that something was wrong by my actions in the postgame speech. I hadn't noticed but most of the parents had begun to gather around me when I gave those postgame speeches so they were able to tell if something was wrong.

Before the night was over I fielded many more calls from parents but none more powerful than the one Mr. Kubb made. When I called him back to explain what happened, he listened to what I said than assured me that he would personally handle it. He told me that he had been hearing good things from parents of my players which made him proud of me. I hadn't spoken to Mr. Kubb in six years but it didn't matter. I felt as though I was on his team all over again. He spoke with my Dad as well at length. One of the things he mentioned to Dad was that he always liked our family because we never missed a game or practice. He said that we were one of the few family's he dealt with that never gave him any problems. As upsetting as the night was it served a further reminder of the positive role models I had in my life when it came to baseball teachings. I was taught well from my father, brother, grandfather and Uncle Pete. It also helped matters that I came from teams coached by baseball masterminds such as Mr. Wheeler and Mr. Kubb.

A few hours had passed with everyone in the house getting ready for bed when the phone rang one more time. This time it was not a supportive voice on the other end but rather Mr. Hill himself. I never had the chance to answer the phone as my Dad picked up before I could. Dad made his point short and simple. His message for Hill was that he was never to speak to me. Dad also insisted in explaining to Mr. Hill that if he got out of line again he would knock him right back in. I have no idea what Jack was saying on the other end but I'm sure it wasn't much. Between whatever Mr. Kubb told Mr. Hill mixed in with what dad said, the man never crossed me again the rest of the season.

The words of Mr. Hill echoed in my head as I tried to fall asleep later that night. I believed in what Mr. Kubb along with my father had told me when they said they would handle it. However, I couldn't help but be nervous. I had given up so much to coach so that the thought of it being taken from me was killing me.

The upsetting ordeal made me realize this could be my only chance to coach for many years to come. If Mr. Hill succeeded having me banned from coaching in North Olmsted, then it meant I would have to wait years later in the hopes of coaching my own children. I was unsure when if ever that would be so I didn't want to take the chance. I was happy coaching the players I had with no intention of wanting to coach anywhere else. The entire experience increased my hunger to win more than I thought possible. The chip on my shoulder was becoming a boulder.

We were not scheduled to play again until Saturday, which meant Friday night I was free to do whatever I pleased. Kathy had to work so I took it upon myself to call up Brad Russell in the hopes that he might want to get together. It had been over a month since I hung out with him so I thought it might be a good idea to call him. The last time we got together was when I wrestled a young man named Wes Brown who outweighed me by over 100 pounds. Brad was in my corner with inspiring words that led me to beat the much bigger and stronger opponent. Since that evening Brad or no one else hadn't made any effort to contact me.

Things came to a head after the tough loss to Coyne's team when I stopped at Brad's house unexpectedly. It had been a tough loss to swallow so I wanted the friendship of someone close to me to cheer me up. When I arrived at his house I found he was not alone. The entire group of people I befriended over the course of my senior year were there hanging out. Along with them was Dave Murphy who was there because of his girlfriend Julie. I will never forget as I walked in with them all laughing and joking until they saw me. They had no intentions on inviting me as the conversation came to a silent halt. I only stuck around for about five minutes until leaving. It was clear I was no longer wanted around so I saw no point in staying.

To most people at age 18 this kind of thing would be a major deal. At that point my head was so wrapped into coaching along with Kathy that it didn't annoy me as much as it could have. I called Dave later that weekend to ask him what the problem was. He explained that he did want me to be there but it wasn't his place to invite me. I thought about all the times I had invited him into the group and it angered me that when he had the chance to do it for me he chose not to. There are many joys that came along in that incredible summer; however, the few pains are every bit as memorable. Sacrificing so many friendships had to result in winning or else it wouldn't have been worth it.

For a while hanging out with Brad that evening actually felt like old times. We spent most of the night driving around filming each other doing crazy things around the city. It was typical young man things such as Brad climbing the flag pole at North Olmsted High School. Brad also filmed me doing jumping jacks in my underwear in the front yard of some total stranger. It didn't matter how stupid the things we did were but just the fact that we were spending time together felt good. I was so stressed out with the Mr. Hill screaming session that it was nice to take my mind off of it for a few hours.

By the time I returned home it was well past two in the morning. I thought I would have been the only one in the house up but my mom was still awake. She was getting things in order for my high school graduation party that coming Sunday. We had scheduled the party for Sunday because of the game set for Saturday. In addition to the many varieties of excellent food she was cooking, there were plenty of pictures to go along with the festivities.

There was one incredible collage of all the pictures taken of me during my Little League days, including the current team I was coaching. Looking at the photos helped inspire me to never let Jack Hill's words see the light of day. I convinced myself that no longer would I let the hurtful words and actions of others affect me. If the little boy in the pictures wasn't scared of anything all those years, than the grown man looking me in the mirror wouldn't be either.

Saturday, July 8, 2000 seemed it would be much like any other day as I was getting dressed for that afternoon's game. The first pitch was set for 3p.m against Mr. Molnar's team, Ohio Envelope, at Little Clague Park. It was important to beat them because they were the only team that we had not beaten. I expected to win because of the major improvements we had made since the last meeting.

I made it a point to get to every game a full hour ahead of first pitch in order to be alone with the field. The solace gave me a certain sense of peace that I needed to help relax before the madness of game time. As I pulled into the parking lot I noticed that my entire team, along with their parents was standing by the dugout waiting for me. It was a total shock because they weren't supposed to show up for another 15-20 minutes.

Walking over to them I felt my heart racing because I was scared something might have been wrong. The closer I got to them they came up to me in groups to slap hands. Billy Graves made his first appearance with the team since his accident. He was unable to play; however, it was great to see him. The strong show of respect was exactly what I needed to put the past few days behind me. It made me realize even more how much this team loved playing for me, as well as how much I loved coaching them. Alex Uhlik spoke on behalf of the entire team by telling me, "Coach, we have your back. We will never play for anyone else as long as you're coaching." It is a moment that I will forever cherish.

Alex had undertaken to let the rest of the team know what had happened. With word spreading that I might never coach again causing panic, it caused the entire team to show up early to show their support. I always felt Alex was one of the team leaders not only by his play on the field but also his behavior off of it. He always carried himself in a respectful manner with this another example of what a great young man he was.

With the team showing me such strong loyalty I decided to let them know the truth. I instructed the entire team to sit down as I sat along with them in the outfield grass. I opened up my heart by telling them everything I felt they deserved to know. I explained to them that I didn't even choose half the team. It was only because the other coaches didn't want many of them that they were playing for me. I told them about how Mr. Hill had given us no chance to win a game. I told them how much my parents were against my coaching, but because they saw how much I loved coaching them they had changed their minds. I let them know how I waited for the phone to ring for months before I knew I was able to coach. I explained that the players I picked I had no clue of who they were but went strictly by the sounds of their names. I could tell by the looks on their faces that they were stunned by all of this. I went on to recall how Mrs. Briggs called me early in the morning just to complain about us. In closing I explained that by us winning it was the ultimate revenge and final word. That if we kept winning that everyone else would have to eat their words. I told them that even though no one else gave us a chance that I felt we had the best team in the league. I filled their heads with the image of someday holding up a championship trophy. The best way to shut everyone up was to keep winning. The more I spoke, the more they began to get filled with motivation. I could tell every word I said was getting through to them in the right kind of way.

When my nearly twenty-minute speech concluded they jumped up chanting "Wildcats!" For five straight minutes they began jumping up and down chanting. Just to add more fuel to the fire I told them that Mr. Hill called them a bunch of lily flowers. He had never said anything of the sort, but I knew by adding that one final blow it would set them off for good. Before I gave that speech I considered it might backfire and depress them, but I also knew that chances were I would get the reaction I did. My team developed so much of my own mentality that when I sold them on the underdog role it worked perfectly. I made them believe it was us against the world, because in many ways it was.

I looked into the crowd when I noticed Mr. Briggs along with Mr. Hill were sitting in the stands watching. Mr. Hill had a clipboard in his hands that he was using to collect signatures, I would assume. If Mr. Hill was trying to start a petition it must have never gotten any further because that was the last I saw of it. I was willing to give him the benefit of the doubt because I believed that Mr. Kubb along with my father would handle any uprising that might occur.

There was a familiar face in the stands sitting next to Don and Abbie, it was Dave Murphy. This was the first game all a season that he showed up to watch so I was happy to see him. I understood that he was busy getting ready for college as well as his new relationship with Julie. Kathy and Brad Russell were sitting next to Dave so it was nice to have support in the crowd for such a big game.

With each game becoming more vital to the overall outcome of the season it was important that the starting lineup I chose gave us the best possible chance at winning. At 6-5 we could not afford to lose another game. The lineup for that game is as follows:

CF Matt Poli
3B Dan Kitko
2B Alex Uhlik
C Brian Leciewski
SS Anthony Poli
LF Mike Hach
1B Kyle Keller
RF Andy Barth
P Ryan Mackey
OF John Rehak

I thought for a long time about letting Brian start at pitcher to give him a chance at redemption from the brutal first game of the season loss. The reason I decided against it was due to Mr. Molnar having an extremely fast team. In the previous two meetings they showed the ability to steal bases, never letting a chance pass without trying to steal one. They were so aggressive on the base paths I wanted Brian behind the plate for his strong arm. I believed that with the new plays we developed coupled with Brian's arm we would have a better chance at stopping their run game. The plan was to get a couple of solid innings out of Ryan Mackey until Alex came into pitch.

Ryan was finally given the chance to face his old team. He wanted to pitch against them all season so I thought that this was as a good of a time as any to let him. It didn't take long for his old teammates to give him a rude welcome. Ryan was hitting the strike zone but not with enough speed to do damage. The boys from Ohio Envelope locked in on his pitches early, jumping out to an 8-0 lead after two innings. Ryan gave it his all so I was proud of him but also knew I needed to make a switch at pitcher.

Our lineup was hitting the ball well but not well enough as after four innings we failed to score. Alex came into the game in the third inning being able to pitch three scoreless innings keeping the score at 8-0. We needed a spark going into the bottom of the fifth so I called a team huddle. I reminded the boys of the pregame speech pointing out that the top of our lineup was due up so this was the perfect time to rally.

Sure enough, my words sunk in as the first three batters reached base setting the table for cleanup hitter Brian Leciewski. Until that point in the season our team hadn't hit a homerun, so when Brian hit the first pitch twenty feet over the centerfielder's head it was a thing of beauty. He hit the ball so far that he was rounding third base when the centerfielder was making the throw into the cutoff man. There wasn't a play at the plate as Brian came home standing. In the blink of an eye we had cut their lead in half. The entire team mobbed Brian the second he crossed home plate. It was easily the biggest moment of the season at that point.

Brian's homerun energized the team by giving them the belief that they could come back to beat Ohio Envelope. After Anthony Poli doubled, Mike Hach and Kyle Keller drew back to back walks loading up the bases for Andy Barth. After a slow start to the season Andy began to improve as the games went on. He had not yet had a big hit but I felt that this would be the perfect time for him to finally break though. As Andy grabbed his bat to walk to the plate I patted him on the back and said, "It's your turn now, son."

Andy stood at the plate with his knees looking as if they would buckle at any second. I was nervous for him but not as nearly as he appeared to be. Danny Molnar was able to get a quick zero balls and two strike count on Andy. I told him to, "Step out of the box to take a deep breath". Andy did what he was told as he usually did when given instructions. The deep breath must have worked as Andy crushed the next pitch farther than any ball I had ever seen hit in Little League. It didn't matter how slow Andy ran because the ball was hit so incredibly far it allowed him to round the bases for a grand slam. We had come back to tie the game only minutes after being down by eight runs.

After Andy crossed home plate I gave him the biggest bear hug of his young life. I couldn't have been happier for anyone than I was for Andy. I felt as though all that hard work we put in had finally paid off. Andy had never given up on himself no matter how bleak things looked at times. The second I let go of Andy his mom was right behind me to hug him. It was such an emotional high that both of them had tears in their eyes. We had gone from not hitting a homerun all season to hitting multiple grand slams minutes apart. These were the only two homeruns we hit all season but they couldn't have come at a better time.

It was moments such as these that make that season standout and become a part of my everyday memory. No matter what Andy or Brian go on to do the rest of their lives, no one will ever be able to take those incredible memories from them. I'm thrilled to say that I was even a part of them. Not only did the two homers tie the game but they also swung the momentum swiftly in our favor. For the first time all season we truly believed that no matter what was thrown at us we could overcome it.

Before the fifth inning ended we were able to score four more runs to take a 12-8 lead heading into the sixth. Any thoughts of Ohio Envelope making a comeback came to an end the second Dan Kitko took the hill. He set down all three batters he faced in convincing fashion.

The Andy Barth hit parade was not over as he came to the plate with two runners on base in the bottom of the sixth. He crushed the first pitch he saw for a bases clearing double. In just two innings he managed to drive in six runs. For the first the time in months Andy had a look of confidence on his face that couldn't be removed. When Ryan Mackey drove in Andy with the next pitch, it gave us a commanding 15-8 lead.

Every player on the team was so pumped up that I had no doubt in my mind that the seven- run lead would be safe. I didn't have to remind them to charge the field in the top of the seventh as they all bolted out to their positions. After every pitch Dan threw they each would scream, "Wildcats". I had seen them excited before but never to this extent. Not only were the players chanting but their parents were chanting as well. When Kyle Keller made a diving stop at first base to end the game the place almost came unglued with excitement.

It was our second win in a row and the fifth win in six games. There was no denying that our team was on a roll. It felt great to finally earn a win over Mr. Molnar's team allowing us to move closer to first place. It also meant that we had defeated every team in our league, which was a huge boost of confidence. My players now understood that there wasn't a team they couldn't defeat. Until that point in the season it seemed as though we had a mental block when it came to playing against Ohio Envelope. A victory over them helped us to get past it.

In what was becoming the normal, the entire set of parents stuck around behind the dugout to listen to my post game speech. I gave out game balls to Andy Barth and Brian Leciewski for the big home runs they hit. I also made sure to give out a game ball to Alex for his three innings of shutout work on the mound when we desperately needed it. Dan Kitko was in receipt of the final game ball because of his mastery on the pitcher's mound. For Dan it was just one of many that he received that season. Andy was excited about the game ball that he was given; however, it was what Dad gave him after the game that made a bigger impact.

Dad found a beat up baseball lying in the grass behind the stands during the game. He proceeded to rip the cover off the ball then throw away the inside. When the game was over he went up to Andy and gave him the cover of the baseball. He told Andy, "You hit the ball so hard that the cover flew off so I grabbed it for you". Andy believed every word my Dad told him, keeping that in his room for years afterwards.

I didn't have much time to celebrate that afternoon because I had to help my parents set up for my graduation party the next day. I was so incredibly ecstatic about the win that setting up countless chairs and tables didn't seem like work. Brad Russell came over after the game to help out. It took a few hours to get everything in order, so after all the hard work was done Brad and I decided to go out to celebrate. It was that night that I realized the different worlds we inhabited.

During the entire time that I spent hanging around Brad that evening I kept thinking about the game we had played that afternoon. While Brad was speaking about things that I had little to no interest in, I continued to talk about coaching, which was boring him. I felt bad that we had grown so far apart in such a short amount of time. It didn't help matters that his girlfriend suddenly wasn't getting along with Kathy that summer. It became evident that our lives were heading in two totally different directions. There's a good chance things such as that may have happened even if I hadn't spent all my free time coaching, but I'm sure it didn't help that I was. I speak of these things not as bad memories, but rather to be truthful about everything that happened that summer. I enjoyed many highs but also certain lows. The only way to grow up is to lose part of your childlike innocence along the way. In the summer of 2000 I was experiencing for the first time that to achieve something I love, many sacrifices would be made along the way. The important thing was realizing if these sacrifices I was making would be worth the prize at the end, there was nothing in my heart or mind telling me it wasn't worth it.

My high school graduation party was held on Sunday, July 9, 2000 at my parent's house. With all the excitement of the season I had not thought much about this special day. My parents had gone all out for it by decorating the entire backyard with signs and canopies for the guests to enjoy. A summer that was filled with rain managed to produce a sunny afternoon which only helped matters. It was my first chance to feel like and adult around my extended family by greeting everyone as they showed up. I was hopeful that my entire family would show up because I truly enjoyed the special times we shared together. My Mother's side alone consisted of over 45 people so this would not be a small party by any means.

As I greeted each family member as they showed up I was surprised to see numerous players from the team appear. My parents never told me that they invited them as a surprise for me. I was extremely pleased to have them their on such a special day. They were a major part in why the summer was off to such an amazing start. The following players with their families showed up in support, Dan Kitko, Brian Leciewksi with Ray, Mike Hach, John Rehak, Alex Uhlik, Andy Barth and Ryan Mackey. Taking into account that I had several younger cousins close to their age the party soon had as many children there as it did adults. It meant a great deal to me to have some of my players attend, I made a point of thanking my parents numerous times afterwards.

Before I knew it I was in the front yard with all of the children playing catch with a tennis ball. Each one of my players brought their glove as well as numerous of my younger cousins. It proved to be quite the scene as I was throwing high fly balls in the front yard with well over 25 children scrambling to catch it. The plans I had of talking with the adults never materialized as I spent the entire day with the younger crowd.

I didn't have to worry about ignoring any of my friends because almost none of them showed up. Dave Murphy and Brad Russell both arrived for the party but left early to spend time with their girlfriends. Again, I don't blame them for doing this because they were rather early into their relationships and wanted to spend time with their ladies. Matt Tomecko was also nice enough to show up for the day's events. Joe Graham showed up early and stayed throughout most of the day. Besides those chosen few most of the friends I had made in high school, particularly in choir chose not to attend. With the large number of other people there it didn't even matter to me. I was very pleased with the turnout. Throughout the course of the day over 200 people showed up.

As the day was winding down with numerous family members starting to leave, I couldn't help but notice not a single one of them asked who the children were that they had never seen before. It was apparent to anyone there that my players were following me around the entire time with us sharing a special bond. Yet not a single aunt or uncle asked me about them. I had been waiting all day for someone to say, "Hey, Vince, I didn't know you coached Little League". Our team picture was up in the garage with the rest of the pictures for people to view, yet none of my aunts or uncles asked me a single thing about coaching. Normally I wouldn't have let something let this bug me if it wasn't for when Don coached that everyone asked him about it. It didn't mean that relatives loved Don more than me, it just meant that human nature lets people care more about something the first time it happens. The second person who does it is rarely ever noticed. It was also a clear sign that no matter what I did I would be seen as Don's younger brother and not an adult in the eyes of my extended family. I'm sure people may disagree with me but I have lived it my whole life and it doesn't change. I do believe that if Pete were there he would have asked about it, however, Pete could not make it that day.

Speaking of Don I couldn't ask for a better older brother than he. It didn't matter to him that my aunts or uncles seemed to not care about my coaching, but Don never missed a chance to show interest in my coaching. We kept the competitive edge between us but it never escalated past that. The other great thing about Don was that even know he seemed to get most of the attention from the extended family, he always made sure to include me into everything he could. When I constantly heard about how great Don was from my aunts and uncles, he made every attempt to tell them about how well I was doing. He always made me feel as if he was looking up to me, when in fact I was looking up to him. With all the intention he received it would have been easier to tear us apart, it was how my parents treated us as equals all the time that kept us as strong as we are today. People have asked if I got into coaching to upstage my brother, when in fact I always felt if I could be half as successful as he I would be happy.

As the night wore down the last people at my party helped me count my graduation cards. The remaining guests included Kathy, Joe Graham and Andy Barth who watched a movie in the basement with me as Bill and Don took inventory of all my cards. Before that day I never even realized that someone received cards with money in them at a graduation party. It was overwhelming to have parents of the players give me thoughtful gifts that I never expected. The Rehak's gave me great seats to an Indians game later that summer. It's what some of the parents wrote in the cards that I will forever cherish. Numerous parents wrote their son was having the best summer of his life thanks to the team atmosphere. I took joy in the knowledge the parents were seeing some of the same magic on the field that I was.

The day following the party I woke up with a terrible sore throat. I had Bill call me in sick from work because both my parents had already left for work. I was nervous because we had a big game with Mr. Coyne's team the next night. I rested the entire day without straining myself in any way hoping that the pain would be gone by game day. The next morning I woke up with the pain ten times worse. I was starting to lose my voice so I rushed to the doctor in hopes of a miracle drug to make it better by game time. I found out I had strep throat and was told to rest at home for several days until feeling better. It was clear that no matter how much I respected Dr. Gosky, I was not going to miss a game. I knew that I would only be contagious for 24 hours so I didn't tell anyone else that I was sick.

The remainder of the day I spent thinking about the game that night. It was a crucial game because another win would put us three full games above .500 tying us for first place. It was a chance to win our third in a row as well as our sixth in seven tries. With the effects of strep taking its toll I tried to take a nap before leaving for the game but I couldn't put my mind at ease long enough to fall asleep. I remember pouring salt into tap water then gargling in the hope I would feel better but it didn't work. Our team had such a big win the past Saturday against Mr. Molnar's team that I was afraid of a letdown. We showed a major letdown before playing Mr. Coyne's team the last time so I was desperate not to have it happen again.

While getting ready for the game I changed into my uniform as usual but without any music playing in the background. It was also the only game all year that I did not drive to. It was at

Little Clague Park so I decided to walk. I broke away from my two standard traditions in need of time to think with no distractions. I didn't want to say anything to make my players overly nervous but I felt that it was a must win game. They had fought hard to come back to beat Mr. Molnar's team a few days before so I didn't want it to go to waste with a loss. It seemed as though every time we built momentum something bad would happen, forcing us to start over. I was determined not to allow that to occur again.

I focused my pre game speech around playing a full seven innings. I reminded them of the last time we played with the 0-14 hole we dug for ourselves. I insisted that we must get off to a fast start without allowing them to get too far ahead of us. I spoke in a low tone of voice because my throat was killing me. It seemed as though the low tone of voice may have helped because the players leaned in extra close to pay attention. It was as if every word I said was now the law for these players. At that point I could have told them to eat grass with them most likely doing it. It showed how loyal they were to me, but also how loyal they were to one another. I remembered the days of playing for Mr. Wheeler, having the same feeling of loyalty to the coach. It is important for a coach to have loyalty from his players because without it nothing can ever be accomplished. All the talent in the world doesn't matter when there is no one to guide the ship.

With Nate Dolesh still on his cross country excursion and Billy Graves far from even being able to ride a bike, our team still only had 11 active players on the roster. I tossed around numerous options in my head for a starting lineup before going back to the one that seemed to be working. I didn't see any major reason to stray from an order that was suddenly red hot. The lineup for that evening is as follows:

CF Matt Poli
3B Dan Kitko
C Alex Uhlik
P Brian Leciewski
SS Anthony Poli
LF Mike Hach
2B Kyle Keller
RF Andy Barth
1B Pat Morris
OF John Rehak

It was crucial for Brian Leciewski to get off to a strong start on the mound to build his early confidence. He didn't look his sharpest early on but also didn't look bad either. After two innings we trailed 0-5. A five run deficit didn't seem like much with the way our team had been hitting the ball as of late. However, we were not happy with trailing. The major thing that our team was developing as the season went on was calmness in tough situations. Earlier in the year we may have panicked when getting behind in a game early without having the experience of making a comeback. That was no longer the case because our team developed a strong sense of maturity in tough spots.

Going into the bottom of the fourth down 0-7 I made a switch by putting Dan on the mound for Brian. I moved him to third, telling him to cover as much room on the left side of the infield as possible. Anthony Poli had been struggling that night so I wanted Brian to take charge on anything close hit to that side. Kitko had no issues using his dancing curveball to put away the side in the bottom of the fourth.

Before taking our at bats in the fifth I called a team huddle in the dugout. I reminded them that a mere two weeks earlier we had comeback against this same team from a deficit twice this size. I reinforced that we needed to play a full seven innings by making the other team play every single out hard. It was important that we didn't give them anything easy.

I looked over to the stands where I saw Dave Murphy sitting with my parents cheering us on. I looked over and saw Don sitting by them. I gave him a look as to say, "Don't worry" although I was worried. I didn't like having to make these large comebacks every game but still had the faith we could. I motioned to Ray and Bill to be extremely aggressive on the base paths since we needed runs in a hurry.

The boys from Pat's Cleaners may have had visions of the 14-0 comeback still in their heads as they came out in the fifth inning extremely flat. Their pitcher, Charlie Templeton, walked the first three batters he faced to load them for Andy Barth. I let Andy know that we didn't need another grand slam but just a simple hit would do nicely. The suddenly confident Andy proceeded to hit the first pitch into deep right field for a base clearing   double. The crowd of parents exploded with cheers as the Bell rang loudly to symbolize the three runs. Andy Barth had caught fire and it couldn't have happened at a better time. I had been preaching to him for months to keep his head up with it finally starting to pay off.

The rally was not over with yet as the boys managed to score two more runs on a John Rehak double a few batters later. Before anyone could blink we had cut the lead to 5-7. We were not able to score any more runs that inning but still had new life injected into us.

I knew that if Dan could mow down the opposing order in the bottom of the fifth there would be no stopping us from scoring more in the top of the sixth. Before Dan could take the mound he looked over and saw his mom standing next to his dad in the crowd. This was a rare sight because of the divorce they normally didn't sit or stand within twenty feet of another. It was also interesting because for the first time all season Dan's mom was focused on the game. She would normally sit away from almost everyone else to read a book or magazine. It was clear that Wildcat fever was finally starting to take over Kim Binder (Dan's Mom) as it did the rest of the parents. Dan looked over to see his parents by each other's side with it giving him a surge of adrenaline as he pitched nine straight strikes to strike out the side.

There was no doubt in anyone's mind that the comeback was far from over. In the top of the sixth, trailing 5-7 we knew it was only a matter of time before we took the lead for good. After Brian walked with Anthony's single to follow, it was time for Mike Hach to come through in the clutch. Mike was not known for his power so it was a shock to all when he tripled to deep center field to tie the game at seven. Kyle Keller was up next and hit an RBI single to give us our first lead of the game at 8-7. In a scary moment, Andy Barth got plunked in the head with the very next pitch. I joked around later that evening with him that his head was the only place on him that couldn't afford any more damage. It just one of those jokes that brothers can have with one another, however, Andy was not my brother though it did feel like it at times.

With two batters on and two out's Matt drew a walk to load the bases for Dan Kitko. I put a hit and run on because I knew Dan would put the ball into play as he often did. The hit and run worked like a charm, Dan was able to triple in all three runs building our lead up to 11-7. As the next two innings went on we built the lead to 13-7 heading into the bottom of the seventh.

With a six run lead and only 3 more outs needed for the win I let Alex Uhlik come in to pitch. Alex had played hard all game so I wanted to give him the chance to close out the win. I also knew that Dan had already pitched three innings so I didn't want to over extend his arm. Alex started off shaky but quickly bounced back from two walks to get three straight outs ending the game. It was much more than just our third straight win, it was a statement that we never gave up on any game despite the score. As much as I would have liked for us to jump out to early leads and keep them we did have the ability to climb our way back into any game.

Mr. Kitko approached me while walking to the perch behind the dugouts to address the team after the big win. He complimented the coaching staff on our ability to keep the players focused on the game even when things looked bad. I told him "Each game was a metaphor for the entire season because no one gave us a chance, so everything positive we did just built more momentum in our favor". I felt in my heart that the best part of the season was yet to come.

As the players drank their juice boxes while eating fruit snacks I paused for a second before I spoke. One reason was that my throat was still killing me, the other was I wanted to make sure I said the right things. I started off by saying, "Three in a row and 8-5 overall, that's not bad for a first year team with a rookie head coach". It became our motto to surprise anyone who said we couldn't do it, that game was a further example that no matter the odd's we were not about to give up. I made a point of telling the team I was happy with the win streak but that we still needed many more wins to accomplish our goal of being the best. As I spoke I made sure to look into their eyes to see if they were paying attention. As always they were hanging on my every word. There is no greater feeling for a coach than the respect of his players.

After addressing the players I made a special point to call over in private the parents who attended my graduation party days earlier. I thanked them for their support throughout what was becoming a challenging season. I reminded them that I was new to coaching which meant I would make my share of mistakes, but also that I loved coaching their sons and nothing would stop me from giving them my full effort. I felt that the parents deserved to be thanked due to their overwhelming support.

By the time I walked home a whiffle ball game was being played by Dave Murphy, Andy Barth and Bill in my front yard. Despite being excited about the win I was too sick to join in the fun, so I just sat on the porch and watched. As I lit up a cigar while going over the scorebook, I realized just how lucky I was. Despite everything I had lost that summer, I still had a best friend, a girlfriend, a great coaching staff and a team that I loved. As for the people who rooted against my team so heavily I often reminded myself of what Eleanor Roosevelt said, "No one can make you feel inferior without your permission". As long as the players continued to believe in themselves I could believe in myself. There was no source strong enough to take that away from any of us. However, a few short days later someone would try.

Chapter 16
Going Down Swinging

"The ultimate measure of a man is not where he stands in moments of comfort, but where he stands at times of challenge and controversy.
~ Martin Luther King, Jr.

At a young age I learned that nothing in life would ever be easy. It became clear to me that the more I wanted something the harder I would have to work to achieve it. Growing up with children around me who had nicer clothes or better things never bothered me because I was happy with whatever my parents provided me. They always put food on the table every night and new clothes on our backs every school year. If there was anything lacking we never noticed because our parents would make it up in love. It was the strong foundation built by my parents that helped keep me grounded when I needed it the most as a manager.

When situations got almost too tough to handle I would remember my days of growing up without a care in the world. Ten years before I ever managed a Little League game I sat in the dirt in my backyard and dreamed of playing in the Major Leagues. A bike ride to nowhere special was more exciting than anything a video game or store bought toy could ever provide. It was that carefree innocence that only a child could have that I sorely missed when I thought about playing Mr. Hill's team again one Saturday afternoon.

The season was coming to an end with this the last scheduled meeting between our two teams. I was not worried about winning or losing as much as I was about him trying to pull another stunt to get me kicked out of the league. I had confidence in things working out in the right manner; however, I was still nervous.

If there was one thing that both life and this season had taught me it was that a person must lose before he can win. As painful as it was to lose some of the games early on in the season, those defeats helped the team grow and prepare to handle difficult situations later in the year. The problem was that I could only control what happened on the field without any major direction of people's actions off of it. It didn't matter how many games we won or by how many runs we won them by, individuals were still going to hate me. They obviously didn't like losing to someone they considered a child. Dad told me several times to focus on coaching and not let anything else bother me. Some days were tougher than others but I always kept that in my mind.

I came to the conclusion that people tend to be only threatened by someone they perceive as superior. If my team was horrible then other coaches and parents would not have cared about my coaching or my team's excitement on the field. It was our success that caused the true hatred to spill out of what may have been normally nice people. I was only exposed to one side of Jack Hill. For all I knew he may have very well been a decent human being. It was sad that I never got to see that side of him.

I was starting to finally realize much of what Mr. Wheeler and Mr. Kubb had gone through many years ago. They both coached winning teams that were hated around the league because of the success their teams achieved. I always looked up to both of them so I hoped that my players would do the same to me. I realized that anyone could stick around when things are going well, but it takes a true champion to survive the bad times and emerge stronger because of them.

I loved coaching because I was given the chance to make many decisions that determine the outcome of each game. However, as a coach I learned the stress of having many things to have to worry about. It was a major difference from my playing days when my only concern was my own performance. I would worry about how my teammates would play, but when it came right down to it the only thing I could control was my own performance. There were plenty of times as a coach that I envied only having the one worry a player does. Having a talented team inspired with heart made my decisions easier.

Heading into the final stretch run of the season we held a tight lead on first place. We enjoyed one more win then Mr. Molnar's team. We still had three games left to play in the regular season and knew that if we won all three that we would receive a first-round bye in the postseason league tournament. Things had changed since the days when I played because so many less children now played Little League. Each league only had five teams in it so the league allowed all of them to play in the postseason tournament. It was a far cry from when I played ball and each league had nearly fifteen teams in it. To my surprise I learned that more children were now playing soccer instead. Those who didn't play soccer decided to join the Boy Scouts or swim team.

Even with the changes the top two teams were still invited to play in the state tournament. The other major change was that the state tournament was held before our own league tournament. The way things worked out, we would play the final three regular season games then compete in the state tournament. When all that was over we would get our chance to play in the postseason league tournament for a chance at the championship.

In a small way the changes were almost beneficial for our team because by the time the post season tournament rolled around we would have Nate Dolesh back on the roster. I could also save my best pitchers for the league tournament if I felt that we didn't stand a chance to advance in the state tournament. I knew that the odds of winning the state tournament were 1000 to 1 because in the entire history of Ohio Hot Stove only one team from North Olmsted had ever done it. That one team happened to be Mr. Kerr's team that I competed against when playing for Mr. Hurley in the summer of 1995. My main goal was to win the League Championship Tournament at the end of summer. I had numerous games to get my players completely prepared both psychically as well as mentally for a run at the league championship.

It became clear that blocking out the many distractions would be challenging but also necessary. The best approach was to focus on the positives and not let the negative challenges of others become overpowering. As Psalm 119:37 says, "Turn away my eyes from looking at worthless things and revive me in your way." There couldn't have been a more appropriate Bible verse than that one.

Driving to the afternoon's game against Mr. Hill's Sedmack Insurance team, I couldn't help feeling extra special at the thought of possibly sweeping the season series from them. It was Hill's initial snide comments weeks earlier that lit the fuse for many things the season was built on. With the sweet sounds of Kenny Chesney blaring from my car stereo, Andy Barth and I drove into Little Clague Park with victory on our minds.

With Andy carrying the equipment bag on his shoulder like a small sack of potatoes, we strode from the parking lot to the field brimming with confidence. I noticed a familiar face waiting to greet me behind home plate, it was Mr. Kubb. I hadn't seen him in five years but he looked the same as the day I had last seen him. As he shook my hand he let me know that he would be sitting behind the opposing team's bench to keep his eye on our buddy Jack. I felt comfortable with the notion of both my Dad and Mr. Kubb at the game just in case Mr. Hill decided to do something stupid. With friends and family in the crowd it would be easier not to lose my temper.

This game would present a challenge because we were missing two of our normal starters Mike Hach and Danny Kitko. Mike had been at every single practice and game all year long so it I couldn't get angry when he missed this one to go to his cousins wedding. I have always said that family comes first so I understood when he couldn't play. I also knew that it was killing Mike not to attend the game because he complained about missing it the rest of the season. The other nice thing was that his parents told me after I gave them the schedule months beforehand. The Hach's were great people who always looked out for the team's best interest.

The reason Dan missed the game was considerably more frustrating. His father Steve had called me a few days before to let me know that he was taking Dan on a week's long camping trip. I understood that Dan was his only son and that he only had partial custody of him, so wanting to spend as much time with Dan as possible was understandable. The fact that he would miss the final three games of the regular season drove me crazy. On one hand I couldn't say anything because I never had a son myself to know how those things worked. On the other hand as his coach, it was a bitter pill for me to swallow. There was no denying that Dan was our best pitcher, losing him for three important games would be tough to overcome.

Luckily for us we had numerous options to use at pitcher that evening. I had promised every player who showed up to pitching practice that I would give him a chance to pitch for at least one inning. It was at that practice when I discovered Johnny Rehak wanted to try his hand at pitching. Until that point in the season no opportunity had presented itself to place Johnny in the game at pitcher. Without Dan for three games I needed to find someone to fill in so I didn't have to put all the pressure on Brian Leciewski and Alex Uhlik.

Johnny was such a quiet boy that it was easy to overlook him at times because he never gave me any trouble. He was one of the most behaved children I have ever coached. I credit much of that to his upbringing by excellent parents. Johnny had talent but I struggled to find the right position for him and felt bad about sticking him in the outfield. It never seemed to trouble him that he always played outfield because he never complained about doing so. He had the look of famous Atlanta Braves pitcher Greg Maddux with his glasses and non-intimidating appearance. I always joked that one day Johnny Rehak, Ryan Mackey and Nate Dolesh would work on the space shuttle because they looked like little geniuses.

Though Johnny never asked to pitch, I could often tell that he wanted too, I decided that his long wait was coming to an end. With Johnny on the mound one major decision had been made, but I still needed to rearrange the rest of the lineup. I had been using the same starting eight in the order with minor switches at the bottom. However, with Dan and Mike both gone I was losing my second and sixth man in the batting order. After much consideration I came up with the following starting lineup:

CF Matt Poli
LF Ryan Mackey
C Alex Uhlik
3B Brian Leciewski
SS Anthony Poli
P Johnny Rehak
2B Kyle Keller
RF Andy Barth
1B Pat Morris

As the skies turned bright blue without a cloud in sight, it was baseball time at Little Clague Park. Johnny showed little to no nerves for his first start on the mound. He stuck to the pitches Alex was calling for him and ran into very little trouble. He didn't walk any batters and only allowed two runs to cross the plate. Going into the bottom half of the first we only trailed 0-2.

David Hill took the mound for the boys from Sedmack Insurance. It wouldn't take long for our potent lineup to get the runs back that Rehak had allowed. With the bases loaded and nobody out Brain Leciewski stepped to the plate. He took the first two pitches before swinging and hitting a long double to left field scoring all three base runners. With the help of RBI hits from Rehak and Keller later in the inning, we took a commanding 6-2 lead into the second inning and never looked back.

Johnny continued to throw everything Alex signaled him without any problems. He didn't show much confidence on the mound, but I believe that was because he was so shy. He kept throwing strikes and letting the opposition put the ball in play for our sure-handed defense to make outs. Kyle Keller was scooping up any ball that came his way at second base while Anthony Poli did the same at shortstop. As the defense played better behind him, Johnny was able to gain confidence and throw more strikes. With missing two key players we knew we had to play a smart game with few to no errors and we were doing exactly that.

The lineup continued to rally around each other in the bottom of the second as we scored seven more runs to take a commanding 13 to 3 lead. We took advantage of Sedmack's sloppy pitching to load the bases with walks then rely on one giant hit after another to drive players in. Mackey had the biggest hit of his season when he slammed a bases loaded triple in that seven run second inning. Ryan had been scuffling at the plate so it was nice to see him come through in the clutch. He always worked hard and did whatever I asked him.

The top of the third saw more excellent defense when Matt Poli dove to catch a fly ball that looked as though it would land five feet in front of him. Matt was one of only two players to never commit an error that entire season. The other was Mike Hach who played in left field. I knew that any fly ball hit their way that stayed in the air long enough was a sure out. With many boys not wanting to play outfield in little league, these two not only looked forward to their time but excelled at it.

The hitting cooled off as we headed into the fourth inning with the score still 13-3. Despite Johnny's pitching well in his first game, I didn't want to send him out for a fourth inning, because I didn't want take the chance of burning him out. I had seen what happened earlier in the year by pitching Kyle Keller too long so I was careful not to make the same mistake twice.

I decided to reward Ryan for his big hit earlier in the game by giving him the chance to pitch. This was a shot at getting through an entire game without having to use my best pitchers

(Kitko, Leciewski, Poli and Uhlik) so I took the chance. He started off rather shaky but relied on solid defense to only allow two runs in the top of the fourth. We still held the lead 13-5 as we came to the plate in bottom half of the inning.

I looked in my Dad's direction numerous times throughout the game. He never hesitated to take his fist and pound it into his other hand as to say, "Don't let up!" We had had no intention of doing so. I told Bill and Ray to let the players' steal as many bases as they could. It was only an eight run lead and I knew in Little League that was never safe. The boys didn't hesitate to pour on the offense by scoring seven more times to take a commanding 20-5 lead heading into the fifth inning.

It was incredible that we were able to score 20 runs in only four times up at bat. The eyes of my players showed the deep desire to make Mr. Hill eat his words. I seldom had to urge them to hustle or play hard, but on this evening it was as if they decided to take it up an extra notch without me even saying a word.

Rehak backed up his three innings on the mound with his best night at the plate all season. Johnny had three hits and seven RBI before the game ended. I was incredibly happy to see Johnny exceed at the plate because he had faced struggles early on. His playing well on the mound helped his overall confidence that evening.

One of my earliest memories of Johnny came during one practice very early on in which I helped him change his batting stance. He had the common problem of stepping out of the batter's box when the pitch was thrown. I used a baseball bat and put it behind his back foot every time it was his turn to hit in batting practice. This is done to control his back foot from jumping out of the batter's box, the trick was to have Johnny pretend that the bat was there in real games. It took a long while for him to succeed but when he finally did I couldn't have been happier.

As a coach I enjoyed no greater feeling than seeing a player I helped finally grasp what I was teaching him and use it to improve. It gave me the feeling that what I was teaching them was actually sinking in. I remember after one of the practice's Mr. Rehak coming up to me and thanking me for taking time to help Johnny's swing. At first I was nervous because I didn't know if he was going to be mad that I changed Johnny's swing. But it didn't take long for me to realize that Mr. Rehak had a coaching background himself and knew when progress was being made. One of the greatest feelings in the world is winning respect from coaching peers. Mr. Rehak coached a different sport (basketball) but it didn't matter, respect from one coach to another is always welcomed.

When Ryan Mackey took the mound to defend a 20-5 lead I took two deep breaths. The first was that as long as he only gave up five or fewer runs we would win by the mercy rule. The other deep breath signaled that we had made it through the entire game until that point with no drama. Mr. Hill had been on his best behavior with my Dad and Mr. Kubb staring a hole through him from the stands throughout the game. So as Ryan Mackey delivered the first pitch of the inning, I should have had no worries about any kind of drama taking place. As luck would have it I couldn't have been any more wrong.

As I stood in the dugout watching Ryan try to wrap up the game, Matt Tomecko came running over to me. I had been so focused on the game that I didn't even realize my extremely tall friend was sitting in the stands the whole time. Before I had the chance to tell him I couldn't talk until after the game he said words I never expected to hear, "Kathy is screaming at some lady."

Kathy had chosen to sit on the other side of the stands because the sun was in her eyes, thus it landed her right in the middle of the lion's den. Although Kathy wore a white tee shirt bearing the words "Coach's girl" on the front of it with "Go Wildcats" on the back, one of the parents on the opposing team either didn't notice or simply chose not to care and proceeded to bad mouth me the entire game. According to Kathy the lady had several negative things to say, not only about my coaching style but also questioned my sexuality. Finally after innings of verbal abuse Kathy could not remain quiet any longer. She stood up to defend my honor by arguing with this woman. Kathy explained about how much I cared about my players and how much time I put in to coach them. By the time I ran over to calm Kathy down and bring her back to our side of the field she was beet red. I had never seen her get that angry at anyone for anything. I was proud of her for sticking up for me. But at the same time I felt terrible that she had been put in that situation.

Soon after the argument in the crowd ended, Ryan was able to get three outs, permitting two more runs giving us the 20-7 win, improving our record to 9-5. It was also our fourth straight win. The four game win streak was our longest of the season as well as our fourth against Mr. Hill's team. It also guaranteed that we would have a winning record in the 16 game regular-season.

Mr. Hill made sure to shake my hand and then both of my assistant coaches in the post-game line. As angry I was with Kathy getting into an argument in the crowd, I knew that I couldn't show my anger in front of the boys. I began the post-game speech by making sure the boys knew that as great as it felt to win that we were still a long way from finished. I emphasized that each game would get harder as we went on. Despite the blowout victory we must stay sharp because closer games were on the way. I finished the speech by handing out game balls to Johnny Rehak and Ryan Mackey for their great performances. It was a clear sign to everyone that on any given night it might be their chance to step up and help the team. I told them it didn't matter where they hit in the lineup or where they played in the field; we needed every one of them to win games. It was a total team effort, the kind that championships are made of.

Mr. Kubb stopped by my car as I was packing it up to congratulate me on the win. He said it was great to see one of his former players' coaching a team in a fundamentally sound way. I let him know that most of the things I preached to my team were things I had learned from him. It was a surreal feeling to have one of my favorite coaches witness a game that I was coaching in, let alone one that we had won so handily without our best pitcher. Mr. Kubb told me to keep focused and that the best way to shut people up is by winning. He mentioned he would try to make it to another game but that his responsibility as head of the umpires kept him extremely busy. I thanked him for coming and promised to take his advice. It felt nice to know I had the support of so many good people.

I never missed the chance to thank Kathy for her support, however that evening I felt bad because it was the hatred that I generated which caused her to get hurt. As many times as I told her not to let it bother her when people said mean things, it was never as easy as it sounded. Before I leaned in to give her a goodnight kiss I reached in my baseball bag and grabbed one of the game balls. I gave it to her because she had earned it for her loyalty to the team. I told her that she was a true Wildcat now and that I couldn't have coached without her support. I felt closer to her than ever before and truly felt we were in it together.

I decided not to go straight home from Kathy's that evening, but rather take a trip to downtown Cleveland. It was the first time I had ever driven downtown alone. It was also after midnight, which wasn't the safest thing to do. I felt that I needed to go somewhere to get away from the mounting drama that each game seemed to present. I was thrilled that we kept winning all these games but I also hoped things would settle down. I hated the drama as much as I loved the winning.

The drive allowed me to clear my mind for a few minutes and just relax. I chose downtown because I wanted to see Jacob's Field where the Indians played at night when a game wasn't being played. It was a great feeling when I got off the freeway, driving circles around the two streets that surrounded the massive stadium. It was the first time I had been downtown at night when the Indians game was already over so there was no one in the stadium but the lights were still kept on. I parked the car on the side of the road on Ontario Street and walked over to the fence by the back entrance of the stadium. I peeked through the fence to see the tarp being rolled onto the field and the stadium workers cleaning out the seats. It was quiet enough to hear a pin drop, but held a certain sense of awe at the same time. It was another reminder of the beauty in the game I loved so much. A stadium can still look amazing when fans aren't present because of the memories that spectators can have from past experiences of it being full. I only had to close my eyes to picture the crowd roaring in game five of the 1995 World Series when Orel Hershiser beat Greg Maddux of the Atlanta Braves. I hoped that the memories I was creating in my players to last as long as the ones I grew up with as a player and a fan. The stadium after dark experience gave me what I needed to clear my mind. It was important because our next game wasn't scheduled for a few days.

Not playing again for a while was a good thing because it gave everyone a chance to relax. Our next game wasn't until Thursday July 20 evening against Mr. Briggs team at Little Clague Park. It was essential to use those days off to regroup for the stretch run. The most important thing to regaining focus on something beloved is clearing the mind first. In order to have the ability to plan for the future, one must first possess a clear mind.

I worked the next four days until having the Thursday of the game off. I decided that going on a picnic with Kathy was the best way to relax and grow mentally calm to face was what sure to be a hostile crowd. My normal game day routine was to sit in my basement and game plan with Bill and Andy Barth. In an effort to calm my nerves this time around I took a break from the normal routine because I had to think about anything but baseball.

Kathy was surprised that morning when I showed up at her house with a picnic basket filled with peanut butter and jelly sandwiches. I could tell she was caught off guard, but also happy that I took time away from preparing for a crucial game to spend time with her. I had put her though so much agony with my coaching that summer that I felt it was the least I can do.

The picnic was the calm before the storm. It always rings true that before every storm the skies are calm. It was pleasant to spend some peaceful time with my loving girlfriend. The relaxation didn't last too long because I only stayed a couple of hours. I told her that I wanted to go home for a nap, although I am pretty sure she knew I was racing home to game plan.

Not a day had gone by since our last game against Wilsons Bike shop that I didn't think about the parents booing me. With that in mind I begged both my parents and Kathy not to attend that evening's game. Kathy was not happy with my request but obliged. I quickly learned that there was no keeping my parents away so I allowed them to come. I knew it was tough on my mom the last time I was booed so I made sure to talk with her for several minutes about not letting it get to her. My Mother is one of the toughest women I know, so I knew she would be okay. I still felt horrible she had to listen to it.

This game gave us a chance to win a season high fifth straight while also clinching the season series against them. After the first time we played them where we suffered the heartbreaking extra inning loss, we had not lost another game against them. Unlike my days when I competed and teams only played against each other once or twice, this league was so small that each team faced each other four times in the regular season. It created some incredible rivalries with plenty of chances to learn opponent's strengths and weaknesses.

With Nate Dolesh wrapping up his cross country field trip soon I was excited at the possibility of adding more power to the lineup. However, he had not yet returned so the team had to continue without him. Billy Graves started coming to games and sitting on the bench to support his teammates but clearly was still in no condition to play. With Dan on his camping trip we were left with ten players to take the field. The lineup for that night's game was as follows:

CF Matt Poli
OF Johnny Rehak
SS Alex Uhlik
3B Brian Leciewski
P Anthony Poli
LF Mike Hach
C Kyle Keller
RF Andy Barth
2B Ryan Mackey
1B Pat Morris

With the way our team had been hitting the ball, the last thing I expected was a pitchers' duel but that is exactly what took place early on. Anthony Poli had his best outing of the year with the help of some solid defense. It started with two out in the bottom of the first inning when Andy Barth made a running catch on a Terry Beach fly ball that looked like it would drop at his feet. Andy was positioned perfectly to make a break on the ball and cut it off a few inches before it could hit the ground. Before the play I had yelled at Andy to take a few steps back in order to compensate for Beaches power. It was common place for my outfielders to play deep because I preached the strategy of having them charge fly balls instead of having them run backwards. I was constantly telling them to keep all balls in front of them because the second they turned their back on a ball it would be passing them by. They were too young to be trying over the shoulder catches. I would rather give up a few soft singles then a long home run or triple on a ball hit over their head. In this case Andy listened to everything I told him and was able to play the ball perfectly to record the out.

After two innings Anthony Poli was looking sharp by only giving up a single run. Adam Sedgmer was pitching his finest game of the season for Mr. Briggs, keeping our hitters at bay. It wasn't until the top of the third inning on hit and run single by Kyle Keller that we scored our first run. Anthony continued to match Sedgmer pitch for pitch keeping the game tied up at one apiece through four innings.

In the fifth inning I replaced Poli with Alex Uhlik in the hopes of keeping the game close enough for us to erupt with some runs for the win. Alex showed early and often that he was up for the task by striking out the side in the bottom of the fifth. While Alex was pitching great for Anthony in relief so was Corey Benkowski for Sedgmer.

Corey was a tall, lanky player with a strong arm and a friendly personality. He was never shy about coming up to me before, during or after any game to talk. He wasn't cocky but just very talkative. He always called me Mr. McKee and never missed a chance to tell me that he wanted me to pick him for my team the following season if I chose to coach again. Going into the top of the last inning the game remarkably was still tied at 1-1.

Emotion was running at an all-time high that evening on the field as well as in the crowd. Every time I left the dugout to speak with a pitcher or make a switch the entire side of opposing parents would get up and shout things at me. It wasn't getting me angry as much as it did the first time because I expected it. It did cause one very interesting counter reaction for the group of parents of the players I coached. Every time they booed, my set of parents and players would get up and start cheering as loudly as they could. It became a loud sight that mirrored the crowd I had imagined about just days earlier at Jacob's Field.

It was in the top of the seventh when Mr. Briggs made a strange switch by replacing the sharp Corey Benkowski with his son Frankie. My only thought was that he wanted his son to have the chance at victory. If that was indeed his motive for replacing a pitcher who was on fire then it backfired on him badly. In what brought back memories of the ferocious rally from the Wheeler team I played on in years past, the Wildcats' erupted for a season high 21 runs in the top of the seventh.

It didn't matter what was thrown, our players crushed the pitches in every direction. We used the same formula we had been using all season of putting runners on base then knocking them in. We didn't hesitate to steal bases any chance we got. By putting so much pressure on the pitcher with constant base running it caused him to make numerous mistakes to the batters. Frankie was unable to record a single out. Mr. Briggs pulled his son with his team trailing 17-1 but it was too little too late.

The highlight of the innings came when we to hit 4 straight doubles. Every single player in the lineup had at least one hit in the inning. Ryan and Andy Barth both stayed hot by driving in four runs each. By the time we finally recorded a third out over forty five minutes has passed. The top half of the inning took so long that the sun had went down and the sky got dark. The umpire Tom Grodek, tried calling the game due to the darkness but Mr. Briggs began screaming and yelling that he was getting cheated so Tom said the game could continue.

Despite the fact that we had taken a 22-1 lead over them, it didn't detour Terry Beach from acting arrogantly. Terry fielded a ground ball at first base to end the inning. However, instead of running to the base to tag it he chose to moonwalk backwards. It was one of the most unsportsmanlike things I had ever seen a Little League player do. I became so angry that I put Brian Leciewski in to pitch the bottom of the seventh just so he could throw at him.

Until that point in the season I had never told a player to throw at an opposing player. While this act is traditional in Major League baseball, it seldom ever happens in Little League. I knew it was the wrong thing to do and very unsportsmanlike to tell my player to do such a thing but I was so furious I lost sight of what mattered. Instead of putting my focus towards closing out the game with the 22-1 lead my sole thoughts turned to plunking Terry Beach. It was the first and only time all season that I lost total control of my emotions without thinking clearly.

The original plan called for Ryan Mackey to pitch the seventh, but when I saw Terry was coming up first in the inning I quickly switched Ryan with Brian. Ray pulled Brian aside before he ran on the field on told him, "Put Beach on his butt!" Brian who was not a mean child in any way looked scared at the request but nodded his head and assured his father he would do so. I felt terrible for Brian that we put him in such a tight spot but he was our enforcer and team leader so it came with the part.

Sure enough the first pitch pelted Terry Beach on his back sending him to his knees. The player began crying instantly as he ran down to first base hunched over. Sometimes revenge can be sweet and bitter at the same time. As great as I felt to get back at a player who gave us so much grief, I knew what I had told Brian to do was incredibly wrong. A couple days later I pulled Brian aside to apologize for putting him in that tight spot. As usual Brian didn't mind and just told me that he'd do anything I asked of him. It was another example of how loyal my players were towards their coaching staff.

In what had been an already dramatic game as part of a hectic season of odd occurrences, the next few moments would become surreal. Things started off innocently enough with our middle infield turning an excellent double play on the first pitch thrown to the next batter. The ball was hit hard but right at Anthony Poli who flipped it to Ryan Mackey covering second base. After receiving the flip and stepping on second base, Ryan turned and threw out the runner at first base. There were two outs leaving us just moments away from a sure victory and a 10-5 record with one game left in the regular season. Two seconds after Morris stepped on first base the most bizarre thing I have ever seen happen in Little League occurred.

At first I heard screaming from the crowd. But this time it was only one woman bellowing insults. A tall dark haired lady with glasses began shouting swear words and insults at me. She was absolutely livid and didn't mind showing it to all who would listen. She was so incredibly loud that it caused the game to come to a dead stop. She ripped the Bell away from Mrs. Hach and began ringing it loudly for no apparent reason. I remember screaming, "Somebody grab my Bell!" The woman had no plan to stop as she ran onto the field. Apparently I made her so angry that she thought climbing up the back stop was a good idea.

The sight of a woman in her mid-forties climbing up a large backstop while screaming obscenities is something I can never forget. It is hard to describe the madness she was causing but it was more than enough to stop everyone in their tracks. It was almost depressing to see a grown woman have a nervous breakdown in front of so many people, most of them strangers. Even Mr. Briggs could not settle the woman down enough for her to climb back from the top of the backstop.

Being only eighteen years old I had not been exposed to anything even close to this nature. I felt bad that I had caused this woman so much anger by something I was doing that it would make her go wild. I never knew I could cause such strong reactions out of adults as I did on this fateful night. I kept asking Bill and Ray if we should do anything to get her down from the cage so we could finish the game but there wasn't much we could do. I felt helpless seeing a grown woman have such a mental collapse caused by the pure hatred she felt for me.

Finally after ten minutes of her screaming on top of the backstop someone used a cell phone to call North Olmsted Police. I can't even imagine how embarrassed her son must have been to have seen this entire performance. When informed the police were called she wasted no time climbing down from the fence. She threw the Bell at me as she ran by our bench. I didn't care as much about the Bell as I did finishing the game. As this mêlée was occurring I noticed the skies growing darker.

By the time the police arrived she had already gotten in her car and sped away. I asked some of the parents along with Bill to handle speaking with the officers because I just wanted the game to end before it got any darker so the win could be official. By this time it was almost pitch dark and we had no business playing in such bad conditions on a field without lighting.

Between our 21 run top of the seventh and the opposing parent causing a massive stoppage with her wild scene, the seventh inning had already taken over an hour. The cutoff time for any game to end is 8:30 and by this time it was a quarter past 9 p.m. Rather than calling the game both coaches decided to let the last out happen so the game could be official. As much as I worried about playing in such dark conditions I knew not to let Mr. Briggs have any reason to protest the outcome.

My worst fears came true when Corey Benkowski smashed the very next pitch off the chest of Brian Leciewski forcing him to the ground in intense pain. Before I could even react Ray stormed on the field to check on his fallen son. It was the scariest thing I have ever witnessed on a baseball field. As Brian lay in the dirt screaming in pain the only thing I could think was how it would have never happened if the lady didn't cause the delay. Meanwhile as I pleaded with the umpire to call the game, Ray rushed Brian to the car to take him to St. John's Hospital five minutes from the park. It became one chaotic scene after another.

In situations like these it comes in handy to have good assistant coaches. In this case I didn't have good ones, I had great ones. Bill not only kept me from completely losing my temper but also agreed to watch over the team for the final out so I could speed to the hospital. I didn't say goodbye or a word to anyone as I jumped in my car to drive to the hospital.

On the drive there the only thing I could think about was how this may have been my fault if Brian was seriously hurt. I was the one who put him in the game to protect a 21 run lead when I didn't need to. I was the one who had put him in a position to get hurt by leaving him on the field when it was far too dark to be playing. I should have taken him and the entire team off the field until the game was called. Perhaps if I would have argued with Tom Grodek the game would have been called. Instead I let it go and it caused of my best players and a great boy to get hurt badly. I simply couldn't stop blaming myself for his injury. The thought of bad karma crossed my mind as well because of making him throw at Terry Beach.

Brian wasn't at the hospital long before they took him in for x-rays. Ray and I met with the doctor a short while later. He explained Brian was going to be okay because it was only a deep bruise. Luckily for Brian nothing had been broken or fractured even though the ball had hit his chest so hard. He would not be able to play in the season finale the following night, but he would be able to play in the State Tournament opener on Saturday morning. Telling Brian that he was unable to play the next night was one of the hardest things I had to do as a coach. Ray explained that it would be better coming from me because Brian listened to every word I said. He was one of the most competitive players on the team so when I told him he couldn't play it broke his heart. I explained to him that State Tournament games were being held that weekend and it was important that he rest up for them. It didn't make things any easier as he continued to cry.

I waited with Ray for about an hour until Brian was released to go home. As awful as it was to lose Brian I realized it could have been much worse. Had the ball struck him on the head he could have had a terrible concussion if not worse. Had the ball landed on his eye there was a chance at blindness. That the ball landed on such a muscular part of his young body was a blessing.

Mrs. Hach had scheduled a pool party for the team that night following the game. As I was driving to it I was racking my brain about who I could pitch in the season finale against Mr. Molnar's team. Dan was on vacation for one more day and we would be without Brian. My options were running low because I had pitched Alex for several innings that night with the opening state tournament game scheduled for Saturday morning. It was a stretch of three games in three days with a chance at a fourth if we won on Saturday.

It was a somber drive to the pool party because I wasn't in the mood to celebrate anything. Thinking about how we just won our fifth game in a row to stretch our record to 10-5 felt good, but it wasn't enough to make me forget about Brian screaming in pain on the ground. I was aware that I needed to stay positive in front of the team so I could emphasize that we were only one win away from sole possession of first place to finish the regular season. I knew it would be difficult not to show how upset I was about Brian.

When I arrived at the party the entire team jumped out of the pool and ran towards my car. They were very anxious to hear about their fallen teammate. I decided to tell them the truth because they would find out soon enough if I didn't. When learning that Brian couldn't play the next night they held their heads low. I told them not to let it get them down because it meant that without him and Dan it would give a chance for other people to step up and lead the team. It lifted their spirits enough to get back in the pool for more fun. I chose not to swim because I was still in a very bad mood after what happened. It was such a strange night that swimming was the farthest thing on my mind.

Before I left I huddled the players up to review plans for the following game. I explained that because we were now down four players that they needed to be prepared to play anywhere I put them. I told them that there was a chance that I might have four or five different players pitch if need be. I left them to enjoy the night but asked them not to stay up to late because I didn't want them tired out for the next night. We had many games left to play in a short amount of time so rest was important. I let them know to get all the need for swimming out of their system that night because starting the next day I didn't want them in a pool the night before a game and never the day of one. I wasn't exactly thrilled that the pool party was scheduled the night before a big game but that was the only night Mrs. Hach was able to schedule it so I didn't make a fuss over it. Her heart was in the right place and for that I could only thank her for the act of kindness.

I was so distraught over what happened that I forgot to call Kathy to say goodnight when I got home. It wasn't until after midnight when she called me to find out why I hadn't contacted her yet. She was angry that I forgot about her but after I explained why she calmed down. It was another example of me putting the team before her and there was no excuse for it. After what started off as a nice day with the picnic ended in agony.

We decided to put our relationship on hold until the season was over. I wasn't doing the best job as a boyfriend because I couldn't balance those two worlds. I told her that I loved her and I would call her in a few weeks. We also agreed not to tell anyone that we were taking a break.

That night I was unable to sleep because of the many things on my mind. I was proud of the team for bouncing back from a rough start to win five straight and eight of our last ten games. The ten wins we had were ten more than most people expected at the start of the season. It had been an incredible summer with many surprises along the way.

The winning had opened up the possibility of finishing the season in first place heading into the playoffs. I always told the boys that if we played the game with hustle and intelligence, we could overcome anything that came our way. We had come so far and improved so much from the first practice that no matter what happened in the end I would be proud. However, that didn't stop us from wanting to win every time we took the field. The main thing was making sure the players still enjoyed themselves without putting too much pressure on them to win. With my team I never had to put the pressure on them because they wanted to win as badly as I did. Maybe the groups of opposing parents saw this and believed I was putting too much pressure on my team. Whatever the reason was for some of the resentment I felt at times that summer I will never know. However, to get the strong reactions I received from players and parents I must have been doing something right.

As bad as I felt that the women lost her temper by creating a huge scene earlier that evening, I knew that there was nothing I could have done to prevent it. I wasn't going to let it deter me from coaching or even cause me to change my approach. The most important thing was that the boys were having an incredible summer and so was I. As for the people who didn't like it or disapproved of a younger man coaching children, Rocky Balboa once said, "Some people hate for no reason."

Waking up the next morning I hoped that working all day would help keep my mind off the game that night against Mr.

Molnar as well as the break with Kathy. Normally on game days if I had to work I wouldn't be able to focus on work at all because my mind was constantly on that evening's game. This particular day I forced myself to think about anything else other than that evening's game or the Kathy break. Surprisingly, work actually helped distract me for a few hours because we were so busy that day that I was forced to focus. I was drenched in sweat while unloading the delivery trucks because I always wore my jersey underneath my work shirt on game days. I thought about taking off my long sleeve dress shirt to unload the trucks but I didn't want to get my jersey dirty before the game. The tradition of showing to a game with a spotless jersey and leaving with it muddy had never left me. Despite being a coach and no longer playing, I would still take a handful of dirt and run it across my jersey a couple times during every game when no one was looking to help relax. The only person who noticed it was my mother who couldn't figure out why I kept coming home with a dirty jersey as a coach. It may seem odd to many people who didn't know me or understood my baseball background, but tradition was and always will be first and foremost. This ritual was just one more way to give back to the game I loved.

I returned home from work with a little over an hour before I had to be at the field for that evening's contest. For some reason no one else was home so I had some quiet time to mentally prepare. As I was trying to make a lineup without my two best pitchers the phone rang but I didn't answer it. I didn't think it was for me and I didn't want to be annoyed by anyone or anything unless it increased our team's chance at winning. The call came from my brother Don. He called to wish me good luck on the game. He also mentioned that I shouldn't be worried about winning because we played hard all season with nothing to be ashamed of if we fell short. It was a very nice message from a great brother and actually helped me relax for a few minutes. Don couldn't make the game because he was obligated to work sales at a rock concert later that night at Cleveland Browns Stadium. He had started the job months earlier so I understood that he needed to be there.

No matter the outcome of the game we still would be entered into two tournaments in the postseason. The outcome did factor into if we finished the season in first or second place. As of that game we had one more win than Mr. Molnar's team with one less loss. A win and we would become outright regular season champs; however, a loss meant that we would finish with the identical record as they. They would receive the tiebreaker because they would've won the season series 3-1. We knew how important it was to get the win to finish first in the regular season as well as secure a first round bye in the league tournament that was held after the state tournament. With the final game of the regular season about to be played the standings were as follows:

Mr. Vince McKee, "Play it Again Sports" 10-5
Mr. Mike Molnar, "Ohio Envelope" 9-6
Mr. Tim Coyne, "Pats Cleaners" 8-8
Mr. Daryl Briggs, "Wilsons Bicycle Shop" 7-9
Mr. Jack Hill, "Sedmack Insurance" 5-11

With the margin for error thin we knew we had to play a near perfect game to beat Ohio Envelope. It was bad enough not having Danny or Brian to pitch but Nate Dolesh wasn't set to return until the next day at the State Tournament. We had enough players to field a lineup. Still it wasn't near the caliber that we were used to it.

The element working to our advantage was the game being played at Little Clague Park. For whatever the reason was we never quite knew, we seemed to play much better at this field. The one time that we had beaten them the game took place at Clague. Most of our wins had taken place in games held there. When the chips are down a team must cling to whatever bright spots to be found so we clung hard to this one.

I decided not to change a thing going into this game as far as pregame rituals went. I still listened to the same music while getting dressed. In this case it was getting undressed from my work clothes while keeping my jersey top on but also putting on my black Nike shorts I wore all year. The car ride to the game was short but I still managed to hear a few chords of a country song. It didn't matter that we were missing some great players. I still felt as though if we played our best game we could walk away with the win.

I was in the middle of finalizing the roster when I looked up to see that my friend Joe Graham was able to attend the game. I was happy to see him there as this was one of the few games in which Kathy or my brother would not be present. It is always nice to have a friend in the crowd before a game begins to bring you a few seconds of joy. I must admit that during the games I almost never noticed a single person in the stands because of how focused I was on what was going on. I looked over to my dad or brother a few times throughout the season, but for the most part the crowd didn't exist unless I was getting booed heavily or my player's parents were screaming with support after an exciting play. It didn't mean that I didn't appreciate people being there for support, I just was so incredible focused on what I was coaching that nothing else mattered.

The lineup was mangled but I felt if I could get at least a few quality innings out of two or three different pitchers that we might be able to keep it close enough to win. The problem was that Brian played so many positions well that losing him felt as if I was losing multiple players. Dan was such a good pitcher that missing him for a crucial game almost felt as if we trailed before the game ever started. I couldn't let the team know how much of a disadvantage we were at because it would have crushed their spirits, I made it seem as if it was the best lineup we had all year. I felt terrible as I looked over to Brian sitting on the bench in full uniform just hoping I changed my mind and put him in the game. The doctor's note didn't clear him to play for one more day unfortunately so we had to go on without him. The lineup for game 16 against Ohio Envelope coached by Mr. Molnar is as follows:

CF Matt Poli
3B Ryan Mackey
P Alex Uhlik
RF Andy Barth
SS Anthony Poli
LF Mike Hach
C Kyle Keller
2B John Rehak
1B Pat Morris

It may not have been the most intimidating lineup of the season, but I felt as though it might be strong enough to get the job done. I didn't like having to move Andy up from batting eighth to clean up. However, we needed his power. Johnny Rehak was also making his first start of the year as an infielder so that was something to be nervous about as well. I believed he had the skills to be good but it's always shaky when starting someone at a position for the first time in a pivotal game. Johnny was a true team player so I knew he would try his best at the new position. When assigning a new position to a player it is important to make sure that not only does the player have the skill but also the heart necessary not to give up if he doesn't succeed at first. There was no doubt in anyone's mind that Johnny possessed both traits.

I wasn't surprised to see Anthony Marflak take the mound for Ohio Envelope to start the game. He was their dominant pitcher, performing well against us all season. The game plan was to match them run for run until he was out of the game and then take over. As plans often do this one went differently. We were unable to score a run on Anthony in the first two innings, barely getting a few hits along the way.

While Marflak kept our hitters baffled the Ohio Envelope offense had no problems with hitting anything Alex Uhlik had to offer. It was the same problem he had encountered numerous times in the season by throwing the ball hard but right down the middle of the plate. Alex was throwing strikes which is the main point of any pitcher that age; however the opposing hitters were able to lock in on his speed and hit the ball at will. He was making good pitches but the opposition was crushing them.

Going into the bottom of the third we still hadn't scored but at least we managed to hold their offense to six runs. We pulled Alex in favor for Anthony Poli to start the third in the hopes that a change of speed and location might slow down the Ohio Envelope offense. Trailing 6-0 is not an admirable situation for any pitcher to get himself into; still Anthony had been in some tight spots that season and made his way through them.

Poli stood tall in the face of a great offense keeping the score fairly close at 9-0 through four innings. It was only one more run then we trailed by in our last meeting against them in a game earlier that season. The big difference was last time we had more fire power in the lineup with a much better chance at stringing together a few runs to get back in the game. My hope was that with the top of our order coming up and Marflak out of the game that it would be the spark we needed.

Matt Poli wasted no time in bunting his way on first base to start the inning. He stole second and third base on the next two pitches thrown to Ryan Mackey. Ryan then faked a bunt on a 2-0 pitch that went off the plate allowing Matt to race home scoring our first run. It was the first time our fans had something to cheer about all night as the Bell rang proudly. After Ryan drew a walk Alex was able to hit a double. This put two runners in   scoring position with still no men out for the suddenly red hot Andy Barth.

Perhaps remembering the grand slam hit off him earlier in the season, Danny Molnar wasted no time in tossing the first pitch at the middle of Andy's upper back. As painful as it was for Andy to run down to first base it was great to see the bases now loaded. Anthony was able to draw a four pitch walk which forced home the runner from third making it a 9-2 game.

I sent a signal to Bill at third base to call for a hit and run on the next pitch. Mike swung away at the first pitch hitting the ball over the head of the charging third baseman down the line for a bases clearing double. The timely double from Hach pulled us closer at 9-5. It wasn't the score I was hoping for so late in the game. Still it was a strong improvement over the nine run deficit we faced moments earlier.

The rally would soon fizzle out as Kyle Keller popped up to the second baseman Jeff Feglemacher in shallow right field. The hit was not far enough for Mike to advance from second base to third. Johnny Rehak managed to hit a line drive single into deep enough left to score Mike from second base. That would be the last run scored in the inning as both Pat Morris and Matt Poli failed to reach base. We had managed to make a small comeback while also batting around that inning.

Heading into the bottom of the fifth inning our hope was to hold the Ohio Envelope offense at only nine runs until we got a chance to get back up to the plate. As hard as Poli tried to find the strike zone he simply kept overextending his arm and throwing balls in the dirt or above the batters head. When I finally pulled Anthony from the mound he had already walked three batters in a row and it was time to take him out of the game. The problem was that without Brian or Dan the pickings were slim to replace him.

I chose to go with Ryan Mackey in the hopes that his unconventional style might throw off the red hot Ohio Envelope batters. It looked at first that the risk might pay off when he forced Chad Brooks to ground out to second base. The out produced a run, making the score 10-6, still very attainable for any comeback. When Danny Molnar sent the first pitch he received twenty feet over Andy's head in right field for a three run homerun it took any wind left completely out of our sails. I hated to see it but it was clear that the three run homer completely demoralized us. By the time the inning ended we trailed 15-6. It wasn't the biggest deficit we faced all season but it certainly felt like it.

My assistant coaches along with myself tried to motivate the players between innings as much as possible. It was a hard task due to the lopsided score. As usual the boys did their best to make it interesting by putting a couple of runners on base to start the sixth with no outs. The rally would be snuffed out shortly with us only being able to put up one more run. Heading into the bottom of the sixth we trailed 15-7.

John Rehak pitched a solid bottom of the sixth by holding the opposition to a single run. With only three outs remaining we still trailed 16-7 which felt as if it was an insurmountable mountain to climb. I was surprised when we went down in order with no one reaching base to end the game. I believed our team was capable of putting up a better fight. In this case I know we would have if we had our full roster. A win is a win no matter how it comes so I was sure Mr. Molnar's team was happy for it despite how it was attained.

It never feels good to lose the first game of the season or the last. It feels even worse to lose it to the same team both times. I truly believed that we were the better team and I made sure to get that point across to the boys after the game. I assured them that the chances of facing them for the league championship were likely and that we would be ready for them next time. As always I told them that I was proud of their efforts all season long from start to finish. We finished up with a 10-6 regular season record which is extremely impressive for a first year team with a first year coach. I told them that even as horrible as losing felt a times, it would only make us stronger in the playoffs. We needed to keep learning from every mistake by finding ways not to do them again.

In closing I left them with the notion that this was not an ending but rather a beginning. The season was merely practice for what they were about to achieve in the post season. I made it clear that our new number one goal was to win the post season league tournament. I stated that our number one goal from that point on was to win it all. I explained that we must use our time in the state tournament as intensified practice for our own league tournament. I explained that the state tournament would provide the best competition we would face all year so if we could play well against them then the teams in our league would seem easier to beat. I mentioned that it didn't matter if we played one game or six in the state tournament that we must play them hard to get in full stride for the league championship tournament to follow.

The best part of what was becoming an amazing summer was about to begin. It was hard to cheer the team up after a tough loss. The speech about getting our players back in time for the tournaments seemed to work on them as they concluded the speech by jumping up and down screaming "Wildcats." Just to make sure that they forgot about the tough loss in time for the next morning's state tournament opener, I decided to take them for ice cream. Taking a team out for ice cream after a brutal loss is something I never thought I would do. It was because I cared about these players so much that I couldn't stand to see their heads hanging down after what had been a great regular season. At times maybe I did focus too much on winning, but Vince Lombardi summed it up best when he said, "If it isn't about who wins and loses why they keep score?"

It was months since I walked into the North Olmsted Recreation Center with the wild dream of coaching my own Little League team. At the time I didn't think too much of it other than it sounded like something I would enjoy and might even be good at. Never in my wildest dreams did I ever believe I would be on the roller coaster thrill ride that a group of ten year olds were taking me on. Little did I know that the best was yet to come.

Chapter 17

Heart and Soul

Men are judged by many measurable qualities. The one quality that is not measured is the one that can move mountains. That quality is heart.
~ Vince McKee, 2010

I felt out of place after returning home following the loss to Ohio Envelope. I had no doubts that my team played its hardest but still felt as though we could have played better despite lacking some crucial players. I was starting to believe that the players were letting the opposition get into their heads every time we played them. I hoped we would get one more shot at playing them in the league tournament a few weeks away. As a coach I cannot accept defeat against a team when the full roster is not available.

After pacing around my room for a few hours, I realized that staying home would be an impossible task so I went for a drive. I wasn't sure where I was going but I felt the overwhelming need to see Kathy. We hadn't spoken in a day because of our break but I couldn't stand the separation so I went over to her house. It may have not been the smartest move because it made me look desperate. I weighed my odds and decided to go for it. I had to talk with someone about how nervous I was for states and also how aggravated I was that we lost earlier that evening.

Arriving at her house I noticed that both of her parents' cars were gone and there were no lights on. It was then that I remembered her parents were out of town for the weekend visiting separate family members. I had been so consumed with coaching that I had forgotten it was a Friday night, which meant she was working. I looked at my watch and noticed it was nearly midnight. The chances of her returning home soon were strong. Without hesitation I hurried to the Giant Eagle grocery store a few minutes away in order to buy some flowers. I had made a habit of going there on trips back from Kathy's to stop off for a wrestling magazine or candy. I knew that I would have enough time to get there and back before Kathy returned home from work. I bought a dozen yellow roses because I thought they looked the nicest; but I didn't realize that yellow meant friendship and not love.

Sitting on her front porch with the roses I hoped that she would forgive me for ignoring her so much though out the summer. When she pulled into the driveway and noticed me sitting there, a big smile came on her face, letting me know that I would be forgiven. I walked up to her car and gave her the flowers along with a big hug. It was something sweet and kind in a summer of growing madness.

Hours passed while Kathy and I sat on her back porch swing holding hands while looking at the stars. We talked about everything that had nothing to do with baseball. As much as I hated to admit it, I needed that night more than I thought I did. My every thought had been so incredibly wrapped into coaching my players that I never took a step back to enjoy certain things with the girl I loved. Everything was happening so fast that I never focused on my relationship; my full focus was completely on coaching. I apologized to her numerous times by promising that everything would be different in the future. The saddest part was that I knew they wouldn't be. I hoped that I could do a better job of balancing the two sides of my life. I knew in my heart that I could never let my love of coaching be interfered with by anything else, but for Kathy's sake I had to start trying.

It was four a.m. by the time I drove home that morning. With the exception of prom night I had never been out that late before. It was a pretty sight seeing the night break into dawn as I arrived home. I sat on my front porch for a few minutes to soak it in before I went to bed.

The game that morning was held in Spencer, Ohio. The drive took 30-45 minutes to get to the field. My last trip to Spencer was when I broke up the perfect game while playing for Mr. Kubb six years earlier; I hoped that this year's events would bring the same luck. The biggest problem with playing a game so far away was that it started at 10 a.m. This meant I had to get there at 9 a.m. I needed to leave my house no later than 8. Considering that I had less than four hours of sleep made for an interesting drive with Bill Meyers to the game. We sat in silence for the first twenty minutes of the trip as I tried to stay awake. I had pulled all-nighters several times that season but always was able to take a nap the afternoon before the night's game. This time I was allowed no such option.

Bill kept the stereo on loud, which helped keep me awake enough to prepare a lineup. It was the first time in over a month that we would have at least twelve active players. It was a big adjustment playing without Billy and Nate all season. But Nate was back for the stretch run which helped. The timing couldn't have been better because we were about to play the most important games.

The state tournament enforced different rules about how many players could be on the field at the same time. The North Olmsted Hot Stove League allowed four outfielders for our age group; the State Tournament went with the normal three. It didn't affect us that we could only have the three because we had played that way a few times already. The hard part was figuring out whom I was going to start in right field. It was set that Mike Hach would play left field and Matt Poli in center. The biggest problem was choosing among four players for the final spot. It was brutal because both Rehak and Barth had been red hot with the bat and glove. With Nate Dolesh returning I also wanted to get him some at bats to remove any rust he might have. I decided that the fairest thing to do was give them each two innings in right field and if a seventh was needed then stick with whoever was playing the best.

One of the toughest things facing a coach is making sure he is able to play all of his players without leaving someone out. The reason it becomes so tough is because of the high importance that comes with winning. The parents of players not only want their son to play but also win. It isn't always so easy when certain players give the team the chance to win more so than others. I give much credit to the parents of John Rehak, Pat Morris and Nate Dolesh for never making me feel bad that their sons sat the bench at times. I didn't even realize it until I looked at all the scorecards at the end of the season, but Matt Poli and Mike Hach never once sat the bench. They played every out in the outfield for every game they were in. Despite that fact, not a single player or parent ever complained. That is when a coach knows he has something truly special.

We arrived at the field about an hour before first pitch which left me plenty of time to finalize the roster. I wasn't at the field for long when the players starting showing up eager to play in their first State Tournament game. It was a thing of beauty never being forced to motivate my players any more than I saw fit because of the incredible willingness they had to play and win. As much as I enjoyed the inspirational speeches I was giving them all season, it was they who inspired me to keep working hard when I saw how much they worked their butts off. Parents of players often praised me that season for motivating their sons; little did they know that it was their children motivating me.

This tournament was compiled of the best 64 teams in each age group throughout Ohio. To win the championship a team must win six games in a row over the course of three weekends. Once a team lost it would then be eliminated. Each bracket had four separate brackets of sixteen teams in it. In our particular bracket we received the twelfth seed due to our regular season record. Our first game would be played against the fifth seeded team from Mogadore with a record of 12-4. Because they only had two more wins than we did, I felt that if we played our best ball we could compete with them. The strange thing was that Mr. Molnar's team, "Ohio Envelope", was also in our bracket. It seemed very odd to have two teams from the same league in the same bracket. Despite them finishing with the same record as we did, they were actually seeded lower than us at thirteen. If we both managed to beat our first round opponents then we would meet in the second round with a spot in the final sixteen on the line. There wasn't a need for it but the chance of a rematch with our rivals gave us extra incentive to win.

Mrs. Hach approached me while I was looking over the lineup for a final time to ask me if I wanted anything from the concession stand. Until that day I had never once tried coffee. For some reason it was the first thing that popped in my head so I just blurted out, "Can I get a cup of coffee?" It was a vain attempt at trying to act like an adult in front one of my favorite parents. I thought by ordering coffee it would make me look older. It was comical when Mrs. Hach asked me, "Are you sure you wouldn't prefer hot chocolate instead?" I stuck to my choice of coffee and never told her that it was my first cup. After receiving it from her I took it back to the stand when no one was looking to add multiple spoonful's of sugar. It was a long time before I had another cup of coffee but it never took away the excitement of my first.

With the sugar filled coffee running through my veins I was pacing around like a mad man getting ready to address the team. It was Saturday, July 22, 2000, and we had a matchup to show the city of Mogadore what Wildcat baseball was all about. I based my entire pregame speech around it being our first chance to show why we finished with the league's best record. I told them that they were considered as one of the finest teams in the state because it was absolutely true. This was the chance to showcase talent that we spent the past several months developing. I preached that our opponents had no idea that we were a team no one else wanted. I sold them on the idea that our best times were ahead of us and that it all began today. We had to set the tone early and jump out to an early lead then never look back. It was our mission to show our opponents who we were and what we were about right from the start. I finished by telling them to play seven innings of Wildcat baseball and there was no way we could lose. I felt my own blood pressure start to rise with my heart pounding in my chest as I spoke every word. I was sold on the idea that we had come too far to go home early.

Often times that season I had been called "tactical" not only by the players I coached but also players I coached against. It was on that day that I took one of the biggest gambles of the season out of pure necessity. With Brian back in the lineup but still very sore and Alex tired from pitching the night before, I chose Ryan Mackey to take the mound for game one of the tournament. We had played two games in the past two nights, if we won that morning it meant a fourth game in four days the next afternoon. With all that in mind combined with the wanting to use Dan Kitko in the later innings to close out games, I couldn't look anywhere else but to Ryan Mackey.

My hope was that Ryan's unorthodox style would throw off the opposing lineup that had never seen him pitch. The rest of our league had grown accustomed to his slow delivery, but this team had no idea whom they were about to hit against. I made it clear to Ryan that he only needed to get through two innings because I planned on using a fresh Dan for five to follow. The state tournament had the rule that a player could only pitch 10 innings in a 48 hour period. This allowed me to use Dan for more than the North Olmsted Hot Stove limit of four innings a game. I also made it clear to Ryan that if he pitched well I would leave him as pitcher. It was Ryan Mackey's game to win or lose and he knew it. He took the opportunity with a look of determination on him that I hadn't seen all year. Ryan was hungry to show what he could do; I was more than willing to let him try. With Ryan on the mound the rest of the lineup appeared as follows:

CF Matt Poli
3B Danny Kitko
1B Alex Uhlik

2B Brian Leciewski
SS Anthony Poli
LF Mike Hach
C Kyle Keller
RF Andy Barth
P Ryan Mackey
Reserves – Johnny Rehak, Pat Morris and Nate Dolesh

We were unable to score in the top of the first. This meant that Ryan had his work cut out for him to keep the game tied. The biggest bonus of having him on the mound was the ability to start my four best infielders behind him. With them in place it gave Ryan the confidence to throw strikes, knowing that the fielders behind him were capable of fielding anything that came towards them. If a pitcher doesn't enjoy the confidence of his defense, then he tries too hard to strike people out which will lead to trouble.

At first it appeared that Ryan let his nerves get the best of him because he walked the first two batters he faced. I called time so I could jog to the mound to settle down my pitcher. I told Ryan numerous times to just throw strikes and let the defense do the work behind him. The message was heard loud and clear when he forced the next batter to ground out to Anthony Poli. Then with runners on the corners he got their next better to ground into an inning ending double play turned by Poli and Leciewski. It was an early sign that my plan was working exactly as I hoped that it would.

We managed to put a couple more runners on base in the top of the second inning but were turned away with no runs. With the pressure mounting for us to keep the game scoreless, we again relied on strong defensive play. Anthony made an incredible diving stop of a hard hit ball to get the first out. After Ryan let up a pair of soft singles we were back in the jam we faced in the first. It was then when Mogadore's first batter crushed a ground ball to third baseman Dan Kitko. He was able to look back the runner at third and get the second out at first base.

With two outs and men in scoring position, I made a gutsy call to have Ryan intentionally walk the next batter with first base open. I only did this because it created a force out at every base giving us multiple options on any ground ball hit. The difference between the fans in State Tournament Ball compared to the fans we played against all year was that they were smart baseball people so they didn't boo this move. If we had walked anyone on purpose in the North Olmsted League, it may have caused a riot. I knew from my days of playing as a youngster that once a team made it to the state tournament it became a completely different atmosphere.

One pitch after the walk it looked as though the move I made would backfire, because the next batter blasted a long fly ball down the right field line. Andy Barth was able to sprint fast enough to track it down in time to make an amazing head high catch. If Andy was playing even two feet closer at the start of the play, it would have traveled over his head, creating a 4-0 deficit. It was hustle and determination on Andy's part that kept the game tied.

With the top of our order due up in the third, I called the boys together for a quick pep talk. I explained that despite our ability to hit the pitches hard, we kept hitting them right at fielders who were able to make outs. I told them that it was time to start using our speed to catch them off guard. With that being said I informed Matt that I wanted him to take the first pitch but then to bunt the second. Telling him to take the first pitch would trick the defense into thinking there would be no possibility of a bunt. Matt did exactly what I told him by bunting the second pitch down the first base line for a single.

I signaled to Bill at third that I wanted Dan Kitko to take the first pitch so Matt would have the chance to steal second. The plan couldn't have worked any better when catcher threw the ball over the head over the second baseman allowing Matt to get all the way to third on just one pitch. Dan was able to single in Matt on the next pitch scoring our first run.

I didn't hesitate to put the hit and run on for Alex who wasted no time hitting a single into shallow left advancing Dan to third with still no one out. Brian Leciewski walked on four pitches loading the bases for Anthony Poli. After working the count full Anthony was able to scorch a double down the left field line to clear the bases giving us the 4-0 lead. The hit by Poli was huge but it turned out that it wouldn't even be his biggest hit of the season.

The manager from Mogadore wasted no time switching pitchers after the four run explosion. His move paid off instantly as the new pitcher was able to strike out the next three batters ending the inning. The damage had been done, however; we took a 4-0 lead into the bottom of the third.

With a four run lead I was tempted to alter my original plan of having Ryan Mackey only pitch the first two innings before inserting Dan Kitko in the game on the mound. I decided to tempt fate by letting Mackey start one more inning. I kept Johnny Rehak behind the dugout to warm up with Ray just in case I needed to make a quick switch if Mackey got into any kind of trouble.

Ryan Mackey walked a tight rope for the third straight inning but relied on his defense to get him out of trouble yet again. With two outs and the bases loaded, Ryan forced the opposing hitter to ground out to Kitko at third base. It wasn't pretty or the way we had planned, but Ryan Mackey had just pitched three scoreless innings in a pressure packed game. I couldn't have been prouder of him and our defense. Fielding countless ground balls in practice paid off when it counted the most.

We had only played three innings but it felt as though we had played three full games because of all the pressure involved in getting through them. Clinging to a four run lead I moved Dan from third base to pitcher. I took Ryan out of the game and placed Johnny into second base with moving Brian Leciewski to play third. I also replaced Andy Barth with Nate Dolesh in right field. I replaced Kyle Keller at catcher with Alex Uhlik. This caused Keller to come out of the game for Pat Morris to finish at first base. It was my way of making sure everyone received their playing time without jeopardizing the defense behind Kitko. The great thing about our team being talented from top to bottom was the confidence it allowed me to play people where I needed them.

If Ryan Mackey played the role of Houdini on the mound, then Dan Kitko looked as if he were the second coming of Roger Clemens. Kitko had zero problems shutting down the opposing offense for the next several innings with a variety of breaking balls and heat. The switch from our slowest pitcher to our fastest was far too much for any team to handle. If they were unable to score against Mackey, then scoring against Kitko was impossible.

Dan showed that his mastery of the mound was not limited to the teams from North Olmsted but also the entire state. In that early Saturday morning in July 2000, our ace pitcher was simply unhittable. In the course of the last four innings he only allowed two base runners. Neither of them crossed the plate. At the end of seven innings we held on to win 4-0. It was the lowest amount of runs we had scored all season; however, it didn't matter because it came with our first shutout.

When the game was over I reflected back on several teams I played on as a youngster that didn't even make it this far and couldn't help but smile. Looking at my team I could tell that they didn't realize the enormity of what they had just accomplished. We had put so much focus on winning our league tournament that this was seen as merely a warm up to them. I had been worried because we played two games in the two days prior, so I was thinking we would have been tired which would have allowed this team to beat us. I was not only surprised that we won but also encouraged because this meant we might be as good as any team in the state. I didn't want to let the excitement of the win go to our heads but it was hard not to let it happen.

In the postgame speech I let the boys know that I was proud of each and every one of them. I reinforced the fact that it was a total team win. I preached about how good the defense was, pointing out that if we were going to win any tournament our defense would have to keep getting stronger by the day. I knew they had to be tired from playing three games in three days with the fourth one just 24 hours away, so I told them to go home and rest. I emphasized that no swimming would be allowed until we had a day off. It was brutal to tell a group of boys to stay inside on a hot sunny day but I needed them to refresh and be ready for round two. It was one of those times when my head and heart couldn't help but disagree.

I concluded the speech by repeating what I had been preaching all season long, that was the fact that no one would determine our destiny but us. "Start believing, Gentleman, start believing." It was more than a slogan but a way of life for us. The odds had been against us from day one but we chose to ignore them by doing things our way. We had just beaten one of the best teams in the state with the opportunity for more in the near future.

The team decided to stick around to watch the next game between the thirteenth seeded Ohio Envelope coached by Mike Molnar play against the fourth seeded team from Canton. We awaited the winner of this game in the second round. I was hoping to play against the Canton team simply because it defeated the purpose of a state tournament to play against teams from our own city league. I also wanted to compete against new competition rated highly to continue to measure our own progress headed into the league tournament in the near future. As the game unfolded the boys from Ohio Envelope were able to come up with a huge upset to beat the team from Canton. It took an amazing pitching outing by Anthony Marflak going all seven innings while holding the opposition to only four runs. The normally high powered offense had no problems once again by scoring 13 runs to win easily. They used a mixture of power with speedy base running to score early and often. Jeff Feglemacher stole home three separate times during the rout.

I was unhappy about having to play against Ohio Envelope again after four meetings in the regular season, but I took comfort in the fact that I truly believed we had the better team. It would be the second time in three days that the two teams would play one another. This time we would have a full roster with nothing to hold back. "There is no way we lose this game," I said quietly to myself when it became official that we would be playing them in the next round.

During the car ride to the game I fought stay awake. It was a much different story on the way home. Bill and I were both so ecstatic to advance in the tournament with the chance of gaining our revenge against our rivals that we screamed along with the loud stereo with every song that came on. Kyle Keller and Andy Barth had chosen to come along for the ride and were not shy about joining the celebration. It was one of the few times that season that I could step away from being their coach to spend some time being their friend. My hope was that the energy of winning would carry the team through the rest of the weekend, masking the fatigue of having to play four games in four days.

Upon returning home I didn't take a nap as I should have done. Instead I chose to go to Burger King and order every desert pie they had to offer. I figured that I was technically an adult so it meant I didn't need to have normal food for dinner. So if I ordered desert pies instead of real food no one could tell me that I was wrong. I was incredibly stupid to order only desert for a meal, but the logic at the time seemed to make complete sense.

It was early evening by the time I had finished my feast and gotten cleaned up from the game so I looked for something to do with the rest of my night. With Kathy working until late and our relationship still on shaky ground I chose to do something relaxing. Over the years I had collected numerous VHS tapes from old wrestling programs. Some of them I had bought and many I simply taped off the TV. I still had all my action figures from years of collecting them. I went up into my attic and brought them down to the basement once again. This was the fourth or fifth time they had been brought down from the attic since originally being put up there. Over the course of the next several hours I played with the action figures by mimicking the same matches that were playing on television. If I didn't like the wrestler who won in real life then I didn't hesitate to change the ending in the make believe world I had created. I'm sure the sight of an 18 year old man playing with toys was something to behold but I simply didn't care. It made me happy which was all that mattered at the time. I had lost several friends that summer so I never felt bad about the times when I could have a great time all by myself.

This activity went on for hours before I finally felt all the sugar from the coffee and pies wear off causing me to pass out on the couch. I slept for a few hours until the phone rang. Kathy was on the other line. I had forgotten to be on the phone with the weather channel so it ended up waking up the entire house. She explained that her parents were out of town for one more night and asked me to come over. She didn't like being alone in a big empty house so I didn't pass up the offer. Relations between us remained shaky so I didn't pass up the chance to patch them up.

We stayed up all night talking about everything under the sun. I told her about the game earlier in the day with the rematch against Mr. Molnars team to come on Sunday. It was the first time in a while that I could bring up the team without it dominating the entire conversation. I was finally learning how to balance the two worlds of serious relationship and coaching.

By the time I returned home after another incredible night it was early morning. The entire weekend was starting to seem as if it was one long day. The so called "break" Kathy and I were on ended up with us spending more time together then when we were going steady. I made the point to her upon leaving that morning that I was no longer satisfied with the break label. I told her that I needed an answer by the time I called her that evening if we were going back to normal or else it wasn't going to work. She understood that with my heart so involved in coaching, I couldn't afford the distractions of a on again off again relationship. She explained that she didn't want to be on the break anymore either and that we could go back to normal. I couldn't have been happier.

With the drama out of the way, it was time for me to focus on beating Ohio Envelope. I woke early the next morning with my mom sticking the phone in my face. My boss Ron from CVS was on the line. Half-awake I greeted him and asked what the purpose of the early morning call was? He explained that fellow employee Doug had quit that morning and he had no one to cover the store. I told him that I had a game scheduled in Spencer, Ohio, and that there was no way I could work a full shift. My parents had taught me to never turn down work so I let him know that I would come in to help him out. However, I could only work until 11.a.m. when I had to leave. Our game was set for 1 p.m. and I didn't want to take any chances of being late.

After scrambling to get ready for work as well as grab my baseball uniform then head out the door, I made sure to wake up Bill who was sleeping on the upstairs couch. I told him what was happening and that I needed him to pick me up from work at 11 with the equipment loaded in the trunk, so we wouldn't have to stop home for anything. He was barely awake enough to understand what I was telling him but I didn't stick around to go over it.

Hour after hour of work went by until it was nearly 11 a.m. with no sight of anyone coming into relieve me. I noticed Ron in the manager's office scrambling on the phone to get someone to come in to work the rest of the shift. As the minutes turned into hours I was becoming more and more nervous that I was going to be stuck there longer than I planned. I enjoyed working there but it wasn't worth missing a game over it if I was forced to quit on the spot. When the clock struck 11:30 and I was still standing at the register, I nearly picked up the speaker phone and told Ron I was leaving. I looked out the big window to see Bill sitting in his car furious. Bill was one of the few people I knew that had a shorter temper than I. I could almost see the steam coming from Bill's ears as he grew even more impatient.

It wasn't until a few minutes before noon that I couldn't take it anymore. I called up to Ron who was cowering in the manager office to make him aware I was leaving. It didn't matter that I had several people waiting in line waiting to check out, I was ready to go. My team came before anyone else and by my standing there I felt as though I was abandoning them. Ron came flying down the steps to try stopping me, but I wasn't about to be held up any longer. To his credit he was able to stop me in the parking lot and even let me know that he wasn't angry with me. He was a good natured man and I felt guilty having to leave him on the spot, but I had more important things to handle. He understood and thanked me for my time. I was lucky that he didn't fire me for walking out; however he was lucky that I even came in the first place. I talked about coaching all the time while at work so he knew my passion for it and understood why I was so desperate to leave.

This was a moment when having two incredible assistant coaches came in handy. Bill drove at the speed of light, risking a possible speeding ticket to get us there by the first pitch. I was changing from my work uniform of a dress shirt with long pants into my baseball uniform while Bill was flying down the highway. I can only imagine what on coming drivers thought as we flashed by them with my butt high in the air getting changed.

Ray had no problems in getting the team ready to play by running all the pre-game drills and stretches. This was a case of both of my assistant coaches doing everything in their power to help myself and the team. Without the help of such great men by my side, our team wouldn't have climbed to the heights in which it did that summer.

Upon arriving at the field, just a mere ten minutes before first pitch I had to rush the scorecard to the scorekeepers table before it was too late. Lineups were due five minutes before first pitch, so if I had showed up a few minutes later we would have had to forfeit. It was a close call but it succeeded.

The news wasn't all good as I walked into our dugout and noticed that Billy Graves was no longer the only player we were missing. Andy Barth had forgotten we had a game that day and didn't show up. He had seen my car parked in the driveway next door and figured that I was still home. My parents dropped me off at work and Bill picked me up so my car never moved from the spot where it was sitting the night before. It wasn't until hours later when I returned home that night and I saw Andy riding his skateboard that he realized he had missed the game.

I asked every parent and player if anyone had seen or heard from him. No one replied that they had. I was incredibly angry that Andy would forget about such an important game that I couldn't even talk without shouting. Frustration was mounting by the second and the game hadn't even begun. It went back to the point of a coach only being able to control so much.

My normal pregame speeches lasted up to ten minutes and the players had counted on them to motivate them for each game. This time we didn't have the time or need for a lengthy speech. The facts were simple and to the point: we were the better team and it was finally time to prove it. It was not only time to prove it to them and ourselves, but now we had the chance to show it to the whole state. My pregame speech lasted all of ten seconds and was wrapped up in one sentence. I gathered the boys up and told them, "We are the better team." Those simple words were all I could come up with but I felt that they were enough.

Before I posted the lineup on the below ground dugout wall for the team to see I needed to speak with Kyle Keller. I asked him, "Are you prepared to play the entire game at catcher?" Without hesitation he replied, "Yes". Kyle never ceased to amaze me with his hard work ethic and loyalty to his teammates. He had worked diligently all year. This was just another example of his willing to do anything it took to help the team win. It was extremely hot that afternoon and with him playing catcher the entire game was a heavy burden. Ohio Envelope was also the second fastest team in the league behind us, so I knew Kyle would have his hands full behind the plate.

Looking out to the stands for my normal pregame scan of the crowd I noticed the entire team and coaching staff of the number one seeded team from La Grange filled up the first two rows. They had gone undefeated throughout their regular season and post season city tournament. They were not only the top seed in our bracket but also the entire tournament. People around Ohio had been referring to them as "The Machines" because of how good they were. It was a take on how well that played, as if they were programmed to do so. I never bought into hype but even I had to admit they looked impressive.

Don and Abbie along with my parents had also made the journey out to Spencer to show their support for the team. It always felt good to know they were there close by even though once the game started I mentally blocked out everything that was not happening on the field. It normally worked with a few exceptions of people who went overboard to make their presence known.

Despite not having the red hot bat of Andy Barth, I still felt that our team had a great shot at winning. When I posted the lineup for the team to see I made sure to write underneath it; "The sweet sixteen is waiting!" It was a simple message that this game would end in nothing but a victory. I wanted to erase any possible thought about losing. The lineup for game two of the 2000 State Tournament against Ohio Envelope from North Olmsted is as follows:

CF Matt Poli
3B Danny Kitko
2B Alex Uhlik
P Brian Leciewski
SS Anthony Poli
LF Mike Hach
C Kyle Keller
RF Nate Dolesh
1B Pat Morris
Reserves – Ryan Mackey, Johnny Rehak

The decision to open the game with Brian on the mound was a tough one because he had been injured his last time out. I hoped that he could mentally get past what happened. It might be easier for him to do so against a familiar opponent. Brian had the mental toughness that most great players possess, but I still worried about pitching him too soon. It had only been four days since he was struck by the ball.

Brian got off to a slow start in the top of the first inning by walking a few batters. His teammates were behind him with words of encouragement trying to help in any way they could. When Brian threw a belt high fast ball to Danny Molnar it spelled doom for our outfield that was playing much too shallow. I had shouted out to them before the play to back up but it fell on deaf ears. The ball sailed ten feet over Mat Poli's head in center clearing the bases for a triple. I was angry that they hadn't backed up when I shouted at them to do so. The next batter was Anthony Marflak who clubbed a two run homer over the fence in right field. Before we could even take a breath we were down 5-0.

With a mixture of exhaustion and anger my outlook quickly sunk. I began screaming at anyone in sight to pay attention and stop making silly mistakes. The next ball was hit at Dan Kitko who juggled what should have been the first out of the game. Instead he never made the throw because he couldn't even get the ball out of his glove. Before the inning was complete Ohio Envelope managed to score three more times placing us in an 8-0 deficit before we even had a single time at bat. I was livid at my team as they returned to the dugout. "You're not going to win by not listening to the coaches," I barked. I felt bad for screaming at them so much but I couldn't stand the thought of another loss to a team I knew we could beat.

Anthony Marflak took the hill for the opposition after pitching seven innings the previous day. I knew the State Tournament only allowed a pitcher to throw 10 innings in a two day time frame. With this knowledge the game plan became to keep it close against Marflak in the hopes of crushing their bullpen later in the game. We knew he could only toss the three innings so we didn't panic when starting the game down 8-0, but it wasn't a good feeling either.

Marflak wasted no time in showing why he was not only one of the best pitchers in the league but now also in the state when he struck out the three batters he faced. It became crucial that we could play the next inning without giving up too many runs digging an even bigger hole to climb out of. I told Brian to relax and just pitch his game. I also used harsh words on my infielders to pay better attention and stop allowing balls to get past them. This was the sternest I had been with them the all season but the time called for it.

Brian took the defense out of the game completely by pitching a shutout inning with three strikeouts. I could tell that his chest was sore from throwing hard after not pitching for a several days. I knew that if I asked Brian if he felt all right that he would just lie, so I wouldn't take him out of the game. He was a fighter with such an incredible heart that taking him out was not an option. I told him that I would let him stay in the game by switching him with Dan at third. He wasn't pleased to be pulled from the mound but he also knew that most coaches would have pulled him out of the game when they saw him wincing in pain. When he came back from his time at bat I handed him a jar of Ben Gay and told him to go to the corner of the dugout and spread some on where it hurt. Between innings Ray asked me not to take Brian out of the game. I told him that he was Brian's father and that it would be his choice.

When Dan Kitko took the mound for the third inning, it was the first time all season I had turned to my best pitcher so early in a game. The simple truth was that I had no choice. We were already down by eight runs and I needed to stop the bleeding. Dan went to work quickly by setting the order down with a great mixture of fastballs and breaking pitches. Heading into our at bats in the bottom of the third the score remained 8-0. Marflak, who continued his brilliance of our batters, didn't allow a single run.

Despite being down 8-0 to start the fourth inning I took a little solace in the fact that Marflak couldn't pitch any more innings. My solace quickly turned to anger upon seeing Marflak jog to the mound to start the bottom of the fourth. I knew that if he even threw one pitch to our leadoff hitter I could challenge it and cause them to forfeit the game. I believe many coaches in that environment would have done just that. However, I didn't want to win that way. Mike Molnar was an honest man so I felt as though he simply didn't realize his pitcher was over the limit. I calmly jogged to the scorer's table to point this out before it went any further. Mike came over to see what the problem was when the official scorekeeper told him the news. He thanked me and apologized for the error then quickly brought in someone else to pitch.

As the new pitcher Ted Kelly entered the game, taking warm up tosses, I used that timeout to huddle with my players. I was angry that they had played poorly in the first four innings and determined that they turn it around right away. Dan had just pitched two scoreless innings keeping the deficit at eight runs. I scolded them for playing sluggishly and not hustling after every ball. I told them that we had come too far to put our tails between our legs and quit. I didn't want to hear that anyone was tired or thought that we had no chance at winning. We had come back to beat numerous teams that season including this one. I was very hard on them because I felt I had to get their attention. I was sick of losing to a team inferior to us and I was sure my players were too. I concluded my rant by demanding they wake up! I shouted so hard that others may have heard me but it didn't matter. Normally I didn't get so upset by losing, rather it was the lackluster effort we were exerting that made me so angry. I was loud and clear: my hope was that the message got through to them before it was too late.

With Dan's back to back scoreless innings combined with our opponents pulling their best pitcher, it was clear that this was our chance to get back in the game. After our first two batters grounded out to Jeff Feglemacher at second base things were not looking good. But when Alex Uhlik hit a two out double our team showed life for the first time. Brian Leciewski drew a walk on four straight pitches that may or may not have been intentional. Anthony Poli made them pay by smacking a two run double over the left fielders head to put us on the scoreboard. After Mike Hach slapped a single down the right field line, the once massive lead was cut to 8-3 giving us much needed hope.

Still trailing 8-3 to start the fifth inning I kept Kitko in the game with the hope he could continue to shut down the Ohio Envelope offense. Dan continued his mastery of the opposition by pitching another scoreless inning. It kept the margin at five with our suddenly red hot bats returning to the plate.

Pat Morris and Nate Dolesh both hit the ball hard but right at defenders for outs. Matt Poli laid down a beautiful bunt single to get us our first base runner. Dan Kitko remained hot at the plate by lining a single to shallow center allowing Poli to score. Alex Uhlik, who was having a tremendous game and tournament, wasted no time hitting a double on the first pitch he saw to score Kitko all the way from first base. I had called for the hit and run and it working perfectly. The score was now 8-5 and we were slowly making our comeback.   Anthony Marflak made a diving stop on a line drive hit by Brian Leciewski to end the inning. We had cut the lead to three runs and stolen all momentum.

I let Dan Kitko take the mound for the start of the sixth inning. It was his fourth inning of work in the game and also his eighth in two days. Any signs of Dan showing fatigue or slowing down didn't appear in that inning. He looked strong early and often in the sixth by using a variety of fastballs with movement to keep the opposing hitters off balance. The crowd would roar with approval at every out Kitko managed to get. The game was taking on the feel of a heavyweight prize fight with both teams slugging it out. I wasn't sure how Dan was able to pitch so well against such heavy hitters but I never stopped to ask. Dan's heart carried over to the rest of the team, inspiring them at a time when we badly needed it.

Heading into the bottom of the sixth inning, we were fully aware that time was running out on us. Anthony Poli stuck out to start the inning. With one out Mike Hach ripped a hard line drive but right at the second baseman. For the third inning in a row we started off with two quick outs. It was becoming a bad habit of putting our back against the wall before we took action. With two outs and no one on base Kyle Keller laced a single into left field. Keller easily stole second base on the very first pitch to Pat Morris. The next pitch was high and inside which hit Morris on the shoulders allowing him to take first base. Nate Dolesh stepped to the plate with two on and two out still trailing by three. I yelled out to Nate that "We only needed a single and just worry about making contact." I was secretly hoping that he was about to hit one over the fence to tie the game. Nate answered any questions we might have had about his being rusty when he crushed the 0-2 pitch into deep left field for a two run two out double. The game was now 8-7 and the crowd came unglued with excitement.

After feeling fatigue and frustration, we were now involved in one of the greatest Little League games I had ever been a part of. It was our third straight inning with a two out rally to draw closer. I was almost in disbelief that we could do it again. I felt it was only a matter of time before we found a way to win even when Mat Poli struck out to end the inning.

Since I trusted my gut many times when it came to pitching changes, I felt that it was telling me to pull Dan from the mound. He looked great in his four innings of work with two innings of availability still remaining. It was the start of the seventh and final inning and I felt that if I left Dan out there again he might become tired and let up runs. It was one of the hardest calls I ever had to make but I went with Alex Uhlik instead of Dan to start the seventh inning. I put Dan at third base and moved Brian over to second base. The biggest reason for the switch was that Dan never went more than four innings in a game and I didn't want to see what would happen by chancing it. There was a good chance that he could have gone out in the seventh and shut down Ohio Envelope again. Still I just thought it wasn't a good idea to risk it with so much riding on the outcome.

I felt confident in Alex Uhlik with his ability to throw strikes. The problem we seemed to have every time he pitched was faulty defense. With Kitko at third, Anthony Poli at shortstop and Brian Leciewski at second base, our defense looked strong enough to support Alex this time. He looked excellent in pressure situations all year, and this one becoming no different. Down by only one run in the final inning of regulation he knew that he must hold our opponents scoreless to give us a chance at winning.

Alex, who continued to have no problems throwing strikes, forced the first two batters to hit weak ground balls for outs. The next batter was Anthony Marflak who had been crushing our pitching all season. Alex pitched Marflak a belt high fast ball that he drove into the right field seats. The only good thing about this was that the right field seats were in foul territory so it was just a long strike. Kyle Keller jogged to the mound to settle him down. Kyle had grown so much in one season that the coaching staff became deeply proud of him. When Kyle was behind the plate he always knew when to settle down a pitcher and what plays to call for the infield without our even having to say a word to him. It was another sign of his hard work that allowed him to mature into an incredible ballplayer.

Alex forced Marflak to ground out to third base on the pitch following the near homerun. It brought the top half of the seventh inning to a close with our trailing by one run. I pulled the team together and let them know that it was gut check time. We only had three outs left and still had to score at least one run to send the game into extra innings or two runs to win the game. I asked them, "are you guys ready to go home? Or do you want to keep playing?" I knew the answer would be a resounding "yes" to keep playing from all of them. We had the heart of our order coming to the plate making me feel confident that a dramatic win was on the way.

Any feelings of confidence quickly lessened when both Kitko and Uhlik struck out to start the inning off of Danny Molnar. We were down to our last out with only one run separating us from tying the game. No one was left sitting on the bench. Every player stood against the dugout fence supporting their teammates at the plate. In heart wrenching drama Brian drew a walk after being down two strikes to keep our hopes alive. Danny Molnar continued his wildness when he walked Anthony Poli on four straight pitches. By this point everyone in the stands was on their feet screaming in support for the Wildcats to keep the game going. Mike Hach also drew a walk to load the bases with two outs.

Mr. Molnar called timeout and strolled to the mound to settle down his son. Kyle Keller was up next to bat, so I used the timeout to ask him if he wanted to hit. I had Ryan Mackey and John Rehak both on the bench that I could have used to sub for him. Since Kyle had played catcher all game in the hot sun I knew he had to be feeling tired. He assured he felt fine so I let him hit with the game on the line. Kyle fouled off the first two pitches falling into the hole 0-2. Danny Molnar's wildness returned when he threw three straight balls in the dirt to make the count full. It was bases loaded with two out in the bottom of the last inning in a one run game. With the count full it was a moment right out of a movie. Kyle then hit four straight pitches into foul territory to keep the at bat and game alive. My shirt was covered in sweat from the drama. Kyle hit the next pitch sharply into the hole between second and third base with the opposing shortstop making a diving effort to knock down the ball. Lazzaro picked it up and threw it to first base in an attempt to get Kyle out, but he was too late. Kyle hustled down the line fast enough to beat the throw. The infield single allowed Brian to score from third tying the game. In an effort to catch them off guard Bill sent Anthony Poli to round third base and try to score to win the game. Anthony Marflak who caught the ball at first turned quickly enough to gun Poli at the plate by a good two feet. This ended the inning but not the game.

Anthony Poli was upset when he came back to the dugout to grab his glove for the top of the eighth. I could tell that he was holding back tears from the disappointment of getting thrown out at the plate. I gave him a pat on the back and told him: "Don't worry about it because you will get another chance." I didn't realize how true those words would soon become.

The game went into extra innings, all tied up at eight runs apiece. We had come from eight down to draw even. I didn't hesitate to send Alex Uhlik back to the mound to start the eighth inning. He had looked sharp in the previous inning so I felt comfortable going back to him. Alex didn't disappoint and set down the opposing batters in order to keep the game tied.

In the bottom of the eighth we only needed one run to win the game and advance to the next round. Danny Molnar managed to control his wildness but not before he loaded the bases with two outs and Brian Leciewski at the plate. We had a decent amount of speed with Dolesh at third base. Mat Poli was at second and Alex Uhlik at first. The only run that mattered was Dolesh at third because if he scored the game would be over. Things looked good for us with our strongest hitter Brian Leciewski at the plate. I was tempted to call for a suicide squeeze believing they would have never expected it. I decided against it because I didn't want to take the bat out of the hands of our cleanup hitter. I quickly regretted my decision to let Brian swing away when he popped out weakly to Lazzaro at shortstop to end the inning. It was a no win situation; if I had let Brian bunt and he got out then I would have to live with the thought of not letting him swing away.

After playing with the idea of letting Alex Uhlik start the ninth inning on the mound I finally decided to let him take the hill one more time. Uhlik had looked great in the previous two innings so I felt comfortable riding on his hot arm. He did not disappoint once again he gave up only one hit and no runs to keep the game tied headed into the bottom of the ninth.

With the score still even I hoped that we could score at least one run to win the game. Sadly after a promising start with both Anthony Poli and Mike Hach reaching base, we were once again denied. Ohio Envelope turned to relief pitcher Jacob Pine to stop the rally. He was able to set down Keller, Morris, and Dolesh in order to keep the game tied heading into the tenth inning.

To start the tenth I switched Uhlik from the pitcher's mound to shortstop and let Anthony Poli pitch. I told Anthony, "Relax and don't worry about anything but throwing strikes." With the top of our order coming up to start the bottom of the tenth I knew that if we could hold the opposition scoreless one more time that we would score to win. Anthony was able to get the first two batters out on long fly balls tracked down by our outfielders.

Anthony walked the next two batters he faced before giving up a single to Aaron Lazzaro that allowed Ohio Envelope to regain the lead at 9-8. It was disheartening that we gave up the lead after working so hard to tie the game. It may have been the slight blow to our momentum that allowed the trick play Mr. Molnar called for next to work. After Anthony threw the first pitch strike to Marflak, their third base coach sent Jeff Feglemacher halfway down the third base line. I started screaming at Keller just to walk the runner back up the line then call timeout. Keller was unable to hear me. He threw the ball five feet over the head of Danny Kitko at third base, allowing Jeff Feglemacher to come home easily. This disastrous play put them ahead 10-8. Anthony managed to settle down enough to get the next batter out but the damage had already been done.

It was the second time that day that our team faced three outs away from elimination. Both Keller and Poli sat in the dugout crying loudly because of the fatal mistakes they had made. I tried my best to console them by reminding them we still had three outs to go, but it didn't do much good. They had enormous hearts and the thought of costing their team the game was too much for them to bear. I felt really bad for Kyle because he had played so hard, never complaining about wearing the heavy catchers gear in the hot sun. The game had been going on for nearly four hours on an extremely hot July day. It was the longest game in both time and innings that I had ever been a part of in my Little League career both as a player and coach.

I huddled the boys up for one last pep talk in an effort to give them hope for another comeback. I mentioned how they fought hard all day. I told them not to worry about being tired because I was sure the other team was every bit as weary as we were. The main message was to take one at bat at a time and we could still win.

Mr. Molnar switched Jacob Pine for Aaron Lazzaro on the mound. It seemed to be an ongoing chess match between Mr. Molnar and myself. I felt confident that I could match strategy not only with him but any opposing manager I might face. I was also confident that with the top of our batting order due up that the outcome was still to be decided.

Matt Poli took the plate as we trailed 10-8 in the bottom of the tenth inning. I took a deep breath before I stepped onto the top step of the dugout to watch. The next few minutes have been played over again in my mind more times than I can count since that epic day. What was about to occur would not only help shape my life but also the lives of every player on our team.

Mr. Molnar ordered his infield to come in close to guard against the bunt. He knew the speed of Mat Poli and took the proper steps to thwart it. With the infield drawn in I gave Bill the sign to let Mat swing away. Our confidence in him paid off when he hit the first pitch barely over the head of the third baseman for an infield single.

Down two runs with Dan Kitko coming to the plate, it was time for the hit and run. I told Dan that if the ball was too far away from the plate not to worry about swinging. It wasn't a typical hit and run because I knew that even if Dan chose not to swing or didn't make contact Matt had the speed to steal second base. Dan made contact on the first pitch he saw by sending it into deep center field for a double. It moved Matt over to third and put both tying runs in scoring position with no outs and the red hot Alex Ulik coming to the plate.

Kitko had the biggest hit of the season until Alex hit a triple on the next pitch clearing the bases and tying the game. I can never remember being happier in my young life than when Alex hit the triple. The bench mobbed Matt and Dan as they came across to score the tying runs. The crowd rose to its feet and roared. The Bell was ringing so loud that teams could hear it two fields over from us. For the second time that game we had come back to tie the game with the chance to win.

I flashbacked to a game my brother Don played in years ago when he stole home to win the game for his team. With the speed of Alex Uhlik on third base unmatched by anyone else in that age group I have ever seen play. It crossed my mind to let him take off on the first pitch in a straight steal. I held back because we had no outs and the worst thing a manager can do is let his team run itself into an out at home plate in a tie game. I also counted on the fact we had our best hitter coming to the plate with solid hitters behind him as well.

The opposing defense was playing at the edge of the grass hoping to knock down any ground ball that may come their way. With the speed of Alex and the depth of the defense, it would have only taken a slow ground ball for us to win the game. Again I was tempted to put the squeeze on by chose not to do so. I kept asking myself over and over about what play I should call. I let Brian have the option to swing away in the hopes that simply making contact would be enough to score the winning run. Brian could not measure up the off speed pitches from Lazzaro, causing him to strike out on three straight pitches.

Brian's striking out was a bitter pill to swallow but one we couldn't quickly overcome. Anthony Poli, who had just seconds prior been crying his eyes out for letting up the go ahead runs, now had the chance to be the hero. As he walked to the plate I calmly told him, "relax and have fun." It had been a four hour game in the hot sun with more momentum swings than any previous contest all season, but the biggest and best moment was about to come.

I looked to Bill at third base and gave him the sign I had been dying to use all season, I called for the suicide squeeze. With Alex's naturally gifted speed on third combined with Anthony's excellent ability to bunt there was nothing stopping us. Two seconds later Anthony swiped his chest to let us know he read the sign. There was only one small problem; Mr. Molnar had read the sign as well. He was about to call timeout but it was too late because the ball had already left his pitcher's hand. Anthony Poli didn't square up to bunt, but chose to slap a swinging bunt down first base line instead.

The first baseman was unable to field the ball quick enough to make a throw. Exhaustion turned into elation as Alex slid home to win the game. It was a moment that took mere seconds but will live in our memories forever. This was the type of game the players used for motivation later on in life. We used a never say die attitude to overcome the odds throughout the game without ever giving up. It was the single greatest win of my coaching career and rivaled some of the biggest wins I had enjoyed as a player.

In many ways the win summed up our season. We had gotten off to a slow start but never looked for excuses. As much as I hated having to come from behind all the time I couldn't deny that we were becoming extremely good at it. I was happier for my players that day than I had been all season because of the emotions involved. There had been times in the game that I felt we would win no matter how many runs we had to score to do so. The team had the attitude that whatever the height of the hill they could climb it.

The team was barely able to take a knee because they were exhausted by the marathon battle. It was a moment when the words came easy to address a bunch of players who left everything they had on the playing field. I told them that I was proud of how hard they fought all season but especially the efforts they gave in these last four days. Because we wouldn't play again until the following Saturday, I told them to go swimming as much as they wanted until Friday when we had practice. In closing I made it clear that this was an enormous win and that if we played them in the league tournament, this would provide the mental edge we needed.

The win had improved our record to 12-6 overall and advanced us into the final sixteen teams in the state. Big as this win was, I wanted more to follow. The run in the State Tournament was fun but I knew that it could end at any time. I hoped that all the experience we were getting in this tournament would carry over into the league tournament to follow. One thing was certain; we had a date with "The Machines".

Chapter 18
The Machines

"I've missed more than 9,000 shots in my career. I have lost
over 300 games. 26 times, I have been called on to take the final shot and missed. I've failed over and over again in my life
and that is why I succeed."
~ Michael Jordan

The famous philosopher Aristotle once said, "We are what we
repeatedly do. Excellence therefore isn't an act but a habit." As
happy as I was about the thrilling comeback victory in round two
of the state tournament, I was not surprised. We had practiced
what to do in tight situations so many times that when they
happened we were ready. Striving for excellence became our goal
every time we took the field. Wildcat baseball was becoming
more than just a motto. By the end of the season it had formed into
a way life for our players and our fans. The passion and desire that
each player carried with him showed every time he stepped onto
the field. The approach was not to wait for something good to
happen but rather make it happen with hustle and disciplined
baseball. A philosophy started by William Sprague which states,
"Don't wait until the iron is hot; but make it hot by striking."

After the incredible come from behind victory that propel
our team into the top sixteen in the state, we barely had the energy
to pack up our gear let alone do much else. When the game
concluded our team stormed the field to celebrate. We never had
the chance to shake hands with the opposing side. Mr. Rehak came
up to me as we were packing everything up and suggested that the
entire team walk over to where Molnar's players were huddled up
to thank them for the classic game we had just played. I decided
that it was a classy idea so I instantly directed my players to walk
over as a team to thank Ohio Envelope for the privilege of playing
them.

Mr. Molnar was still addressing his team when we
approached them. His son Danny shouted out, "Hi, Mr. McKee." I
felt bad because he completely cut off his dad's speech so I told
Mr. Molnar to finish what he was saying and we would wait
patiently. It was the first time I heard an opposing player refer to

me as Mr. McKee. It had a nice sound to it and I hoped to hear more of it someday. The rest of the players on other teams had always called me Coach McKee. All of my players either called me just plain Coach or Vince. It was the first time I had ever heard the name Mr. McKee without it referring to my father.

After Mr. Molnar finished up his speech to his players, we spoke for several minutes as the players shook hands. We both agreed it was the greatest game we had ever been a part of. Mr. Molnar even claimed to be grateful that his team wouldn't have to face the boys from La Grange in the next round. He like many others had been well schooled on the legend of the team people referred to as, "The Machines." To listen to people around the tournament speak about them it was as if Paul Bunyan and Bigfoot had come together to form a Little League team. I was never one to buy into hype so I knew it would be important not to let my players feed into it.

I was approached by Jeff Feglemache'rs grandmother as I was loading up Bill's trunk with the equipment. My first reaction was to expect the worst with an opposing parent confronting me with an issue. It turned out that she was simply coming over to thank me for coaching such wonderful young men. She went on to explain that our team always looked ready to play and have fun every time. She went as far as to ask me to pick Jeff to play for our team if I returned to coaching the following summer. I had expected the worst but received some of the nicest compliments someone could want from an opposing side.

Later that evening my Mom, who had been at the game and spoke with Jeff's grandmother, told me an extremely interesting story about how she played a role in my birth. I was born at Fairview Hospital on January 14, 1982. Because I was a premature baby I had to spend the first several nights of my life in the intensive care unit. The nurse on duty those nights watching over me was none other than Jeff's grandmother Colletta Carl. The coincidence that she was the only opposing parent or grandparent to thank me for coaching, was a miracle. It was one of many signs that summer that made me feel there was a higher purpose for what I was doing. Anytime I felt like giving up or letting the negative get the best of me, something like this would occur and restore my faith that there were some good hearted people left. I tried not to stress the negativity from the opposing coaches and parents; however the first time I received a little praise it felt incredible. Colletta was a generous woman for spending the time thanking me and relaying the story to my mother.

The intensity of the emotional day with its many ups and downs finally started to catch up with me on the way home. With Bill driving only slightly slower than he did on the way to the game I had the chance to sit back and reflect on the craziness of the past four days. Our team had experienced the agony of defeat but also the thrill of victory. It was a line that ABC Sports used but our team had just lived it. While my heart felt like the man holding up a gold medal, my body was feeling as if I crashed down a snow hill on skies.

Upon arriving home I made sure the first thing I would do was address the Andy Barth situation. I had made a habit of saying, "Andy Barth, what are you doing?" There was never a better time than that moment to try and figure out exactly what he was thinking. He explained to me his car theory as to why he didn't believe we had a game that afternoon. I proceeded to scold him for several minutes before eventually letting him off the hook. I told him, "Don't ever let it happen again!" He knew his mistake and I felt it wasn't intentional so I gave him a pat on the back and retired for the evening.

It wasn't until 2 p.m. the next day that I awoke. I was so worn out from the previous four days that I didn't even set my alarm. Later on that evening I spent the majority of the night lying by Kathy's pool relaxing. I hoped that most of my players would follow my lead but somehow I knew that wouldn't be the case. I couldn't blame them if they were out running around and getting dirty all week because they were children and that's what they are supposed to do. I would rather have them outside playing than inside on a computer game. The only things I asked of them was not to swim the day before or of a game, and not get hurt. After the freak accident with Billy Graves, I started to become a little cautious.

Our next game wasn't until Saturday afternoon against the number one seeded La Grange Knapper Burners. The good thing about having so many days off in a row was that it gave time for our pitchers to rest. We had pitched just about everybody we could over the last several weeks so the time off was just what the baseball gods ordered.

The bad part about having so much time off between games was that it left me with plenty of time to become anxious. The first couple days off were relaxing because they gave me time to spend with Kathy. By the time Tuesday evening rolled around I was chomping at the bits to get back on the field. It started earlier that day when I took her to the zoo and we walked past the tiger cage. Seeing the tigers made me think about the Wildcats. Kathy even bought me a small figurine tiger from the zoo gift shop. It was a nice gesture on her part but did little to sooth my eagerness to get on the field.

The next day it was still only mid-week so I called for practice at Little Clague Park that evening. We practiced for a solid two hours. Mainly we covered hitting and fielding just to keep ourselves sharp. I didn't schedule any pitching because I didn't want to run the risk of anyone hurting his arm. It was a good practice because we mainly kept things loose but still maintained the same intensity that we needed to stay ready.

I knew the team we were playing against had not allowed a run in the previous two rounds so we extended batting practice a little longer than normal. Ray had the great idea of having a team batting session at the cages on Friday night. Bill and I both agreed with Ray so we scheduled it and told the boys if they came we would buy them ice cream afterwards. I apologized to the parents for the short notice, most of them understood.

The team gathered at Swings "n" Things the Friday evening before the big game against La Grange. The fastest pitcher we had faced all season was Anthony Marflak, who was pitching near 60 miles per hour. Chris Gore whom we faced numerous times as well was also pitching at nearly the same speed. I assured my players that the pitching we were about to face was going to be consistent with what Gore and Marflak had been throwing against us. With that being said I allowed some of the hitters to try hitting in the cages throwing 70 miles per hour. The coaching staff tried everything we could to get them mentally and physically prepared.

Later on that evening as the boys ate their ice cream and ran around the indoor game center the coaches sat trying to come up with a game plan. Bill had the great idea to move Alex to the outfield for this one game because of the hitting power La Grange possessed. The thought was that the chances of the ball being hit to the outfield increased and we needed another player with speed and skill out there to chase down fly balls. Alex had both of those qualities as well as the natural leadership that our outfield lacked at times. It wasn't that Matt Poli and Mike Hach weren't great outfielders, because they were very good. It was a move based upon Alex's ability to take charge out there and allow the coaching staff to worry more about coaching the infield. I felt bad about moving Andy out of his starting role in right field but this was more than likely a one-time deal so I was okay with it.

I was determined not to allow my team to be intimidated by the massive opposition. The first step to losing occurs when a team allows its competition to psyche them out before the game even begins. I stressed to them over and over again that the score would be 0-0 at the start of the game and we had just as much say as they did to its outcome. I tried to keep their focus on strictly playing our brand of baseball and not worrying about toppling a giant.

The team from La Grange had won its season and post- season city tournament prior to entering the State Tournament. Their league was run like most where the league games and post season finished before State Tournament play began. North Olmsted was one of the few leagues not to complete a city tournament before the State Tournament began. Entering their game against us they had compiled a total record of 22-0. I wasn't ignoring the fact that they were good, but I didn't choose to focus on it. The key to winning was to neutralize their strengths as best we could without weakening anything that we did well.

I was fully aware that if we lost on Saturday the first round of our League Tournament would begin the next day. With this in mind I had to prepare for that possibility as well as if we won. If we played in another extra inning affair in which I had to use many pitchers and still end up losing it would seriously jeopardize our chances in the League Tournament. As much I was wanted to go for broke I knew I needed to keep something reserved just in case we couldn't defeat the heavy favorite. It was as if I was forced to play a chess game with my own mind on how I wanted to attack the weekend. My biggest fear was to give full effort and come up short against the Machines, causing us to have nothing left in our tank risking an early exit from the league tournament. My competitive pride got the best of me in the end when I decided that we would start Dan Kitko and leave him in for as long as it took if he did well. I felt I owed it to the boys to put out the best lineup I could.

Our roster of twelve players was cut down to eleven because Ryan Mackey would be missing the rest of the season to go to swim camp. I knew it was coming because his parents had told me about it weeks earlier. I was not angry about this because Ryan had been a solid contributor to the team and helped us win numerous games. I wished him the best and promised him that he would have a championship trophy upon returning home. I wasn't exactly sure if it would be the State Title or the League Title but I was sure we would win one of them. With Ryan out of the lineup and Alex moved to the outfield the lineup appeared as follows:

CF Matt Poli
P Dan Kitko
RF Alex Uhlik
3B Brian Leciewski
SS Anthony Poli
LF Mike Hach
C Kyle Keller
2B John Rehak
1B Pat Morris
Bench – Nate Dolesh, Andy Barth

I felt comfortable with or lineup because I believed it gave us the best chance to win. A lineup is one of the few things the manager has control over throughout the course of a game so I always took pride in filling out the lineup card.

I made sure to instill confidence in my players one last time in the pre-game speech. I tried my best to give them hope and remind them as to how hard they had fought to reach this point. They hadn't backed down from any obstacle all season so I was positive they would give their best effort. It was a tall task but I couldn't ask for a better team to manage then the one I was given. As we gathered hands to scream out our rally cry of 1-2-3 "Wildcats", I truly believed we had a chance to win. Sadly, the confidence would not take long to disappear.

I knew we may be in trouble when the barely four foot tall Matt Poli stepped into the batter's box to face the almost six foot tall opposing pitcher Steve Griffin. La Grange Knapper Burner had made a habit of blowing out teams early with strong pitching combined with massive hitting. If we stood a chance against them we were going to need to bring our best from the very first pitch.

Matt was a tough player who never let size get in the way of anything; however, this time he simply could not time the pitchers incredible speed. The opposing player was throwing the ball a good five miles per hour faster than anyone we faced all year. Matt tried as hard as he could but couldn't avoid going down on three straight pitches.

Dan Kitko stepped into the batter's box to face the hard throwing lefty from La Grange with a look of determination to hit the ball. Dan was able to make contact but not nearly enough as he grounded out weakly to the third baseman. Our last chance for a base runner in the first inning rested on the shoulders of team leader Alex Uhlik. He was able to work the count full until striking out swinging. It was an unimpressive top half of the inning. Little did I know that the bottom half was about to get worse, much worse.

Dan Kitko had been one of the most dominant pitchers at the age of ten years old in the entire city of North Olmsted. I was even willing to bet he could match up with any pitcher in the neighboring five cities. For the boys from La Grange he was just another pitcher seemingly serving up the ball on a silver platter. Dan gave up five runs in the first inning before recording a single out. The out that he managed to get was on a beautiful diving catch in deep right field by Alex Uhlik.

I sent Ray to the mound in an effort to calm down Danny but it didn't do him any good. He continued to allow hitters to reach base. With the score 8-0 and two outs I was hopeful that Dan could get us out of the horrible inning without any more damage being done. My hopes were quickly dashed when the next batter smacked a two-run double, putting La Grange up 10-0. As hard as it was to not show anger I was able to restrain myself. I knew my players were trying hard but were just simply overmatched by a phenomenal team that had been together for years. The inning came to a merciful end when Dan managed to force the next batter to line out to Pat Morris at first base.

In the blink of an eye were down several runs so I took the team aside and told them to relax at the plate and focus on making contact. I told them we couldn't make up all the runs in one at bat so we needed base runners to establish a rally. The message got through when Brian managed to hit a soft single to start the inning. Anthony Poli ended any chance at the rally when he grounded into a double play on the next pitch. With two outs and no one on base Mike popped out to the shortstop to end the inning.

Already down 10-0 I decided the time was right to make a switch. I couldn't help but look ahead to the League Tournament that might start the following day. I didn't have a great feeling that keeping Dan out there would change anything so I decided to switch him with Brian. My fear was that by leaving Dan out there longer I ran a major risk of having his confidence and stamina both destroyed. Because I needed him to be sharp for the league tournament, I took him out of the game before even more damage could be inflicted. I switched with him with Brian Leciewski at third base.

I told Brian to "have fun and let them fly" as he took the mound. I wasn't hoping for a miracle comeback; rather I wanted to get Brian some experience pitching against hitters of that caliber. Brian stood tough as I knew he would. He didn't shut down the competition but he looked strong by striking out two of the batters he faced. The only problem was everyone else he faced seemed to zone in on his pitches and hit them all over the park. Brian was able to get through the inning only giving up four more runs; still a 14-0 deficit was no bargain.

In the top of the third I hoped that we could start taking control of the opposing pitcher. I knew that if we could just get a few hits off of him that we might be able to shake his confidence and start scoring some runs. The opposing pitcher Steve Griffin would have none of that as he shut down the bottom three in our order on just seven pitches. It was demoralizing.

I decided to let Alex have the next chance to pitch against the machines. Alex had looked very sharp at times but also shaky on the mound. He had been a hard worker all season so I wanted to give him the proper chance to test his skills against the best. Alex showed heart as he gave up four more runs allowing the deficit to grow to 18-0.

When the team returned to the dugout for the start of the fourth inning, I knew I needed to do something to cheer them up. It was brutal seeing a team that worked so hard all year get crushed this badly. My assistant coaches and I tried everything we could to get them fired up but it simply wasn't working. After Matt Poli and Dan both struck out, I signaled for Alex to lay down a bunt. I would normally never signal for a bunt when down by so many runs but I wanted them to have a spark of some kind. Alex laid a beauty down the third base line for a single. The third baseman on La Grange had been playing back on the edge of the grass and had no chance to catch the speedy Alex.

With Brian stepping to the plate I called for signal for a hit and run. Brian had been crushing the ball all season so I hoped we could generate some excitement. The first pitch was in the dirt and Brian swung and missed because he was disciplined to the signs we gave him that he still swung and missed at a horrible pitch. This allowed Alex to steal second base easily. I took the hit and run sign off and put in for a straight steal of third base for Alex. The next pitch was a high fastball that Brian had no chance of catching up to. Breaking for third base during the pitch Alex slid in ahead of both the tag and the throw. The umpire saw it differently and called Alex out.

It was clear to anyone with even halfway decent vision that Alex was safe by a mile at third. The umpire took one look at the scoreboard to see a team down 18-0 and made the decision that the sooner the game was over he could escape the hot sun. I was positive from my angle that Alex was ahead of the throw. It didn't matter that we were down by eighteen runs with the chance of the mercy rule looming. I was determined to fight for my players no matter what the situation was if I felt that they had been slighted. I argued with the umpire for several minutes until he finally threatened to throw me out of the game if I didn't return to the dugout.

Upon returning there I saw the entire team was smiling for the first time all day. It was the first time all game that they had fun. Apparently seeing me get in the face of the umpire gave them a reason to relax for a few minutes and enjoy the scene. I was glad I finally could find something to take their minds off the hammering that was taking place. It was the first time all year that we didn't care about the score for at least a few minutes.

It was at this moment that I made a decision that even I never would have thought possible. I told them not to worry about winning or losing but to simply have fun with the remainder of the game. Already down 18-0 I knew that the chances for a win were slim to none so I asked them what positions they each wanted to try. When I heard their answers I let them play in the positions they wanted. Such switches included Brian Leciewski going to center field so Mat Poli could pitch. It was unlike anything I had ever done before or would do again.

The main reason behind the jumbled line up was to give the players something to keep their spirits up heading into the League Tournament the following day. I knew that they would need that after the brutal pounding we were taking. As I looked at the infield and saw them smiling I knew I had made the right call. Keeping in mind that the next several days would most likely be the most stressful and important of my entire life, I wanted to make this one somewhat fun despite the eventual outcome of a blowout loss. I also took into consideration that if I had gotten angry with them about the horrible loss it could have killed their momentum and enthusiasm heading into a time when they would need it the most.

Before the bottom of the fourth inning could end, I let every single player pitch who had wanted to. I could tell that the opposing manager and both umpires were getting angry with the constant pitching changes but I didn't let it stop me. By the time the inning came to an end we were on the south side of a nail-biting 25-0 score.

The game came to a merciful end after the top of the fifth inning when we failed to score. It was the only time all season that we failed to score a run. It made some sense that our highest of highs might be followed by our lowest of lows. I shook the hand of the eventual State Championship Winning coach after the game. He didn't say much to me but I made sure to tell him good luck.

I wasn't sure how to address my team when I walked behind the dugout after shaking hands. I didn't have time to think because the second I approached them they start throwing water at me from their water bottles. They proceeded to tackle me to the ground and dump their water all over me. They were acting as if they had just won the championship of the world instead of suffering the worst loss of the season. Making matters even more bizarre was the opposing team walking by us shaking their heads. One of the players even said to their coach, "Do they know they just lost?" It actually got under the skin of the Machines that losing to them wasn't the end of our world. The fact remained that we still had our coveted League Tournament to play in and felt as though we would enter it as the favorites.

When the boys finally calmed down I addressed the situation at hand. I pointed out that we made it farther than forty eight other teams despite the outcome of the game we just finished. I made it known that our number one goal of winning the League Championship hadn't changed. I pointed out that no matter the outcome of that day's game we had still been playing our best baseball of the season coming in. Our last game against each team we might have to face in the tournament ended in us beating them. We had drawn last blood on every potential opponent we would possibly face. I reminded them of an old saying, "The lord doesn't close one door without another one opening". The chance to win the State Tournament was over, but it gave us more time to focus on the primary goal of hoisting up League Championship gold.

As painful as it was to lose to a team as talented as La Grange, it was the best team to lose to. It showed us the hardest competition we would have to face. The analogy I gave the boys was taking the donut off the baseball bat. This means that when a player places a donut shaped weight on the bat it makes the bat seem heavier. Thus when the player takes it off the bat appears lighter than it actually is, allowing the batter to increase his bat speed. Facing such a tough opponent it would make our normal league opponents appear much weaker. I concluded the speech by telling them that our season of hard work and sacrifice would pay off with one of the sweetest gifts if we could play our best ball over the next several days. I wanted them to fall asleep that night with nothing on their minds other than winning the championship.

Chris Scarl, who was the commissioner of North Olmsted Hot Stove Baseball, attended the game that day. He entered our post game huddle to inform us that our first game in the league tournament was set for the following afternoon at 2 pm. against Sedmack Insurance which was coached by Jack Hill. The Ohio Envelope team was awarded the number one seed and would play the winner of the game between Pats Cleaners and Wilsons Bike Shop. The winner of our game would play the winner of that game in the championship on Tuesday night.

The gauntlet was thrown down and my players were set to storm through it. It would only be a matter of time before we realized our dreams or watched as they became a nightmare. The choice was ours and the future was now. It was time to apply what nineteen games had taught us into one sole purpose. That purpose was to win the championship. With our backs against the wall and no room for losing, the time to shine when it mattered most was upon us.

With the brackets set I now had time to create a game plan to defeat Mr. Hill for a fifth and final time. The worst thing I could have done was taken them lightly and not prepare as hard as I did before every other contest. I was fully aware that we had routed them several times during the regular season. But I knew that the playoffs could result in a completely different outcome. One motto that always rings true in the playoffs is that every team that reaches them starts fresh. It no longer mattered that we had beaten them several times because we both stood at the bottom of the same mountain needing to be climbed. It was evident that Mr. Hill displayed serious anger issues towards our team so we had to prepare for their best.

It became increasingly difficult to fall asleep that night because I couldn't relax long enough to doze off. I couldn't cope with the possibility that if we lost it meant the end of our season. We had come so far that I would hate to see it end with anything other than us winning championship trophy. I finally fell asleep after tossing and turning most of the night. The thought of win or go home couldn't leave my mind.

I awoke on Sunday July 30, with as much anguish about the game as I had when I went to bed. I hoped that going to church would be enough to settle my nerves down. I walked into St. Brendan's Church, the same place in where I had spent my Sunday mornings for the previous ten years with the hope that I could take my mind off baseball for an hour. I didn't want the mass to end, unlike when I was a child and wished that mass would go faster so I could go home and watch football or play with my toys. This time I was hoping for a long mass because it was the only place I felt at peace.

I received a few quizzical looks from the patrons in the same pew as me because I had my baseball uniform on along with my glove tucked beside me. It was a far cry from the normal church clothes parishioners were used to seeing, but I felt that I needed to wear them. I honestly thought that if I wore them to church God might be on our side.

When I returned home I went over the lineup one last time. The tournament was a single elimination so we couldn't afford to take any chances. I decided to start Dan on the mound because I felt he was our most consistent pitcher and would give us the best chance at winning. It was important that we start off the game on top and never look back. Dan gave us the best chance to keep the opposition scoreless while we built a lead. My only concern was that Dan might have had his confidence rattled the previous day by the La Grange team. The best way to prevent it was putting him on the mound before he had too much time to dwell on it. With Dan selected to be our starting pitcher the rest of the lineup was composed as follows:

CF Matt Poli
P Dan Kitko
2B Alex Uhlik
3B Brian Leciewski
SS Anthony Poli
LF Mike Hach
C Kyle Keller
RF Andy Barth
OF John Rehak
1B Pat Morris
Reserve – John Rehak who entered in the third for Nate Dolesh

My unsettled stomach finally began to calm down when I pulled into the parking lot at North Olmsted Middle School and saw who the umpires would be that afternoon. The umpire for our first round tournament game against Sedmack Insurance was none other than Karl Kubb. Standing there with a smile from ear to ear, I knew instantly that he personally chose to umpire this game. I shook his hand and told him to "go easy on us, blue". He laughed and promised me that if Mr. Hill even thought about getting out of line he would personally toss him from the game. It was a comforting feeling to know we would have a fair umpire in such a big game.

I began my pre game speech to the team by pointing out all the reasons why we must not take the opposition lightly. I expressed to them how I felt about coaching them and that it had been an honor to do so. I let them know that all their hard work and sacrifice led to this tournament. I reminded them to take one inning at a time without getting ahead of themselves. It was important that we stuck to our solid fundamentals, using speed and defense to win.

Towards the end of my talk I remembered a classic line from former Cleveland Browns coach Marty Schottenheimer. The legendary coach had addressed his team before playing against the Denver Broncos in the 1986 AFC Championship game. While the game was famous for the John Elway lead touchdown drive that sent it into overtime, it was the head coaches' pregame speech that I had mimicked in my room countless times. "There is a gleam men, there is a gleam. Let's get that gleam!" Schottenhiemer was speaking about the possible gleam from the Super Bowl if they had gone on to win that game instead of losing it. I used it in my speech for much the same purpose. I was trying to implant the idea that we were one win away from playing in the gleam of the championship game. At first I couldn't understand why none of my players had heard of the famous speech. Then I realized that it occurred several years before they were born.

I could tell they wanted to win as badly as I did but didn't seem nearly as nervous. This was a good sign. My only fear was that they would come out flat. It was crucial that Dan throw strikes early and often allowing our defense to do its work. I couldn't believe my eyes when Dan threw twelve straight balls to begin the game. It was a clear sign that he had lingering mental effects from the shelling he received at the hands of La Grange one day earlier.

I wasted no time in calling time-out and sending Ray to the mound to calm down our pitcher. Kitko was known around the league as one of the best pitchers and I could tell that with every walk it allowed Mr. Hills team to gain confidence they normally wouldn't have when facing him. Confidence is one of the most important mental skills a hitter can have. One reason Dan had excelled all season was because he didn't allow batters to gain confidence. A game started with three straight walks ruined any intimidation factor he had going in. The game had just begun and we were already in a dire situation.

Cleanup hitter Jacob Brooks slammed a bases clearing triple to make the game 3-0 only four batters in. What was once a nightmare was slowly becoming reality when Dan went on to walk three of the next four batters he faced, forcing in a run and once again loading the bases. We had only given up one hit but still trailed 4-0 with the bases loaded and just one out. As bad as things looked I refused to pull the plug on Dan's start because he had performed well in clutch situations all year and knew that he could get out of this jam.

It was at this time that Brian, Alex and Kyle stepped up as true leaders by encouraging Dan after every pitch. They were vocal in their support and it seemed to help him as he rebounded to strike out the next two batters and get out of the inning only trailing 4-0. I was proud of the boys because they stood behind each other through thick and thin. This was another example of how tight they were with one another even when the chips were down.

I made sure not to lose my temper but to remain calm and positive when the team returned to the dugout. I reminded them that we had played well against this team all season and that we needed to settle down and focus. I tapped Dan on his cap and told him not to worry about it because we would get it back. To his credit, Dan didn't look nervous or even shaken. It was his second rough start in two days but he seemed calm and ready to get back to business.

It was crucial that my gut feeling would prove to be right about Dan settling down because we were unable to score any runs off opposing pitcher David Hill in our half of the first inning. We managed to get Kitko and Alex Uhlik to reach base but were unable to drive them in. Dan knew that he had to shut them down to start the second inning and keep the game close.

As the boys took warm up for the second inning I looked over at Mr. Kubb, who just nodded his head as if to say, "It's a long game, hang in there." Even after years had gone by he was still coaching me in his own way. My gut feeling about Kitko turned out to be right as he set the Sedmack Insurance team order down in a mere five pitches. He forced the first two batters to ground out to Anthony Poli. He then struck out their third batter with three cut fastballs that I don't believe I could have even hit.

Dan's return to dominance seemed to light a fuse with the rest of the team as they returned to the dugout like a house on fire. First up to hit was perennial singles hitter Mike Hach. David Hill decided to throw at Mike's back after falling behind in the count three balls and no strikes. David had now hit Mike with the ball every time we played them all season. It was clear the child was doing this on purpose. I don't know if Mike had been mean to David at school or what exactly his motivation was but we were always happy to get a runner on base by any means.

Kyle Keller walked on four pitches, putting two men on base with no outs for the lumbering Andy Barth. He had broken out of his slump midway through the season and stayed hot. I had Kyle and Hach steal second and third base on the first pitch so Andy could have two men in scoring position with no outs. Andy rewarded my faith in him when he belted the next David Hill pitch into deep center for a two run double. His big hit cut the lead in half while swinging the momentum back into our favor.

Johnny Rehak followed with a walk putting two men aboard for Pat Morris. Pat was unable to capitalize on the momentum and grounded out to the first baseman. His groundout did allow Andy and Johnny to move up one base each. This put two men in scoring position with only one out for Matt Poli. I called for the suicide squeeze because Matt was an excellent bunter and with Andy's slow speed at third base I figured that Hill would have never seen it coming. The strategy paid off when Matt laid down a perfect bunt allowing Andy to score and make it a 4-3 ballgame with still only one out.

Any fear of not taking the lead disappeared on the very next pitch when Dan Kitko tripled in both runners on base giving us a 5-4 lead. The crowd cheered loudly in favor of the action on the field. I could tell that every ring of the Bell was slowly getting under the skin of the opposing team and management. Mr. Hill pulled his son David from the game after he gave up another walk to Alex Uhlik. It was clear that the Hall team was cracking like a brittle rock; meanwhile the Wildcats were heating up.

With men on the corners and still only one out I called for the double steal. I knew that third base coach Bill was smart enough to call Dan back to third if the catcher didn't throw down to second. Alex was fast enough to make it into second base so I wasn't worried about him getting tossed out. The play worked to perfection when the catcher made an awful throw in attempting to get Alex out at a second base. This throw allowed Dan to score from third base on his end of the double steal. The throw was so bad that it skipped away from their shortstop and rolled into shallow center field. Alex used his speed and mental awareness to get up and hustle down to third base. The score was now 6-4 with still just that one out.

Brian kept the Wildcat players and fans on their feet when he crushed the next pitch into deep right field for another double. The mammoth blow allowed Alex to score our sixth run and give us what was becoming a commanding 6-4 lead. When Anthony hit a double into the gap between left field and center the crowd went wild, as did our bench. With all the extra base hits we took a 7-4 lead. When Mike Hach came up to the plate for the second time that inning it meant we batted around. Hach continued to keep the rally alive by hitting a line drive single into center field scoring our eighth run.

The four run lead seemed much bigger than the four run deficit we faced merely minutes earlier. We went on to score four more runs before the inning was over and took a 12-4 lead heading into the top of the third.

Dan continued to perform well by setting down the opposing line up in order one more time. Any nerves from the first inning were gone and Dan was cruising.

The Wildcat bats refused to cool off when Andy Barth, Johnny Rehak and Pat Morris led off the bottom of the third with singles. No matter who Jack Hill put in to pitch against us his plan simply wasn't working. Our batters remained focused at the plate and closed in on every pitch thrown their way. Numerous times we were able to put several runners on base then drive them in with big hits. Before Sedmack Insurance could catch their breath we had increased our lead to 18-4 after only three innings.

I was proud that my team was playing so well in a game that Mr. Kubb was actually umpiring. It would have been unfortunate to play poorly in front of a coach I had admired for such a long time. I never told any of my players that I knew the umpire. I didn't want them to get nervous or affect their mindset in any way. I told them after the game but I was sure not to mention it during play.

Holding a comfortable fourteen run lead I decided that Dan had seen enough action for the game and replaced him with Brian Leciewski. I was confident in his ability to shut down the opposition long enough for us to win by mercy rule after five innings. I told Brian to throw hard but make sure that he threw strikes. I didn't want to let them crawl back into the game by getting free bases with walks. Brian was comfortable protecting the lead and had no problems keeping them scoreless in the fourth.

I pulled the team aside before we could take our at bats in the bottom of the fourth. Already ahead by fourteen I saw no point in running up the score. I explained to my base coaches and players that I only wanted them to steal if it was a passed ball. I wanted them to keep their intensity level up but not run up the score. It was hard to tell them to take their foot off the gas for a few minutes, but I knew it would be smart. One thing Mr. Kubb had always preached was to win with class. As much as I wanted them to keep stealing home and pour on the runs, I knew the smartest thing to do was not make a huge scene about it. For the first time since we had the Bell I went over to the stands and asked the parents not to ring it for this one inning. I knew Jack Hill was looking for any reason possible to get me thrown out of coaching and I didn't want to give him any more incentive. It didn't matter what we did or said people were still going to find reasons to dislike us.

We managed to score three more runs and take a commanding 21-4 lead into the top of the fifth. I knew protecting a seventeen run lead would not be a problem for anyone, however; I kept Leciewski on the mound in the hopes he could get them out quickly. I was anxious to get the game over as soon as possible so we could begin focusing on the championship game. Brian didn't disappoint us and had no problems shutting down the order.

We won due to mercy rule by a final score of 21-4. With twenty games in the record books our record stood at 13 wins with 7 losses. We were about to play for the League Championship in a few days. It was further than anyone could have imagined us going just months prior. The only people who believed we could make this far were our players and their parents. It didn't matter what anyone else believed because the individuals who mattered the most were the ones who stood behind us. Legendary Indians broadcaster Tom Hamilton once said, "The season of dreams has become a reality". He was talking about the dream season of the 1995 Cleveland Indians. In many ways our season of dreams was just one win away from becoming reality.

The team was serious instead of the overly joyous mood they normally showed after wins. I could tell that they knew this was simply a stepping stone to get where they needed to be. They were happy to win but knew that the biggest game of their young lives was on the horizon. They kept the same look of intensity they had all season. They never strayed from it despite how good or bad things had been going. It was easier for me to keep their minds focused on winning because they wanted it every bit as much as I did.

I kept the post-game speech to a few short minutes. I concluded by telling them that in a little over 48 hours they would have the chance to achieve something that would mold their lives. They knew I was proud of them but they also knew the job was not yet done.

The next playoff game was scheduled in an hour between Wilsons Bike Shop managed by Darryl Briggs against Pat's Cleaners managed by Tim Coyne. It was at Little Clague Park so I had to hustle if I was going to make it in time to see the first pitch. I did take time to thank Mr. Kubb for umpiring the game. He was very complementary about what he had seen and also offered a few pointers. I was happy to take any advice he had to give me. It dealt mainly about adjusting my infielders to different spots depending on what kind of player was hitting. His ideas made good sense and I intended to use them. I thanked him again for all the years of dedication he had given to coaching. I let him know I never understood how much work it took until I had to do it myself. It was a truly gratifying moment to thank someone who had helped me so many times with such important advice.

It started to rain lightly as I drove to Little Clague Park to watch the next game which was already in the first inning by the time I arrived. I was hoping for a long, drawn out game that went extra innings. I wanted whatever team that won to be tired by the time they played against Ohio Envelope the following evening. It didn't matter who won because we had beaten everyone several times, I simply hoped that the path they took to get there would be long and tiring.

To my great dismay the game was called after only two innings with Wilson's Bike Shop up 2-1. The shocking fact was that the League called the game a victory for Mr. Briggs team. They only had the fields on loan until the third of August so they couldn't afford any delays in the tournament. It was an even bigger shock when Mr. Coyne didn't even fight this rule and simply took the loss. I felt bad for the hardworking players on his team like Chris Gore and Tyler Counts. I could tell that those two children were sad at the outcome. The rest of the team didn't seem to care. The premature end simply meant an early start to the rest of their summer.

The semi-final match up was set to take place the next night between Ohio Envelope managed by Mike Molnar against Wilsons Bike managed by Darryl Briggs. Each possible outcome presented a different challenge. We had played some classics against Mr. Molnar's group. I knew that any game against them would be a battle. A matchup against Mr. Briggs team would present a much different challenge. They had one solid pitcher in Adam Sedgemer. They also had the powerful yet cocky Terry Beach to contend with.

I stayed up for hours that night analyzing every inning we played against both teams that season. I looked at every possible matchup both with their pitchers and ours. I even went as far to figure out the personal batting averages of each player against each pitcher faced from each team. It was a grueling process but one that was completely necessary and fun. Bill even stayed up to help me every step of the way.

We had had success against several pitchers from Ohio Envelope, but the thought of facing Anthony Marflak one more time was daunting. They also had heavy hitters on their team with Danny Molnar and Marflak. They had speed with Jeff Feglemacher as well as with the Lazzaro brothers. I was positive we could beat them again but knew that it would most likely be a close game.

Mr. Briggs team presented many of the same qualities. It didn't matter who we would eventually face it was shaping up to be a close game. Again, my only hope was that the game went long and both teams would be exhausted by the time it was over. The championship game was set for Tuesday night so the winner wouldn't have any time to rest before facing us.

The game plan was set in place for both teams. I had two different lineups in mind as far as positions in the field would go. I did keep the original eight in the lineup in the same order I had them most of the season. The main differences revolved around who would start at pitcher against either team. If we played against Mr. Molnar then Johnny Rehak was set to start on the mound with Dan Kitko coming in to relieve him. If we played Mr. Briggs it would be Brian Leciewski starting with Dan Kitko or Alex Uhlik first to relieve him.

The deciding game turned out to be a huge disappointment when only four players from Mr. Molnar's team showed up. I never found out the exact reason why but almost his entire team decided that their season was over and they were done playing. This meant that Wilsons Bike Shop won by forfeit. They had only played two innings in almost a month and yet they were awarded the chance to play for a championship. I was livid that my team had played three grueling State Tournament games and a League Tournament game only to face a team that had been resting for weeks.

Driving home I was furious that Mr. Briggs and his team had been given a free pass to the biggest game of the year. It took me awhile to cool down but when I finally did I looked on the brighter side. We had beaten them three times in a row. They only had one great pitcher to have to contend with. I knew that if we could jump out to an early lead, they didn't have the heart to make a comeback. It was also one more chance to overcome the extreme negativity coming from their fans and turn it into the sweetest revenge possible.

My parents both asked me why I was home just minutes after I had left. I explained to them what happened and that I would need the phone for about an hour to call the team. I made sure to spend several minutes with each player on the phone talking about what I wanted from them the following night. I even spent time going over their stats with them against the numerous pitchers we had faced when playing Mr. Briggs's team that season. Each player sounded excited and promised to get to bed early that night so he would be well rested for the next evening. I made a point of telling each player to sleep with their glove that night for good luck. It may have seemed corny to some, but every player did it without question.

I went over Kathy's house to relax after I made the phone calls. At my request we watched Rocky. It was my favorite movie and I wanted to see it for inspiration. She agreed to do this because she knew it meant so much to me. I watched with more passion than I ever had in the past. I couldn't help but find so many similarities between Rocky and my team. They were both true underdogs who fought against the odds to achieve what they once dreamt for themselves. I wanted my players to win so badly for themselves, I could taste it. I wanted them to have the feeling of achieving greatness because I knew that they would carry it with them the rest of their lives.

After saying goodnight to Kathy I got in my car to drive home. It was about a twenty minute trip between her house and my parents because it was all one road with twenty three different stop lights. I had counted one time on the way home because I noticed that I was constantly stopped at a light. That night marked the first time I drove home without turning the radio on. I didn't want to hear any music or even listen to the Indians game. I was thinking about the game and nothing else. I felt as though there weren't any other cars even on the road. My mind was focused on one thought and one thought only, winning!

I worried that perhaps I didn't teach them as much as I could have. I considered calling an early morning practice just to go over things one more time. I knew it would have been crazy to call a practice the same day as a championship game but that was how nervous I was. For the first time all season I wasn't nervous about winning. Instead I was scared about losing. If we lost then that would have meant I let everyone down.

I went over the game plan one more time before crawling into bed. Every time I closed my eyes I saw images of holding up the championship trophy when I played for Bill Wheeler nearly ten years earlier. I closed my eyes again and envisioned holding up two separate championship trophies while playing for Mr. Kubb. It was becoming clear that sleeping was not a viable option.

With everyone in my house already fast asleep I climbed into our attic and starting looking around. I found the box with all my Little League gatherings in it and rummaged through. Taking a short trip down memory lane was fun and actually helped me relax.

With the game plan and all other preparations for the championship game taken care of there was only one thing left to do. As I crawled out of the attic I felt the baseball gods pulling me towards the only appropriate place I could go the night before such a huge game. Minutes later I was pulling out of my driveway en route to my destination.

Chapter 19
Champions

**We all have that fire but never have the chance to use it than it
goes away. But you can, you have this opportunity, so do it!
Why not? This is who you are and who you will always be.
You don't move aside for nobody until you're ready to move.
It doesn't matter how this looks to other people, it only
matters how it looks to you! Rocky, how it looks to you! If this
is something that you want to do and something that you have
to do then you do it! Fighters fight!
~ Little Marie, Rocky Balboa-2006**

The clock had just stuck midnight as I pulled into the parking lot
at Terminal Field. It had been nearly ten years since I had set foot
on the sacred grounds. The last time I was there I was holding up
our championship trophy with my teammates. I never thought I
would return as an eighteen year old recently out of high school on
the eve of coaching a championship game. Life had pulled me in
many directions over the past nine summers but it led me back to
where it all started.

The foray onto the field wasn't as easy as I thought it
would have been because the fence was locked. It was only about
fifteen feet high so I had no problems climbing it. The field was
located behind the Holiday Inn in a neighborhood that wasn't
exactly safe. Scaling a fence to a closed park late at night
wasn't the smartest thing I could've been doing with my time;
however I felt it was the right place to be. I walked to home plate
on the field where the championship game took place. I jogged
around the bases until I slid into home plate face first. After
getting up I knelt back down and kissed home plate, touched my
heart and pointed to the sky. It was my way of saying "thank you"
to the people who created the memories over my years of playing.

I owed much of what I learned of the game from those
days of playing at Terminal Field. If Mr. Wheeler wasn't such a
good coach I might have never developed the love for the game
that I did. Having the blessing of good coaching from a young age
helped the love for the game I had developed. If I would have
played for a bad coach, there is a chance that may never
have happened. As I looked up at the stars I could almost feel the
great games and people I had played with on the field years ago. It

was easy to close my eyes and think back to that championship after focusing on nothing but for two straight summers.

Before I left I made sure to reach down and grab dirt near home plate and put it into a zip lock bag I had brought with me. My plan was to get to the field early before the championship game my team was set to play in so I could spread that same dirt near the home plate of our field. I never told anyone that I did any of this. It was a secret I wanted to keep with me for years until I felt the time was right to reveal it. At that time I felt that if anyone knew what I did it might freak them out or make my players nervous. I didn't want to hear safety concerns from Kathy or my family about being out so late in a bad part of town. Technically what I did could be considered trespassing. Despite the chances that I took that night I was happy that I did. Not a day has gone by since that I haven't thought about that night.

I had thoughts of driving past the neighborhood where I used to live on my way home that evening but decided against it. It was nothing but big open fields of dirt and weeds since the airport had bought it out a few years after we moved. I did take the long way home with the windows rolled down on my car so I could soak in more of the night. With all the noise that the day brings along with the evenings, it is nice to listen to the quiet symphony that is the late night. I was aware that the following evening had the potential for hellfire and brimstone so I wanted to soak in as much calmness as possible.

I fell asleep only moments after crawling into bed that night. I thought that I would be up all night pacing around but the trip to Terminal Field helped calm me down. It was nearly 2 a.m. when I went to bed and I didn't open up my eyes again until it was time to. It was the best night of sleep I had gotten in months and it came at the perfect moment.

The next morning as I filled my bowl with the sweet taste of Corn Pops, I went over the lineup a few more times. Mrs. Rehak had called earlier that morning to let me know Johnny was sick with the flu and wouldn't be able to play. They would still be there to support the team and for him to sit on the bench. I also knew that Ryan Mackey would not be there due to prior commitments. It left me with a roster of ten players meaning that no one would have to sit the bench. As much I hated for Rehak and Mackey not to play, I felt better about not having to bench anyone in the championship game.

It was while I was making the lineup that Don called from his job with an excellent idea. He suggested that I call Billy Graves and invite him to show up in full uniform. We knew Billy couldn't play but he shouldn't be kept from taking part in the festivities of a championship game. We decided to have Billy show up in full uniform and insert him into the starting lineup. Our plan was to have Billy play in deep right field for the top of the first inning than pull him from the game when the inning was over. It was vital that Billy didn't have physical contact in any way with anything. I had to promise his Dad numerous times on the phone that we would pull him from the game the second the inning was over and tell our other outfielders to cover more territory. The purpose was to have Billy's name on the final scorecard for the championship game. He had come to every practice and worked hard before getting injured, so it was the least we could do. After convincing Mr. Graves that we wouldn't put his son in any serious danger, I filled out the rest of the lineup. The plan was to switch Billy with Nate Dolesh after the top of the first inning.

I decided to start Brian Leciewski on the mound for the final game. Brian had pitched well against them all season and I was confident that night would be no different. Brian was just waiting to get revenge for being knocked out of the game by the line drive the last time we played them. I wasn't about to hold him back when his desire to perform well was at an all-time high. Brian had a giant-sized heart on a team that thrived on it.

I penciled in Brian Leciewski to start with every intention of his going the first three innings. There was no doubt in my mind as to who I would put in to close out the game. Dan Kitko had emerged to become one of the most dominant pitchers in the league and state. I was positive that if Brian could keep the game close, Kitko would bring us home. If both pitchers played their best then there wasn't a team in the league that could stop us. I was more than confident we had the best one two punch in the league.

With my parents, Don and Bill all at work, I had the house to myself all day. There wasn't much I could do to keep myself from getting overly nervous so I decided the best thing to do was read a book. I chose my all-time favorite book called Have a Nice Day by Mick Foley. It is an inspirational tale of an incredible journey by one of my favorite wrestlers. It is one of the best tales anyone who is struggling to fulfill a dream could read. His book is the greatest I have ever read because he details things in a manner that allows the reader to put themselves in his shoes. I became so deeply engrossed into the book that numerous hours passed until I realized it was time to get ready for the game.

Getting ready for this game was no different than most others as I made sure not to change a thing. I kept playing the same few songs until they finished off with my usual selection of "Higher" by Creed.

I couldn't help but notice that I still wasn't becoming nervous. I felt calm throughout the day with no signs of the pre-game nerves I suffered before our last game. I was more relaxed for this one because I knew it was our last no matter what the outcome. Before our last game I worked myself into a panic from worrying about our season being cut short. There is much to be said about controlling one's own destiny. Not having to worry about tomorrow is the best strategy for playing for today. Often some of the most classic World Series Games take place in the final Game Seven because both teams give every ounce of energy they have left in their bodies. This championship game had the Game Seven feel to it.

As much as I would have liked the game to take place at Clague Park it was not to be. The game was scheduled for the field behind North Olmsted Middle School. It didn't have the familiar feeling that Little Clague gave us but we had played well there so I didn't mind it too much.

The fifteen minute drive gave me more time to think over the game plan. In my mind I had gone over numerous times about my plans for the game. It has been said that numerous all pro quarterback's in football tend to do the same thing. They visualize themselves throwing touchdown passes hours before each game, then go out and do it on the field at game time. Major League pitchers do the same type of thing. If a coach can mentally game plan well enough to beat the opposition, it becomes easier for him to sell that winning idea to his team.

By the time I arrived at the field there wasn't a single person who could tell me that we wouldn't be victorious. I firmly believed that we were going to win and there wasn't anything anyone could have done about it. Years of playing champion style baseball had brought me to this moment and I was sure to inspire my players. Having worked their butts off all season they deserved it more than any other group of players I had ever seen. It was our time now and the championship was too close not to reach out and take it.

There would be no need to worry about the umpires. Tom Grodek would call the balls and strikes while Scott Pogros worked the field calls. They were my two favorite umpires that season and deserved the honor and responsibility of calling the championship game. I didn't hesitate to shake their hands before the game. Some people may not realize just how stressful it is for an umpire to call a championship game. They realize the importance of the outcome just like everyone else and want to do their best. Having this knowledge I made sure to wish them good luck.

It wasn't much longer after I arrived at the field when my players began to show up. I tried to look at each one of their faces to get a sense as to how they were feeling then gauge my pregame speech around it. If they looked nervous I would try a different approach than if they looked focused or even over confident. It didn't take long to notice they seemed like their normal focused and confident selves. Having a team that came ready to play and win every time out was a huge blessing. Having the players focused and determined to win made my job ten times easier.

With the team going through their normal warm ups I was approached by League Commissioner Chris Scarl. He congratulated my team on a fine season, making sure to point out that if we were victorious I would be the youngest manager in City history to win a League Championship. The calm I had felt all day disappeared briefly when he pointed out that fact. I never gave much thought about what my age would mean if we won the championship. Hearing someone mention it out loud sent shivers of excitement down my spine.

Chris Scarl was just one of many luminaries in the crowd that evening. Numerous figure heads from the league decided to watch the action. Not only were their people from the league board at the game but also fellow coaches Mike Molnar, Jack Hill and Tim Coyne. It reminded me of my younger days playing for Mr. Wheeler in the classic games against Brooks and Bebe when the entire league would turn out to watch. I took it as a compliment as a coach the same when I did in when I was a player. Anytime a crowd shows up to watch you perform at your best, it is real praise. It doesn't matter to me if they are rooting for or against my teams, the effect is still the same.

As I looked out on the crowd I noticed many familiar faces including my brother and Abbie. Both of my parents as well as Kathy were in attendance for this important game. I was pleasantly surprised to see that my Aunt Anna had shown up for the game accompanied by her two young sons Emerson and Christopher. Her newborn baby, was only a couple months old, Joseph, remained at home with my uncle Chris. Matt Tomecko showed up for the game and even brought his mom and younger brother. It was a pleasure to see Matt again because I had so few chances that summer to spend time with him. He was the only friend that showed up for the big game. Joe Graham had made plans to be there but he had been called into work. I honestly believe Joe would have made every attempt to be there if he could. I called a few of my other friends but they either didn't get the message or simply didn't care.

The more I thought about things with friends and family, the more it reminded me of all the people a victory would have been for. Mr. Wheeler and Mr. Kubb were the obvious two, but there were still other coaches who had helped mold me. I believed I had to go through that 0-16 season with Mr. Klien to show me how painful losing was so I would try even harder to win. The summer of 1995 spent playing with Mr. Hurley's team showed me the importance of teamwork and the ability to come from behind in games. It also showed me that winning is a total team effort and that we didn't have to keep relying on the same few players. I felt that the outcome of our game had a lot to do with what all those experiences had taught me.

It wasn't only the baseball memories that I was coaching for but also the non-baseball ones as well. It was for all the countless times in the backyard playing with Don. It was for the numerous times hanging out with Steve Pecatis or Paul Hut. It was as if every bike ride to nowhere led me to this moment. All those things helped shape who I was at that time and why I was able to connect with my team in the way that I did. Because I had such a great childhood, it was easier to connect with children as a coach when I had to.

The past can make persons become who they become; the past is not to be ignored but to be cherished. Every loss and every victory made our team who they became that season. Our team had gone through the rigors of a long season which helped us become stronger. I felt that we compared to a piece of tempered steel. We may have been burned a few times, but these setbacks only led us to become stronger as a unit. In the winds of adversity many teams would have crumbled into ashes. We took that adversity and turned it into a driving force for victory.

This game was for every player who wasn't picked and ended up playing for me because of it. This game would once and for all silence anyone who said we weren't good enough. We were the team no one wanted with the coach no one believed in and we were about to shock everyone. We wanted to win for every boy not picked on the playground. We not only accepted the underdog role but we thrived on it. This David was carrying a large rock and more than ready to sling it.

With all these thoughts running through my mind, I called the team over for a pre-game huddle. Before leaving the house earlier that night I grabbed the championship trophy I earned playing for Mr. Kubb in the summer of 1992. I earned it when I was ten years old, the exact age of most of my players. I had three championship trophies to pick from but I chose that one because I it was the most appropriate. I gathered the team in a big circle and told them to all close their eyes. They did exactly what I said to do and closed their eyes. When I noticed that they were all shut I pulled the trophy from my bag. I explained that I wanted them to keep their eyes shut until the object was handed to them. Then they would have to kiss it before opening up their eyes and hand it to the next player.

The team had never shown me anything but their utmost trust and respect all season and this wasn't any different. It took plenty of trust for them to kiss something that they had no idea what it was until they opened their eyes. Each player was smiling from ear to ear after he figured out what it was. The thought of wide spread germs never crossed my mind and I was glad no one brought it up. Our team had been less than hygienic all season so this wasn't much worse than anything else that happened.

After the trophy was passed around to everyone in the circle, I began my speech. It was one of the shortest speeches that I have ever given; it was also one of the most direct and important. I have played it over in my head more than a thousand times since that evening and can still recite it word for word today. "Gentleman, this is the Hot Stove Little League Championship trophy that I won playing on a team at your exact age. Play hard and smart for seven innings tonight and you are all going home with one of these!" The speech was less than a minute long but produced the impact that lasts forever. Years later Alex Uhlik told me that my speech stayed with him for a long time and that it made him focus harder than anything ever before that night. I kept it short and simple because I knew it would be more effective that way. We were ready and they needed to know one last time that I believed in them and what was at stake. With Brian Leciewski on the mound to start the game, the rest of the lineup appeared as follows:

CF Mat Poli
3B Dan Kitko
2B Alex Uhlik
P Brian Leciewski
SS Anthony Poli
LF Mike Hach
C Kyle Keller
RF Andy Barth
1B Pat Morris
Deep Right Field Billy Graves
Not in attendance- Ryan Mackey
Sick- Johnny Rehak
Bench – Nate Dolesh (only for the top of the first inning)

"1-2-3 Champs" was the chant we shouted before taking the field for the start of the first inning. Brian had a look of intensity on his face that made him look as if he would run through a brick wall. I loved seeing that. I felt every muscle in my body tense up as Brian took his warm up tosses. The calm before the storm was over and now we were set to battle for the gold. I looked into the opposing dugout to lock eyes with Darrly Briggs. I shot an intense look right through him as if to say, "Your team is done!" It wasn't that I didn't like Darryl, rather it was about the taunting his group of parents had given me all season long. This was the final chance to silence them for good. We weren't about to let it slip through our fingers.

Brian looked as good as ever when he struck out the first two batters he faced on only eight pitches. He was also throwing harder than I had ever seen him. Terry Beach stepped into the batter's box with two outs and no one on base. I was quietly saying to myself over and over, "Please, God, don't let him hit it to Billy." It turned out that Brian didn't even give him the chance to swing the bat as he threw the first pitch right at his lower back sending Beach down in pain. As Terry Beach lay on the ground crying in front of everyone for the second time in as many at bats against us, we realized that we never told Brian he didn't have to throw at him anymore. Brian was such a good player when it came to taking instructions that he honestly thought we wanted him to throw at Beach every time the boy came to bat.

As Beach trotted down to first base line in pain I called time and had Ray jog out to the mound to speak with his son. He was able to let Brian know that we just wanted him to focus on getting guys out and not throwing at anyone. It was a short meeting and the game was quickly restarted. Upon restarting I couldn't help but try a play to catch Beach napping at first. I signaled to Kyle for nip one. This was the play for him to throw down to first base after the pitchout to catch the runner on first base leaning too far off the bag. Kyle went on to perform the play brilliantly catching Terry Beach straying too far from first to get the final out of the inning. It was an excellent way to end an impressive top half of the first inning.

I held true to my word given to Mr. Graves and took Billy out of the game as soon as he returned to the dugout. Billy was smiling ear to ear that he had played even a small bit in such an important game. I was happy we could give him at least one small bright spot in what had been a rough summer.

I kept the same batting order we had been using since starting our winning ways earlier in the season. The players were comfortable hitting in their normal spots so I found no need to change anything. To our surprise it was neither Adam Sedgmer nor Frankie who started the game on the mound; it was our old buddy Terry Beach. I was shocked because he had not pitched against us all year. I had seen him pitch in only one of the several games I scouted them that season. I am not sure if they wanted to intimidate us with his size or what exactly the motive for their move was.

We didn't alter our original game plan despite the new pitcher on the mound opposing us. I had told Mat Poli that I wanted him to bunt in his first at bat before the game even started. I told the first three players in our lineup to bunt in the hopes of catching the opposition off guard. I was counting on them staying back on their hills because of the power of the early part of our lineup.

Mat did exactly was he was told as he laid down a perfect bunt on the third base line to start the game reaching first. Dan Kitko bunted the next pitch down the first base line sacrificing Mat over to second base in place of our first out. Alex let the first pitch go by him so Mat could have a clear chance at stealing third, which he did without a problem. Alex then bunted the next pitch down the third base line so slowly that it allowed Mat to score from third without them even getting a throw off to first. We drew first blood by taking a 1-0 lead with only one out.

Alex Uhlik had no problems stealing two bases as Brian Leciewski worked the count full against Terry Beach. Brian drove the payoff pitch into deep center field where it was caught for the second out of the inning. The ball was hit far enough that it allowed Alex to tag up from third base and score another run putting us ahead 2-0. We had played small ball well enough to gain the early lead. It caught the opposition off guard giving it something else to have to worry about the rest of the night. Anthony Poli followed with a good at bat against Beach but eventually was forced to ground out to the shortstop to end the inning. After one full inning of play we held a close 2-0 lead.

Brian looked a little shaky as he let up a walk and a single to the first two batters he faced, putting runners on the corners with no one out to start the second. He eventually was able to settle down after Kyle Keller went to the mound to speak with his pitcher. I'm not sure what Kyle said but it worked as Brian went on to strike out the next two batters. With two outs and two on he was able to force their next hitter to line out softly to Mike Hach in left field, holding them scoreless. It was a shaky inning for Brian but he showed true heart by getting out of it without allowing a run. Heading into the bottom of the second we looked to improve upon our two run lead.

Mike Hach led off the bottom half of the second inning with a ground ball single through the hole between the first and second basemen. Keller followed with a single of his own to put men on the corners with zero outs. I told Andy Barth to focus on making contact in his turn at bat. It didn't matter how hard he hit I just wanted him to connect with the ball. His hitting skills had improved dramatically all season so I was confident he could get the job done. Andy hit the second pitch hard, but right at the second baseman for a line drive out. We were in danger of leaving men stranded on base after Pat Morris struck out for the second out. Nate Dolesh was able to draw a walk which loaded the bases for Mat Poli with two outs.

With the third baseman and first baseman both playing far up the line to guard against the bunt, I gave Mat the sign to swing away. My hope was that he would be able to pop the ball over the infielder's heads. He had been able to do such things all season so I knew he was more than capable. Terry Beach's first offering to Mat was low and outside. The ball skipped away from their catcher and rolled up the first base line. Mike Hach was alert enough at third base to witness this and come charging home. Mike slid into home well ahead of the tag and handed us a 3-0 lead. That miscue on their part proved to be crucial because Mat lined out on the next pitch. We were able to steal a run with the wild pitch instead of leaving the bases loaded and not scoring. With a three run lead and the way Brian looked dominant on the mound, I felt my confidence grow.

Brian began the top of the third the same way he had started the second by allowing two men to reach base. This time he gave up back to back singles through the gap between the third baseman and shortstop. He was able to strike out the next three batters in a row with an incredible display of fastballs. It was the second straight inning he was able to strand two opposing runners on base and keep Wilsons Bike Shop scoreless. It wasn't fancy but it certainly was effective. With the Wildcats set to bat in the bottom of the third, we clung to a 3-0 lead.

Dan Kitko led off the bottom half of the third inning with a sharp line drive single to left field. Wilsons Bike Shop had not yet proved they could stop the bunt, so I signaled for another one. Dan was off with the first pitch as Alex Uhlik laid a beauty back to the pitcher, allowing him to advance to second base. With only one out and a runner on second I told Brian to work the count one strike deep, allowing Dan to steal third. What this means is that the batter doesn't begin to swing until he has at least one strike on him. It worked perfectly as Dan was able to steal third base with Brian working the count in his favor. Brian was able to hit the one ball one strike pitch deep enough into left field that after their left fielder caught the ball Dan had no problems tagging up and scoring from third. It expanded our lead to four runs and gave us a strangle hold on the game.

Our team was proving that we could play small ball smart enough to be effective. This is a term used for teams that use speed and sacrifice hits instead of relying on the long ball. Our strategy was working to perfection as Darryl Briggs clearly did not have his team ready to defend it. I game planned that they would have their fielders back all game because of the power we had in our lineup, thus by playing small ball and laying down timely bunts they would never expect it. Than when we needed a powerful hit we had the batters at the right time to do so. Brian had already shown that he had what it took to hit deep enough fly balls to score runs.

Terry Beach was shaken up by our furious style and showed signs of cracking when he walked the next three batters in a row. With the bases loaded and Andy Barth stepping to the plate, the situation was looking very good. I told Andy to focus on making contact and not worry about crushing the ball. I was secretly thinking to myself how fine it would be for Andy to hit another grand slam and put the game out of reach. Andy was over anxious at the plate and made the classic mistake of swinging at the first pitch. The ball was two feet out of the strike zone and Andy was only able to get the tip of the bat on the ball. It was a soft ground ball back to Beach who made the smart play by picking it up and tossing it back to the catcher for the force out at the plate to end the inning. We had tacked on another run and with three innings in the books we led 4-0.

With momentum on our side I saw no reason to stray from the original game plan of switching pitchers to start the fourth inning. Brian had looked good in his three inning stint but I felt we needed Dan to come in and keep the opposition scoreless. I pulled Dan aside before he took the mound and said, "Don't let them breathe". It was a line that Rocky Balboa's trainer Mickey gave him during his fight with Apollo Creed for the title. It was appropriate for this situation because we had smothered all the life out Wilsons Bike Shop with our hot start. If we could keep putting zero's up on the board it would deflate any momentum or motivation they would have at making a comeback. I was confident in Dan's ability to go out and shut them down.

Any doubts I may have had about switching pitchers quickly evaporated when Dan struck out the side. His pitches were moving brilliantly over the plate and away from the plate when needed. He would throw an incredible fast ball then come back with a hooking curveball ten miles an hour slower. His changing of speeds and locations left the opposing batters with rubber legs.

He had all the poise of someone twice his age with the confidence of a seasoned major leaguer.

In the bottom of the fourth inning we were unable to expand our lead despite getting a few runners on base. They had made the switch to Adam Sedgmer on the mound. He was tough against us all season and I knew that things wouldn't change that night. I told my team to hang in there against him and just try to make contact. I knew that Briggs team had a less than stellar defense so if we could keep hitting the ball hard that things would happen.

Dan continued his brilliance in the top half of the fifth when he struck out the side once again. I can't remember someone even getting as much as a foul ball hit off of him. He was throwing the ball so hard at times that people twenty feet away could hear the catcher's mitt pop. It was one of the sweetest sounds my ears have ever experienced. Between every batter that Dan got out Brian and Anthony led the cheers in the field. They were both yelling, "1-2-3" with the rest of the team following it with, "Wildcats"! In the midst of all the action we had the Bell blaring in the background with the loudest cheering section North Olmsted Hot Stove had ever witnessed.

We were unable to score again off Adam Sedgmer in the bottom half of the fifth inning. It was a little disheartening because we sent the heart of the order to the plate. I have to give full credit to Adam. He was on his game that night. We sent Uhlik, Leciewski, Anthony Poli and Mike Hach to the plate but each came up empty. Poli managed to get on base with two outs but we could not drive him in. As Dan took the mound for the top half of the sixth we still led 4-0.

The sixth inning wasn't any different for Kitko then the previous two. He was able to strike out all three batters he faced. It was becoming one of the most brilliant pitching outings I had ever seen a young player have. He was able to get ahead of every batter then work both sides of the plate to keep them guessing. Kyle Keller did an amazing job behind the plate giving Dan good target locations throughout the game. Keller and Kitko had grown up together that summer in the numerous times I had them work the battery. They developed a great chemistry with each other.

With the bottom of the sixth about to begin, I pulled the team aside and let them know that this would be the last time they would bat that season. It meant that we would wrap things up in the seventh and not have to bat in the bottom half of the inning. They understood what I meant and decided to make it count.

Kyle Keller hit Adam Sedgmers one ball one strike pitch into shallow center field for a base hit to start the inning. He then stole second base and advanced to third after a rare wild pitch. Andy dug his cleats in and choked up on the bat down in the count one ball and two strikes. He sent the next pitch clear over the right fielders head for an RBI double. It made the score 5-0 and brought the crowd to its feet once again. As much as I tried to ignore the people in the stands, there was simply no way to ignore how loud and enthusiastic our fans had become. The excitement may have gotten to Andy because he took off on the next pitch without us signaling for him to do so. Even with his long legs he was still not a speed demon by any measure, thus he was easily thrown out at third for the first out. As Andy strolled back to the dugout I couldn't help but say for one final time, "Andy Barth, what are you doing?"

Pat Morris and Nate Dolesh both drew walks with the top of the order now coming to the plate. I couldn't resist going to the well one more time as I signaled out to Bill at third base to have Mat lay down one more bunt. We had a five run lead with only one out and two of our slower runners on base. I wanted to do whatever possible to get them into scoring position for Kitko or Alex Uhlik to drive them in. Mat set down another nice bunt with the pitcher having no play other than throwing to first to get the sure out. This allowed both runners already on base to advance into scoring position as planned.

With two on and two out Dan Kitko stepped into the batter's box. With first base open they were going to pitch very careful to him. Having Alex Uhlik waiting on deck if Dan did draw a walk was an advantage for us. If they did end up walking him it would just load the bases for the red hot Alex Uhlik. It was a case of pick your poison for Darrly Briggs. After working the count to three balls and one strike Dan stepped out of the box. I motioned for him to swing away if it was over the strike zone. I didn't mind him drawing the walk but I didn't want him feeling afraid to swing. I trusted his bat and knew he had a good eye at the plate.

Dan awarded my confidence by lacing a sharp line drive into shallow center field. It allowed Pat Morris to score from third but was hit too hard for Nate Dolesh to score from second base. Pat Morris slid into home face first when he didn't have to. There was a chance that the opposition may have seen this as us showing off, but it was simply Pat showing some hustle and excitement. The crowd on our side had become so loud and excited about the game that even if the opposing fans were booing I did not hear them. As much as I tried to block them out in the previous games I never could. This game was much different because of how loud and raucous our fans were.

The crowd didn't sit down or stop cheering even after Alex Uhlik popped out to end the inning. Our fans were pumped, my players were pumped, and I was more focused on winning then at any other point in my entire life.

With the team set to take the field for perhaps the final time, I had to take the opportunity to give them encouraging words. It is a moment that I have relived in my head over one thousand times since. I had them put their hands in the middle of a huddle and gave them these words, "This is our season, our night, and our field. Now go get your championship!" It was the first thing that came to my mind and the only thing I could have possibly felt at the time. Speaking with players after that night they have all said the words sent chills down their spine.

I meant what I said because I believed that it was our time. We had worked so hard for that moment all season and it was time for it to pay off. We held a 6-0 lead with only three outs separating us from glory. Our team deserved that moment and if those words helped them enjoy it more then I'm glad I said them.

Sometimes three outs can seem like an eternity. I walked over to my brother Don who was sitting in the front row with his girlfriend Abbie. I reached out and gave him a hug and told him quietly so only he could hear me, "I'm scared to death." We were so close and it would have killed me and my players if we blew it. Don told me to relax and just take it one out at a time as I walked back to the dugout.

Dan Kitko had set down the first nine batters he faced, but now Wilsons Bike Shop had the top of their order coming back up for a second crack at him. I knew he had to be getting tired from all the strikeouts so I had mentally prepared myself to pull him if he got into major trouble. I was set to throw Alex Uhlik if need be. Bill had commented to me earlier after warm ups that when he was playing catch with Alex that he was throwing serious heat. It was good to have a solid back up plan just in case things got out of hand.

Dan forced the first two batters he faced to ground out to shortstop Anthony Poli on the first pitch they saw. Less than two minutes after he took the mound we were one out away from winning the championship. Brian was yelling "Wildcats" so loud that I thought he was going to lose his voice. I have never seen them excited as they were at that moment.

The bad news was that Terry Beach was coming to the plate. The good news was that it was with two outs and no one on base. They also trailed by six runs so it didn't matter if he hit the ball to Chicago we would still be in the lead. Dan looked into the dugout as to ask what he should do. We had been pitching around Beach all year when Brian wasn't throwing at him. I yelled out to Dan, "Go after him!"

As Kitko wound up to throw his first offering to Terry Beach it was the first time all game that it was quiet enough to hear a pin drop. The tension over the possible final out was so thick that it could have been cut with a knife. Dan grooved a fastball right down the middle of the plate belt high. Hogan let it go right by him for strike one. If he chose to swing I am not sure if the ball would have landed in the same time zone. It is what happened on the next pitch that will live in the memories of many for years to come.

Beach swung at Kitko's next offering and bounced the pitch a couple feet to the right of the mound. Dan dove off the mound and fielded the ball on his knees. He turned from his knees to try to throw Terry out at first base. The ball reached the outstretched glove of Pat Morris at first base just ahead of the lumbering runner to get the final out of the game.

When umpire Scott Pogros signaled that Beach was out at first base and we won the game, it was the happiest moment of my life. It was the type of euphoria I believe people feel on their wedding day or when their first child is born. My entire body felt as light as a feather, almost as if I could walk on air if I wanted to.

I dashed out of the dugout and joined Kyle Keller and Dan Kitko in a huge bear hug. Kyle had picked up Dan in a hug and I went ahead and picked up both of them at once. The rest of the team joined to create a massive pile of players. It was a wild scene as even a few parents charged the field in celebration. Moments such as these can never be bought. They are God's gifts to people who earned them.

A couple of the players managed to hold me down long enough for the other players to dump this enormous water bucket Don brought to the game over my head. I was soaking wet with ice down my back but I couldn't have been happier.

I never took time to go over to where Kathy was sitting at the time of the celebration. I often felt bad about not sharing the moment with her, but at the time the only people I wanted to be around were my players and coaches. The moment was for them and their families. Kathy understood that and never gave me grief about not going over to hug her.

After drying off with a towel that Mrs. Hach handed to me, it was time for the trophy presentation. Each age group had a separate league coordinator who had the responsibility of handing out the championship trophies. God blessed me with an extra special treat that day as our league coordinator happened to be my good friend Jack Hill. Out of all the people in the world to hand me a championship trophy, I knew it had to anger him the most. I was gracious about it and made sure to thank him with a big smile on my face.

The standard procedure was to pull the team aside and hand them their trophies individually. I felt as though my team deserved much better than that. I asked everyone to stand on the first base line because I felt that they deserved public recognition. I also asked Mr. Briggs to line up his players as well so he could hand them their trophies for taking second place. It turned out to be a nice impromptu ceremony as each of his players ran up and got their second place trophy.

When it was our turn I made sure to call up each player by not only saying their name but also their nickname. It was the proudest moment of my life as each player picked up his trophy. I felt better in that moment than all three of my championships as a player combined. In a way I sensed that I had just inherited thirteen younger brothers for life.

I had planned on talking to the parents and team as a whole one final time after the trophies were presented. The players decided to cover me in silly string before I could even begin my speech. I still have no idea who brought the silly string, but the players had a blast covering me and each other in it. The pictures that were taken that day of the different festivities looked like we were at a birthday party instead of a baseball game.

I was glad that the boys were celebrating but I felt it important to thank everyone. I had Bill and Ray call everyone over to form a giant circle. With each player and parent standing in the circle, including my own parents, I became choked up. It was the first time all season that I went to say something after a game and couldn't get the words out. I was lucky enough that no one noticed it because I had sunglasses on. I took a deep breath and then said, "Thank you, everyone. We have just shared one of the greatest summers of our lives. I'm proud of every one of you and I love you all. Thank you!" With that I threw my fist in the air and walked off. The championship was for them and I wanted them to have the final moments as a team with each other.

What had started off by my waiting by the phone hoping that I would have the chance to coach turned into the greatest summer of my life. Too many things in this world happen without the single aspect of the human spirit. The story of the 2000 Wildcats and the incredible journey is one that thrives on the human spirit. This is an incredible comeback story in a world that loves the underdog. If I listened to a single person who said it couldn't be done then it never would have been. It was a team of destiny from the first practice on. For every extra ground ball thrown to Andy Barth in my parents front yard, there was a time that doubt crept into our minds. We never let doubt and naysayers control our plan, and in the end that is what shone through.

No one player was any more important than the other. We were the only team in the league to place teamwork in front of everything else. Our team wasn't about having two or three all-stars but more about having a team that believed in each other.

For every person who let the weight of the world get them down, the Wildcats story gives them something to believe in. It is story of hard work and faith, one of believing in yourself when no one else will.

It was our destiny to win the championship, but to do so we had to find each other. It was because no one else wanted us that gave us the chance to find each other. Carl Jung once said, "I am not what has happened to me. I am what I chose to become". Our team chose to become champions.

Biography

Vince McKee grew up in Northeast Ohio as an avid sports fan. He enjoys spending time with his wife, and his nephew Matthew. Vince hopes this work will be the first of many he can share with sports fans everywhere. He would love to hear your thoughts on the book and listen to ideas. You can contact him at coachvin14@yahoo.com.